'A great deal of writing on art and politics these days is interested in arts only as a form of political resistance. Alternately, there is a strain of study which circumvents big P politics, concentrating on 'community' and 'conversation' and 'process' as ends in themselves. In *Aesthetics and Political Culture in Modern Society*, Nielsen does something different. He reaches back to classical democratic and aesthetic theory to argue that art can facilitate the necessary conditions for democratic politics on a macro scale. For anyone interested in moving past resistance, or creating change that goes beyond micro-communities, this approach is essential.'
– Stephen Duncombe, Co-Director of the Center for Artistic Activism and Professor of Media and Culture, New York University

'Criticising neoliberal technocratisation and the overall process of aestheticisation while at the same time showing the potentials of aesthetic practice in generating genuine political judgement, this book is an eye-opening analysis of different kinds of current aesthetic intervention within public space. Theoretically brilliant and powerful.'
– Birger Steen Nielsen, Professor, Roskilde University, Denmark

Aesthetics and Political Culture in Modern Society

Do aesthetic appeals to senses and emotions in political debate necessarily marginalise political reason and reduce citizens to consumers – thus dangerously undermining democracy? Or is sensuous-emotional engagement, on the contrary, a basic fact of the political process and a crucial precondition for revitalising democracy?

Aesthetics and Political Culture in Modern Society investigates the current interrelationship between aesthetic practice and political practice in Western democracies, focusing on its impact on democratic political culture. Henrik Kaare Nielsen argues that aesthetic interventions in the political process do not by definition undermine politics' content of reason. Instead, a differentiation must be made between a multiplicity of aesthetic forms of intervention – some of which tend to weaken the political judgement of citizens while other forms tend to stimulate competent judgement.

This book will be of interest to scholars in the fields of political science, sociology, media studies, and cultural studies.

Henrik Kaare Nielsen is Professor of Aesthetics and Culture at Aarhus University, Denmark. He is an interdisciplinary researcher working in the field between the humanities and the social sciences. Author of 11 research monographs in Danish and numerous articles and chapters in academic journals and edited volumes, he is the editor of a number of academic books, including *The Democratic Public Sphere: Challenges and Prospects* (Aarhus University Press, 2016).

Routledge Innovations in Political Theory

For more information about this series, please visit: www.routledge.com/
Routledge-Innovations-in-Political-Theory/book-series/IPT

74 Democracy Beyond the Nation State
Practicing Equality
Joe Parker

75 Reclaiming Representation
Contemporary Advances in the Theory of Political Representation
Mónica Brito Vieira (ed.)

76 Dignity and Human Rights
Language Philosophy and Social Realizations
Stephan P. Leher

77 A Conceptual Investigation of Justice
Kyle Johannsen

78 Compromise and Disagreement in Contemporary Political Theory
Christian F. Rostbøll and Theresa Scavenius (eds)

79 Democratic Political Tragedy in the Postcolony
The Tragedy of Postcoloniality in Michael Manley's Jamaica and Nelson
Mandela's South Africa
Greg A. Graham

80 Epistemontology in Spinoza-Marx-Freud-Lacan
The (Bio)Power of Structure
A. Kiarina Kordela

81 Aesthetics and Political Culture in Modern Society
Henrik Kaare Nielsen

Aesthetics and Political Culture in Modern Society

Henrik Kaare Nielsen

NEW YORK AND LONDON

First published 2018
by Routledge
711 Third Avenue, New York, NY 10017

and by Routledge
2 Park Square, Milton Park, Abingdon, Oxon, OX14 4RN

Routledge is an imprint of the Taylor and Francis Group, an informa business

© 2018 Taylor and Francis

The right of Henrik Kaare Nielsen to be identified as author of this work
has been asserted by him in accordance with sections 77 and 78 of the
Copyright, Designs and Patents Act 1988.

All rights reserved. No part of this book may be reprinted or reproduced or
utilised in any form or by any electronic, mechanical, or other means, now
known or hereafter invented, including photocopying and recording, or in
any information storage or retrieval system, without permission in writing
from the publishers.

Trademark notice: Product or corporate names may be trademarks or
registered trademarks, and are used only for identification and explanation
without intent to infringe.

Library of Congress Cataloging-in-Publication Data
A catalog record for this title has been requested

ISBN: 978-0-8153-5642-4 (hbk)
ISBN: 978-1-351-12318-1 (ebk)

Typeset in Times New Roman
by Wearset Ltd, Boldon, Tyne and Wear

Contents

List of Figures		viii
Acknowledgements		ix
1	Introduction	1
2	Politics and Democracy	19
3	Public Space and Late Modern Forms of Public Practice	43
4	Political and Aesthetic Discursive Practice	74
5	Power-Oriented Aesthetic Interventions in Politics	92
6	Artistic Interventions in the Field of Political Practice	113
7	Current Developmental Perspectives of Public Discourse	133
	Index	141

Figures

1.1	Eugène Delacroix, *La Liberté guidant le peuple* (1830)	5
1.2	Rudolf Henneberg, *Die Jagd nach dem Glück* (1868)	6
1.3	Constantin Hansen, *Den grundlovsgivende Rigsforsamling* (1860–1864)	6
1.4	Hyacinthe Rigaud, *Portrait of Louis XIV* (1701)	9
1.5	Versailles	10
1.6	Hitler Speaks to the Reichstag on the Jewish Question, Berlin, 30 January 1939	11
1.7	NSDAP Reichsparteitag in Nürnberg, 8 September 1938	12
1.8	US President George W. Bush and Danish Prime Minister Anders Fogh Rasmussen at the End of a Joint Press Conference on 3 March 2008 at Bush's Ranch Near Crawford, Texas	13
5.1	Meeting in the European Council, 18–19 December 2014	94
5.2	Activists at International Women's Day, 8 March 2015 in Toronto	95
5.3	All Lives Matter Slogan on American Flag Background	96
5.4	Debate Podium	100
5.5	Twitter Website for Possible Republican Nominee Donald Trump, 5 May 2016	104
5.6	Former Labour Shadow Chancellor Ed Balls with Professional Partner in *Strictly Come Dancing*, 2016	107
6.1	John Heartfield, *Der Sinn des Hitlergrusses* (1932)	116
6.2	Adbusters, 'What Is Our One Demand?' (2011)	119

Acknowledgements

I am very grateful to Senior Editor Natalja Mortensen and Editorial Assistant Maria Landschoot at Routledge for their encouraging and competent guidance and support throughout the publication process. I also thank other team members at Routledge for their friendly and professional assistance.

Further, I warmly thank the friends and colleagues who have commented on parts of the manuscript, not least the staff of the interdisciplinary research centre *The Democratic Public Sphere – Current Challenges and Prospects* (2012–2016), which I had the pleasure of leading.

Special thanks to librarian Jette Bohn from Æstetikbiblioteket, Aarhus University Library, for her immense and competent help in providing the necessary materials.

Last, but not least, thanks a lot to my wife, Lotte Philipsen, for encouraging me to write the book and for backing me morally in the process.

This book is to some extent based on my Danish book *Æstetik og politisk offentlighed* of 2014. However, the present volume as a whole has been written and prepared thoroughly in order to constitute a new, coherent entity. The argument has been condensed in some parts and elaborated in others. Further, new empirical examples have been added, some specific Danish material has been replaced by international parallels, and some chapters have been rewritten entirely.

I am very grateful to Aarhus University Research Foundation for funding the clearing of permissions for copyrighted illustrations and the preparing of the indexing.

1 Introduction

Basic Themes and Overview

This book aims to revitalise the discussion on democracy and political culture and to point out the democratic challenges and the prospects of the present situation of Western democracies. The aim is to throw new light on the complexity and the importance of society's public interactions and specifically to analyse and estimate the potentials and risks for democracy represented by aesthetic interventions in the political public sphere.

It is a core principle of Western democracy that political decisions at any time should be able to be legitimised in relation to the ongoing public opinion formation that emerges from communicative struggles and dialogic exchange among free, autonomous citizens. And correspondingly, for the ordinary citizen, engagement in public debate on common concerns of society represents the legitimate way of influencing political decision-making. This principle holds a central position in modern political philosophy, and it has been implemented widely as the normative foundation of the institutions of democratic nation-states.

This core principle has been facing challenges in recent years that stem from a variety of changing conditions for the political process. Also in well-established democratic societies, the legitimacy of the political system appears to be unstable. Conditions of political practice in which wide-reaching decisions are presented as being 'without any alternative' and in which public political communication has been conquered by spin and strategic positioning, seem to discourage citizen participation. This disengagement and the accompanying erosion of institutional legitimacy occasionally result in anti-democratic, populist currents.

Extensive research in both the social sciences and the humanities has identified a variety of developmental tendencies that represent major changes in the conditions for establishing democratic legitimacy: the development of new media technologies is transforming the terms of social interaction both in everyday life and in the interrelationship between citizens and professional politicians; similarly, globalisation is transforming the political process: today, a multiplicity of economic, technological and politico-administrative relations transgress the boundaries of the nation-state; consequently, the associated

2   Introduction

decision-making is taking place beyond the classic, nationally defined public sphere, and a transnational public sphere able to match these developments has not yet been established; in this process, the nation-state's traditional, relatively homogeneous cultural frames of reference are being challenged by the increasing cultural complexity stemming from migration and transnational media contents.

As further democratic problems, research has pointed to unequal opportunities of participation on the basis of gender, class, and minority status; increased occurrence of non-democratic political movements; tendencies towards technocratisation of state policy-making and the growing importance of non-public forums of decision-making (governance networks, expert systems); the professionalisation of party politics and the simultaneous increased commercialisation of the media public and tendencies towards addressing the public as self-centred consumers rather than universally committed citizens; to the latter process belongs a slide in public exchange from reflective dialogue to attempting to obtain political power by way of fascinating the public and appealing to emotions. Under these conditions, so the predominant diagnosis, democratic legitimacy suffers, and civic engagement appears to be at risk.

The present analysis focuses on one of these contemporary tendencies that seem to challenge the dialogical nature of public interaction, namely, the tendency towards *aestheticisation*. The analysis investigates the relationship between political and aesthetic practice as it presently unfolds in public life in well-established Western democracies. To be sure, the focus of interest is neither aesthetics in the narrow art sense of the term nor the question of 'politicising art', but on the contrary, the role that *aesthetic practice* – in the broader sense of appeals to senses and emotions – plays in the democratic political process.

We have a long tradition of critical analysis of this issue: from Walter Benjamin via Theodor W. Adorno and Max Horkheimer, Jürgen Habermas, Zygmunt Bauman and Jean Baudrillard to Richard Sennett and Benjamin Barber – just to mention a few prominent examples. A common feature of these critical diagnoses of the general state of modern politics is that *form* increasingly tends to replace *substance*, that staging overshadows political content, that emotions are addressed instead of reason, and that citizens in this process are being reduced to a state of stupidity and degraded to consumers.

The present argument stands on the shoulders of this critical tradition, but theoretically and analytically it attempts to dig deeper, move beyond dichotomous thinking in either–or terms, and develop a more nuanced understanding of the contemporary interrelationship between political and aesthetic practice, including the risks as well as positive potentials and developmental possibilities that this relationship may presently entail. In other words, the unequivocal diagnoses of decay will be challenged – not in the form of denying problems, but by developing a theoretical and analytical approach that does not regard emotions and reason as mutually excluding entities.

The investigation will be based on analyses of selected, marked tendencies in contemporary political communication as they manifest themselves in the media's representation of politics, in political agents' own communicative

Introduction 3

approaches, in citizens' public participation in the media and in urban space, and in artistic interventions in politics. A central focal point will be whether a given aesthetic appeal contributes to undermining or to supporting the potential of reason in public debate and political practice – and to discuss on which premises the aesthetic appeal in question is liable to have either problematic or constructive effects on the debate.

If we initially, on the basis of common sense, understand politics as a question of organising societal power, and aesthetics as a question of form and expression, the matter appears quite uncontroversial: like any other kind of social practice, political power must necessarily assume a form, express itself, in order to become a societal reality. In other words, in this overall sense aesthetic designing is a condition of political practice in general, and the interesting question is therefore not whether we are dealing with an intentionally shaped expression (we always are), but, on the contrary, which specific forms are at stake, which weight and status the concrete practice ascribes to expression in proportion to political content, which type of dialogue the recipient of a political approach is invited to engage in, which socio-cultural and historical experiences are forming the context, and which implications the given staging of political practice may have in the context in question.

In the following chapters, a theoretical frame of reference will be outlined for the analysis of contemporary developmental tendencies in the interrelationship between political and aesthetic practice. This Introduction gives an overview of what will follow. After that, some basic themes of the book will briefly be elaborated in a historical perspective. Significant historical examples of traditions and developments in the aesthetic staging of political power – both in artworks and in the self-presentation of power holders – will serve as illustrations of the complex ways in which aesthetic forms are interwoven with and play a role in their specific historical contexts. Finally, the basic theoretical and methodological frame of reference of the book will be outlined.

Chapter 2, 'Politics and Democracy', proposes a conceptual framework for understanding the democratic political process that integrates the perspectives of conflict and consensus, leading to a complex conceptualisation of political culture. Further, the tradition of deliberative democracy is characterised as a congenial position, and in a critical discussion of previous debates on the public sphere, an alternative conceptual distinction between *public discourse* (in various modalities) and *public space* is suggested. Finally, late modern identity work is analysed as a complex resource for public interaction and politicisation.

Chapter 3, 'Public Space and Late Modern Forms of Public Practice', takes its point of departure in an understanding of *public space* as an open arena in which a variety of conflictual interactions continuously take place, and it suggests an overall distinction between the different types of publics that engage in these interactions. The chapter further characterises basic contemporary conditions of practice in public space such as neoliberal technocratisation and an overall process of aestheticisation, and it outlines specific conditions of physical, medial and virtual spaces of practice, including social media.

4   *Introduction*

Chapter 4, 'Political and Aesthetic Discursive Practice', integrates elements of Immanuel Kant's aesthetics and the work of a number of contemporary aesthetic theorists and suggests basic definitions of aesthetic discourse and aesthetic experience. Further, conceptualising modern society as a discursively differentiated entity characterised by conflictual interplay of discourses, it theoretically elaborates differences and compatibilities between aesthetic and political discourse. It introduces the concept *political judgement* as a composed entity and discusses the potentials and limitations of aesthetic experience in relation to the democratic political process.

Chapter 5, 'Power-Oriented Aesthetic Interventions in Politics', analyses, on the basis of the developed theoretical framework, a variety of examples of aesthetic interventions in politics with a special focus on the type of public termed 'the public of parliament-oriented mass media'. The analysis distinguishes between interventions at the concrete artefact level and atmospheric interventions concerning the creation of general moods. Finally, the chapter discusses the possible consequences of this type of aestheticisation in regard to democratic political culture.

Chapter 6, then, is entitled 'Artistic Interventions in the Field of Political Practice'. Whereas the types of aesthetic interventions in politics that are analysed in Chapter 5 are power-oriented by nature, this chapter deals with interventions that do not relate directly to concrete conflicts and power issues, but intervene in the established formations of meaning in more subtle, artistic ways. A variety of contemporary examples are analysed – again with a distinction between an artefact level and an atmospheric level. The examples have been selected on the basis of their respective potentials for generating critical public discourse by way of indeterminate aesthetic intervention in political issues. The examples do not claim to exhaust the field of such interventions, but they cover a broad variety of genres and types of approaches, and each of them has by way of its specific aesthetic characteristics gained considerable public attention and provoked debate.

Chapter 7, 'Current Developmental Perspectives of Public Discourse', concludes the analyses and discusses the situation of contemporary Western democracy in regard to civic engagement, the scope for public discourse, and the prospects of political culture. Based on the analyses of the previous chapters, it is argued that reflectively processed sensuous-emotional engagement is the foundation of the political in a genuinely democratic sense of the term – and that non-power-oriented, artistic interventions in political practice hold a significant potential to initiate this reflective processing.

Artistic Representation of Political Power

The following two sections will very briefly characterise some significant continuities and changes in the interrelationship between aesthetic and political practice in the West over the past two centuries.

One traditional type of aesthetic staging of political matters occurs in *artworks'* reflection and processing of contemporary issues. The following three examples (Figures 1.1–1.3) were all created in the 1800s and represent significant artistic interpretations of the period's broad democratic rising in Europe, but the respective national contexts of experience are reflected in the shape of quite different aesthetic adaptations of the issue of political power.

Eugène Delacroix painted *La Liberté guidant le peuple* [Liberty leading the people] in 1830 (Figure 1.1), inspired by the July revolution in Paris the same year. The painting depicts a battle scene in which the revolutionary forces are moving forward towards victory, led by an idealised female figure with the banner of the revolution, the Tricolore, in one hand, and a rifle, in the other. We are dealing with the Marianne figure that symbolises the victory of the republic over absolutism and thereby incarnates the modern French nation. Marianne represents liberty and reason – and simultaneously holds an element of object of desire as implied in her uncovered bosom.

This specific staging of a power-political showdown interprets and gives form to the French historical experience that a popular revolutionary rising can succeed and lead to crucial changes in the constellation of power and the political conditions. However, repercussions may occur with which one has to wrestle, but the politico-cultural sounding board has an optimistic tone: if the

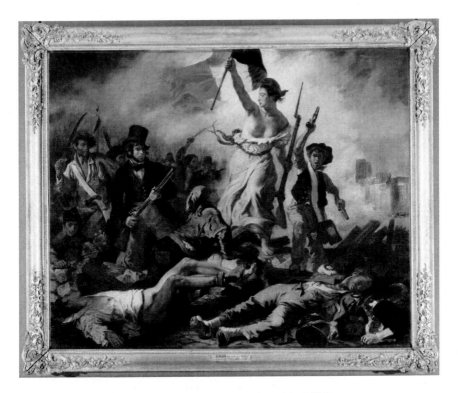

Figure 1.1 Eugène Delacroix, *La Liberté guidant le peuple* (1830).
Source: © RMN-Grand Palais (Musée du Louvre)/Hervé Lewandowski.

Figure 1.2 Rudolf Henneberg, *Die Jagd nach dem Glück* (1868).
Source: bpk/Nationalgalerie, SMB/Klaus Göken.

Figure 1.3 Constantin Hansen, *Den grundlovsgivende Rigsforsamling* (1860–1864).
Source: Det Nationalhistoriske Museum på Frederiksborg Slot. Photo: Ole Haupt.

Introduction 7

people let liberty and reason lead the way, the democratic struggle will prevail. It is further a significant feature of the painting's depiction of the revolution that the agent is a fighting *collective*, and that the symbolic Marianne figure is not presented as an abstract vision but as an active part of this collective.

A quite different staging of the issue of power is presented in *Die Jagd nach dem Glück* [In pursuit of happiness] of 1868 by the German painter, Rudolf Henneberg (Figure 1.2). This work does not hold the same canonised status as Delacroix's painting, but it illustratively addresses basic patterns in the understanding of politics and power that were representative in a German context in the nineteenth century.

Here, the collective struggle for liberty is replaced by an individualised and internalised striving for happiness. Further, happiness is depicted as an unattainable, spiritualised female figure whose appeal holds promises of both power, wealth and sensuous joy, but who deceitfully seduces the wishful lover into crossing the edge of an abyss in his grasp for the objects of his desires (the crown of power, gold coins, and the inviting, uncovered female body). On this ride towards the abyss, he is further driven forward by Death who breathes down his neck, swinging the red banner of revolution, while a potential worldly happiness in the shape of the prone woman is trampled down in the hectic, headlong attempt to realise a fantasy vision of happiness. In the portrayal of this endeavour, the striving for individual happiness and the ideal of political liberty are fused and presented as illusory and doomed aspirations. The only thing that appears to have authority and to stand on solid ground, in this scene, is the feudal lord's castle in the background.

The painting is an exponent of a predominant tendency in the politico-cultural tradition in Germany. In contrast to France, the German proponents of political liberty and reason never achieved sufficient strength and support among the population to make them able to seriously challenge absolutism and the privileges of aristocracy – and when it actually did come to open rebellion, for example, in 1848, the democratic movement was bloodily crushed by the armies of the monarchs. In other words, German history from the Enlightenment and until the democratic revolution in 1918 was first and foremost characterised by the experience of *obstructed liberation.*

Since a political realisation of the desire for liberty held by the bourgeoisie, the artists, and the intellectuals was associated with mortal danger, this desire was sublimated into aesthetic forms. The vision of liberty was maintained, but in mythical, spiritualised shapes whereby it was depoliticised, thus avoiding confrontation with the prosaic reality of non-liberty. Genuine liberty and true humanity were to be realised in the shape of an individual formative process (*Bildung*, cf. Chapter 4) in a special, lofty sphere, a power-protected inwardness ('machtgeschützte Innerlichkeit', according to Thomas Mann) which was to be sought beyond the wicked game of power and interests. Henneberg's aesthetic staging of the pursuit of happiness as tragic and self-destructive builds on this sublimated vision of an authentic, harmonious spiritual freedom that is totally undefiled by the conflicts of the material world. Against this backdrop, by

8 *Introduction*

reaching out for power, wealth, political liberty, and sensuous pleasure, the individual sells his soul to the material world and thereby embarks on a ride to death.

In contrast, it is neither grandiose heroism nor mythical tragedy that characterises the aesthetic staging of the political struggle leading to democracy in Denmark. The best-known and most representative artistic treatment of this process is Constantin Hansen's depiction of the Danish Constitutional Convention, portraying the assembly that worked out the Constitution of June 1849 (Figure 1.3). The painting merely presents itself as a sober documentation of a solemn event in Danish history.

That this epochal shift in the organisation of political power has not been reflected in the shape of a more dramatic artistic expression, is due to the fact that the conflict experiences, to which the democratic struggle in Denmark gave rise, were of a quite different nature than in the French and German cases. The background was not least the specific development of societal power relations, initiated by the abolition of serfdom in 1788 and the subsequent establishment of a major class of freeholding peasants, who during the first half of the 1800s achieved considerable wealth and eventually were able to contest the position of aristocracy as the economically leading class. Due to the peasants' control of approximately half of the economy, the demands for influence and democratic reforms that they were making in alliance with the liberal bourgeoisie of the capital, had a weight that the monarch could not ignore. Therefore, the transition to the early version of democratic rule happened peacefully and relatively unspectacularly in the shape of the King's acceptance of the abolition of absolutism and the formation of an assembly to work out a Constitution.

In the Danish context, the idea of political liberty is therefore not endowed with connotations of revolution and the associated pompous heroism or tragedy, in the same way as in France and Germany. The Danish conflict experience affirms a reform-oriented engagement in that it demonstrates that when humble people stick together, they are able to peacefully achieve major changes. In this perspective, political liberty is not about soaring ideals but about creating practical institutional opportunities for influence, and correspondingly, reason is not ascribed the status of an absolute, abstract entity, but on the contrary, is considered a concrete, pragmatic mode of creating balanced compromises that distribute resources and opportunities as equally as possible.

The Aesthetic Self-Presentation of Power

In contrast to the French and German examples, Constantin Hansen's work was commissioned and therefore, in reality, it represents the middle ground between the autonomous artistic reflection of contemporary societal issues and the type of aesthetic staging that we can term the *aesthetic self-presentation of power*. In the latter category that we shall concentrate on in the following, we are dealing with the forms of representative public appearance in a broad sense that are chosen by the holders of political power themselves. Having to stage oneself as a power figure is a general condition for political leaders in any society of a certain magnitude and complexity, but as indicated by the examples below, quite different, context-specific principles of self-presentation of power characterise the history of modern society.

Absolutism's separation of power from the immediate relations of social life and its concentration of the societally legitimate execution of power in the hands of the monarch and the associated state apparatus were the foundation of the issue of political power on modern terms. In the era of absolutism, however, the struggle over political influence was confined to the court where noblemen competed with each other for the favour of the monarch. The King's power was considered God's gift, and therefore absolute, which clearly marks the aesthetic self-presentation. As illustrated by Hyacinthe Rigaud's portrait of the French Sun King, Louis XIV, of 1701 (Figure 1.4), power displays itself monologically in all its wealth and might. The aesthetic staging cements the King's status as indisputable and self-sufficient incarnation of power whom the spectator is not kindly requested to recognise, on the contrary, he/she is commanded to unconditionally submit to the authority of the King. The King does not need the people – they need him.

Figure 1.4 Hyacinthe Rigaud, *Portrait of Louis XIV* (1701).

Source: photo © RMN-Grand Palais (Musée du Louvre)/Stéphane Maréchalle.

Correspondingly, the architectonic achievements of the absolutist kings, for instance, the chateau of Versailles of that same Louis, are first and foremost aesthetic demonstrations of power: the grandiose gesture that this huge and extravagant reshaping intervention in physical space represents, exposes a power that in its self-conception is omnipotent and self-reliant. The chateau and the park are monological articulations of this power (Figure 1.5): the immense proportions are being displayed – again, not angling for recognition, but in order to inspire with awe. The subjects are mercifully allowed to use and admire the park, but this is an incidental circumstance, not the intended purpose of the park.

With regard to the aesthetic staging of power, modern totalitarianism and absolutism share certain features. In both contexts, the citizen is not invited to engage in a critical dialogue, but on the contrary is ordered to submit to power. In the examples in Figures 1.6 and 1.7, power appears partly as the spectacular organisation of crowds of people in a physical space of enormous proportions, partly as a stylised representation of the dictator – to be sure, not the private individual, Adolf Hitler, but the monumental figure of power, the Führer (Figure 1.6).

But whereas the absolutist King staged himself self-sufficiently, in full assurance not only of *possessing* power but also of *being* power – cf. Louis XIV's *bon mot* 'L'état, c'est moi!' – the power holders of totalitarianism are deeply dependent on the recognition and confirmation of their status by the population.

Figure 1.5 Versailles.
Source: photo: Wikimedia Commons (CC BY-SA 3.0).

Figure 1.6 Hitler Speaks to the Reichstag on the Jewish Question, Berlin, 30 January 1939.

Source: Shutterstock.

12   *Introduction*

Figure 1.7 NSDAP Reichsparteitag in Nürnberg, 8 September 1938.
Source: Shutterstock.

Thus, the little men in the foreground of the photo of the NSDAP's Reichsparteitag in Nürnberg in 1938 (Figure 1.7) only gain significance due to their postulated unity with the immense, uniformed crowd that has drawn up in ranks in front of them – and that also only derives its meaning from the aesthetic forming of the staging.

Soviet totalitarianism was staged similarly in the shape of thoroughly organised processions, military parades, and stylised representations of the leaders as monumental incarnations of an asserted unity, strength and common will of the people. The recipients of this propaganda are not invited to express themselves as citizens, but the staged, insisting reference to the interests and the common will of the people is crucial to the maintenance of the totalitarian rule's narrative of its own legitimacy and grandeur.

The monumentalising staging of power figures also occurs in modern democracies, but first of all as one communicative element among others in election campaigns and in government leaders' demonstration of will and resolution in situations of critical conflict. In less tense situations, politicians' general staging of themselves in the present time is rather characterised by a strong *personalised* appeal that serves to warrant the fact that they represent the democratic will of the citizens. As we shall elaborate further in the following chapters, it is crucial for politicians in late modern democracies to present themselves with personal integrity and credibility – as a person who demonstrates both matter-of-fact competence, drive, determination, and a heart in the right place; a person who as a whole appears sympathetic and thereby trustworthy in the eyes of his/her voters. Today, the main tendency seems to be that a politician is expected to master the role of power figure competently and with authority and at the same time be 'one of us', an equal to whom common citizens can feel personally attracted.

In the present historical context, it may apparently even be considered relevant by both politicians and the media to stage a working meeting between the leaders of two allied powers at war as an intimate gathering of bosom friends (Figure 1.8). As key co-designers of public communication, the mass media have played a crucial role in establishing this personalised relationship between

Figure 1.8 US President George W. Bush and Danish Prime Minister Anders Fogh Rasmussen at the End of a Joint Press Conference on 3 March 2008 at Bush's Ranch Near Crawford, Texas.

Source: photo credit: /ritzau/AP.

14   *Introduction*

politicians and citizens, where the appeal increasingly aims to fascinate and please the senses and emotions of the recipient rather than to involve him/her in a dialogue on substance.

But also in social media, where politicians in principle have the opportunity of communicating directly with citizens on political content – without interference from journalists, editors, and competing media industries – this depoliticising tendency continues and even accelerates: the success of a politician is increasingly measured according to his/her number of 'friends' on social media platforms. A private type of relationship has taken over and marginalised the relationship of publicly interacting citizens.

This tendency towards personalisation/privatisation and other significant characteristics of present design of politics and power will be investigated further in the following chapters. The main thesis is that aesthetic interventions in the political process do not by definition undermine politics' content of reason. Instead, a differentiation must be made between a multiplicity of aesthetic forms of intervention – some of which tend to weaken the political judgement of citizens while other forms tend to stimulate competent judgement. The thesis is developed in critical discussion with classic and contemporary theoretical positions, and it is investigated in analyses of selected examples of political communication in mass media and social media, in political agents' own public approaches, in forms of public participation by citizens and social movements, and in artistic interventions in the political public sphere.

Theory and Method

The following argument is first of all theory-based. The central research question concerns the implications which an increasing tendency towards personalised, emotionally appealing aesthetic staging of politics may have for society's democratic political culture. This question calls for qualitative rather than quantitative methods, since 'democratic political culture' is not an empirically observable, clearly delimited entity. It can only be addressed and projected by way of a theoretical-analytical discourse that in terms of empirical material draws on a multiplicity of symptoms and indications of tendencies. Correspondingly, the interrelationship between aesthetic staging and democratic political culture cannot meaningfully be analysed using quantitative, standardised methods, but has to be addressed in the shape of qualitative analyses of tendencies on the basis of a plurality of context-specific types of material. In the following, this will be considered a basic methodological condition of this type of research question, and this means that we will not be dealing with analyses that are based on a homogeneous, formalised method oriented towards a classic empiricist ideal of truth, but, on the contrary, with a complex searching process that is, first of all, theory-based and necessarily holds an element of speculation qualified by the history of academic knowledge in the field. Possible answers established this way can at best (and hopefully) claim to be *plausible*.[1] The estimation of plausibility, evidently, will depend on the knowledgeable academic public.

Introduction   15

On the basis of a critical processing of existing theories and analyses in the field, the following argument will develop an elaborate theoretical frame of reference for the understanding of the interrelationship between political and aesthetic practice in late modernity. Where it is considered relevant, results of existing empirical analyses (both qualitative and quantitative) will be integrated in this theoretical discourse.

By way of concrete examples, predominant patterns in contemporary political communication will be described and analysed with special regard to possible effects on the formation of society's political culture. The empirical material has been selected according to the principle that the examples cover a variety of prominent tendencies in the public self-presentation of politicians, in the communication of politics by the media, and in artistic interventions in the political field of practice. But the examples do not claim to be exhaustive nor representative in a quantitative sense.

Methodologically, the analyses build on *reception aesthetics* which means that they deal with the empirical examples as *proposals for reception*, i.e. the analyses address the nature of the *invitation* to experience and meaning formation that, for example, a piece of election propaganda or a political TV show offers the receiver. In other words, this type of analysis does not include the actual reception of the examples by concrete recipients, but is based on the thesis that communicative approaches are endowed with an implicit model of reception, according to which the empirical process of reception is orientated.[2] The present argument regards analysis informed by reception aesthetics as crucial for understanding aesthetic communication, but at the same time recognises as an important point that the empirical process of reception is complex and idiosyncratic by nature and that we therefore cannot, on the basis of an analysis of the implicit reception model, draw generalising conclusions as to how all empirical recipients would actually understand the aesthetic approach in question. We shall return to this issue later.

Theoretically, the present argument derives its basic inspiration from German critical theory (especially the second generation of theorists: Jürgen Habermas, Oskar Negt, Alexander Kluge, among others) and attempts to develop this inspiration further towards a still more nuanced understanding of late modern culture and society. With this point of departure, the book develops a novel theoretical perspective on public discourse and the constitution of the political, including an analytical approach that nuances the distinction between reason and emotion, rather than regarding them as mutually excluding entities. The aim is to develop a more differentiated and operational conceptual and analytical understanding of the interrelationship between aesthetic and political practice than previous attempts have accomplished.

The book critically reflects and combines theoretical positions that generally operate separately (cultural theory, aesthetic theory, and political science). The aim is to extract the respective rational cores of these theoretical positions and combine them in order to inspire each field to engage in new critical and cross-disciplinary analyses. As pointed out above, there is a long tradition of addressing

16   *Introduction*

the interrelationship between political and aesthetic practice, but the positions tend to either insist on politics as a matter of pure reason, thus viewing aesthetic interventions as basically problematic; or to grant aesthetic discourse a monopoly on constituting meaning and motivation for acting, thus marginalising human reason as a relevant factor.

The first position was clearly stated by the early work of Jürgen Habermas.[3] The latter position comes in a variety of forms ranging from the immediate revolutionary potentials that Herbert Marcuse ascribes to art[4] to the, in some respects related, analysis by Jacques Rancière,[5] in which true political practice concerns the struggle to change the aesthetic conditions of what we perceive, i.e. changing 'the distribution of the sensible'. Vitalistic theorists such as Michael Hardt and Antonio Negri,[6] took this aestheticising line of thinking to extremes when they found the revolutionary political potential of the so-called *multitude* on notions of 'spontaneous creative energies', 'bio-power', and 'joy of life'.

But also a number of more nuanced sociological analyses of late modern society tend to totalise the position of aesthetic discourse by way of reducing meaning formation and motivation for acting to questions of *taste.* For example, in the work of Pierre Bourdieu,[7] in which class-specific, habitually rooted preferences of taste organise the orientation and positioning of individuals in the social space of meaning, and determine their lines of action. Similarly, in Gerhard Schulze's analysis,[8] the aesthetic orientation has, due to general wealth, advanced to an overriding societal condition, thus submitting the collective space of meaning to a 'psycho-physical semantics' and the accompanying striving for 'positively charged psycho-physical states of emotion'. Michel Maffesoli's analysis of late modern community formation as a new, aestheticised version of a tribal society[9] is likewise an exponent of this tendency towards generalising aesthetic discourse as the basic principle of social behaviour and meaning formation.

In contrast to these predominant positions, this book regards the *interplay* between rational and sensuous-emotional capacities of individuals as the basic generator of meaning and motivation for acting, including the formation of political engagement. In this perspective, the crucial question in relation to political practice and political culture concerns the nature of this interplay in the concrete case in question, i.e. whether the balance between aesthetic and political discourse contributes to stimulating judgement on political terms, or whether the balance tips and marginalises political reason.

This point of departure has evident consequences with regard to terminology and basic assumptions. In contrast to the post-structuralist tradition that denies the experiencing human subject relevance as a factor in understanding cultural and societal processes, the following argument regards the human subject as a crucial factor. However, the subject cannot reasonably be understood in accordance with the classic idealist tradition as an autonomous self-relying entity pregnant with Olympic insight. The post-structuralist tradition is right in its critique of this classic conceptualisation of the subject, but in post-structuralist theory this productive point ends up in a general dismissal of the subject.

Introduction 17

The notion of the human subject as a singular, autonomous entity originated as an early-modern philosophical anticipation of the social and cultural unbinding of the individual and as a radical interpretation of the perspectives associated with this process by classic idealism. Evidently, this conceptualisation of the subject represents a specific historical construction to which no universal status can be ascribed. But less will do: in spite of being a construction, the subject remains a very well-established *reality* in the relations of modern society both juridically, socially, culturally and psychologically, and it therefore makes no sense for a contemporary analysis of culture and society to disregard the subject as a factor.

However, such an analytical endeavour is confronted with the task of secularising the concept of the subject, i.e. of dismantling the aspirations of omnipotence with which idealist philosophy of history had equipped the subject. In this secularised sense, human subjects are neither autonomous nor singular entities nor do they possess any privileged access to a sublime truth. Instead, they should be regarded as in many respects contradictory agents, whose multiplicity of choices and actions continuously creates, recreates, and changes social and cultural practice. These choices are not made on the basis of any overall view of societal totality but from the perspective of individual or group-specific everyday life experience: on the basis of a complex, situated balancing of relationships and affective dynamics in the immediate social interaction, considerations of the common good, special interests, private preferences and desires, unconscious wishes – and with a broad variety of life-historical experiences as horizon.

As Anthony Giddens has put it in his interpretation of Karl Marx, we act as social agents on existing conditions that we have not chosen ourselves and which we are by far not always able to assess, and on these premises, our actions often have unintended consequences.[10] Nevertheless, social agents can be considered knowledgeable, self-reflective subjects who have their more or less qualified reasons for choosing and acting as they do – and in doing so, they continuously contribute to creating, recreating and transforming their mutual life context. In this perspective, the concepts 'empowerment' and 'emancipation' refer to gradual processes in specific social contexts in which the actions and experiences of concrete agents dialectically form the individual and collective conditions of possibility, and do not refer to the notion of once and for all releasing the universal properties of an autonomous subject.

In accordance with this understanding of the subject, the term *discourse* is used as an implication of the actions of human subjects. In other words, discourses are defined as coherent patterns of thinking, speaking and acting that are constantly being produced, reproduced, and transformed as dialectic conditions of human social practice.

18 *Introduction*

Notes

1 Henrik Kaare Nielsen, 'Kritisk teori', in Svend Brinkmann and Lene Tanggaard (eds), *Kvalitative metoder* (Copenhagen: Hans Reitzels Forlag, 2010).
2 Reception aesthetics was developed by the Konstanzer Schule (Hans Robert Jauß, Wolfgang Iser, *et al.*).
3 Jürgen Habermas, *Strukturwandel der Öffentlichkeit* (Neuwied: Luchterhand, 1962) (English translation: *The Structural Transformation of the Public Sphere*, Cambridge: Polity, 1989).
4 Herbert Marcuse, *The Aesthetic Dimension* (München: Carl Hanser Verlag, 1977).
5 Jacques Rancière, *The Politics of Aesthetics* (London: Continuum, 2004).
6 Michael Hardt and Antonio Negri, *Empire* (Cambridge, MA: Harvard University Press, 2000).
7 Pierre Bourdieu, *Distinction* (London: Routledge and Kegan Paul, 1984).
8 Gerhard Schulze, *Die Erlebnisgesellschaft* (Frankfurt am Main: Campus, 1992).
9 Michel Maffesoli, *The Time of the Tribes* (London: Sage, 1995).
10 Anthony Giddens, *The Constitution of Society* (Oakland, CA: University of California Press, 1986); Karl Marx, 'Der achtzehnte Brumaire des Louis Bonaparte', in *Marx und Engels Werke*, vol. 8 (Berlin: Dietz Verlag, 1960 [1852]).

References

Bourdieu, Pierre (1984) *Distinction*, London: Routledge and Kegan Paul.
Giddens, Anthony (1986) *The Constitution of Society*, Oakland, CA: University of California Press.
Habermas, Jürgen (1962) *Strukturwandel der Öffentlichkeit*, Neuwied: Luchterhand (English translation: *The Structural Transformation of the Public Sphere*, Cambridge: Polity, 1989).
Hardt, Michael and Antonio Negri (2000) *Empire*, Cambridge, MA: Harvard University Press.
Maffesoli, Michel (1995) *The Time of the Tribes*, London: Sage.
Marcuse, Herbert (1977) *The Aesthetic Dimension*, München: Carl Hanser Verlag.
Marx, Karl (1960 [1852]) 'Der achtzehnte Brumaire des Louis Bonaparte', in *Marx und Engels Werke*, vol. 8, Berlin: Dietz Verlag.
Nielsen, Henrik Kaare (2010) 'Kritisk teori', in Svend Brinkmann and Lene Tanggaard (eds) *Kvalitative metoder*, Copenhagen: Hans Reitzels Forlag.
Rancière, Jacques (2004) *The Politics of Aesthetics*, London: Continuum.
Schulze, Gerhard (1992) *Die Erlebnisgesellschaft*, Frankfurt am Main: Campus.

2   Politics and Democracy

In critical dialogue with prominent positions in the field, this chapter develops a theoretical frame of reflection that proposes an integrated understanding of the democratic political process, including an elaborate conceptualisation of political culture, the characteristics of public discourse, and the political potentials and risks of late modern identity work.

The Democratic Political Process

One classic definition of politics was delivered by Max Weber in 'Politik als Beruf' of 1919.[1] Weber conceptualised politics as a distinct societal area with an associated professional role and a specific form of practice whose primary rationale is the striving for power and influencing the distribution of resources in society. In other words, politics is understood as a separate field of action in which professional agents' participation in the political process is analysed in terms of conflict theory as a constant struggle to optimise one's own position of power.

Another classic definition is represented by structural functionalism. Talcott Parsons defined politics as an institutionalised sub-system that performs decision-making as a specific partial function within society as a whole.[2] Parsons, in other words, views politics from a perspective of consensual totality, as a system that rises above the level of contending agents and makes its specific contribution to the coherence and functioning of society at large.

Undisputedly, both definitions point to important characteristics of politics, but at the same time they both appear to be one-dimensional and unable to conceptualise the complexity of the political process in late modern democratic societies. One of their mutual limitations is that politics is analysed as a merely institutional entity.

The renewed discussion of the relationship between 'politics' and 'the political' can contribute to nuancing the picture.[3] These terms are not consistently defined in different positions in the debate, but the common point of departure is an analysis of the political process that basically differentiates between, on the one hand, institutionalised power and administration of institutional political decisions (mostly called 'politics') and, on the other, conflicts and politicised

20   *Politics and Democracy*

issues of everyday life, and non-institutional political practice (mostly called 'the political').

The concept 'the political' adds a dimension to the understanding of the political process that was absent in the analyses of Weber and Parsons. Also in the conceptualisation of this non-institutional dimension, however, the debate splits into conflict-oriented and consensus-oriented positions. For instance, Ernesto Laclau and Chantal Mouffe, in the tradition of Carl Schmitt,[4] define the political as conflictual in the sense of the antagonistic friend-foe dichotomy, i.e. as characterised by struggles that are fought without any common normative framework.[5] In this interpretation, the political contains no element of community, but only particularised discursive positions, each struggling for its own agenda.

Opposing this is a line of tradition that includes, among others, Hannah Arendt[6] and Oskar Negt and Alexander Kluge.[7] A common denominator of these theorists is their understanding of the political as associated with an obligation to reflect the common good of society. In this sense, an utterance of will only qualifies as political if it relates to the general public and legitimises itself accordingly. Thus, the political represents a reflective interconnection between, on the one hand, issues, emotions, and interests from the local contexts of everyday life and, on the other, the conception of an overall societal community. In this definition, 'the political' forms the condition of possibility of joint action on a sociopolitical scale and, at the same time, represents a normative standard for the forms that 'politics' can legitimately assume.

The latter understanding of the political further points beyond the predominant tendency of the tradition of political theory to polarise the perspectives of conflict and consensus. The present analysis joins this endeavour and suggests a conceptual framework that explicitly addresses conflict and consensus as not mutually exclusive but, on the contrary, as always present dimensions of the political process. The following line of thinking serves as a point of departure that will subsequently be elaborated: on the one hand, a strong argument can be made – as in the traditions of Weber and Schmitt – that societal relations are conflictual by nature and that obtaining power is the central rationale in the struggle of political agents in both the institutional and the everyday life dimensions. In this perspective, political struggle is guided by a discourse of power, and the basic motivation for action is the ambition of each agent to determine the order of society on his/her own ideological premises, including the distribution of material resources and life opportunities, as well as the nature of the overall horizon of cultural meaning and interpretation.

On the other hand, in both a functionalistic and a normative sense, the reflection of society as a whole likewise holds a rational core. It remains a basic fact of political practice in democratic societies that no single agent is able to monopolise power, that compromises have to be made, that institutions must be established and that all agents have to recognise both differences/diversity and the existence of common concerns, common problems that need to be solved, and generally obligating principles of legitimacy. In order to face reality, a political discourse must, in other words, also be able to reflect its own particularistic projects of order in the universalistic perspective of the common good.

To be sure, for quite a number of years, predominant currents in the academic debate of the humanities have regarded the notion of universalism as highly problematic. The universal perspective of reflection has generally been viewed as intrinsically associated with a totalising philosophy of history, conceptualising the historical process as a teleologically defined, monocultural entity driven forward by transcendental necessities – and, consequently, any thinking in universal terms has per se come under suspicion of representing a totalitarian threat to cultural diversity and to humanity at large.

Considering the multiplicity of latent chauvinisms and manifest historical disasters that have been legitimised with reference to a proclaimed perspective of universalism (colonialism, racism, sexism, homophobia, etc.), this critical assessment evidently has a point. However, this generalising identification of universalism with a totalitarian, teleological approach narrows the scope of reflection in an unsatisfactory manner and thus marginalises positive potentials in the perspective of universalism which should rather be regarded as valuable and crucial resources for the development of an inclusive democracy based on the recognition of diversity. The present argument therefore suggests that we view the chauvinisms and historical disasters of universalism as concrete, specific processes, first of all, contextualised and propelled by special interests and specific constellations of power, not as necessary implications of universal thinking as such.

In other words, as opposed to the perspective of a totalising philosophy of history and the accompanying monocultural teleology, the attempt will be made to reflect universalism in a perspective of social action and experience formation, in which universalism is viewed as a *potential*, always contextually conditioned quality of the historical process of experience. Hence, the diversity of local, national, and global political communities of practice offers a variety of conditions of action and formation of experience with correspondingly different terms for the emergence and unfolding of a universal perspective of reflection. Universalism and particularism should not be regarded as abstract ideals that we can choose to affirm or reject, but as immanent dynamics in late modern social practice, and the crucial question is how society deals with this conflictual condition.

Further, 'the common good' should not be understood as a substantial, unequivocally defined entity but as *a discursive framework for practice*, an overriding, universal horizon of reflection to which the contending positions in public debate are committed and which they take into account in their struggle to influence the development of society. This horizon of reflection presupposes the recognition of the existence of common concerns of society – as this was also implied in the above conceptualisation of 'the political'.

A satisfactory conceptual framework, in other words, has to reflect the necessary interplay between the conflictual and the consensual aspects of the political process. For this purpose, I introduce a model that I have presented earlier in

22 *Politics and Democracy*

greater detail, concerning the basic relations of the political process of modern, democratic societies:[8]

A: (social and cultural conflicts ↔ power relations) → compromise

↕

B: collective historical experience → consensual ethics/political culture

The model conceptualises the political process (including the dimensions of both politics and the political) as an integrated interplay between two levels. On the one hand, a level of conflict (A), characterised by non-violent struggles of interests being settled in the form of always temporary compromises, and mediated by the current relationship of power between the contending parties. 'Power relations' is to be understood as a complex category comprising not only the question of a majority position in parliament but also the backing of a political position in broader, more or less organised extra-parliamentary forums and interest groups, and its legitimacy in general public opinion formation. At any time, the dynamic interaction between these circumstances constitutes the political power relations, and shifts in the power relations have immediate consequences for the nature and content of compromises (be it in the shape of legislation or other kinds of formalised agreements).

On the other hand, a level of consensus (B). This level should not be understood as a guarantor that universal agreement can in reality be established on the substance of any given debate. The term consensus, in other words, does not suggest that difference and conflict disappear. Instead, it refers to an underlying dimension of political interaction which continuously processes and condenses the ongoing, collective formation of experiences of conflict from level A to a consensual ethical framework. This framework is not up for discussion in the concrete political disputes, but serves as the evident, common standard of social interaction in accordance with which the ongoing struggles of interests and the formation of compromises must at any time be able to legitimise themselves.

In other words, this 'tacit' ethical consensus is shaped in society's processing and adaptation of the experiences of conflict that it historically gains in internal struggles between different classes, interest groups, and social movements, as well as in external conflicts with other nation-states. These experiences are inscribed as memory traces in the citizens' bodies and minds, in the cultural forms of interaction, and are reflected in the shape of institutions and collective narratives. The level of ethical consensus dialectically functions as a civilising, normative sounding-board under society's handling of conflicts and thus constitutes the core of the democratic political culture which is continuously being created, recreated, and transformed as part of the broader societal formation of experience. The developmental rhythm of this consensus, however, is slower than that of the conflicts and the formation of compromises on level A.

Public debate is the central forum for discursive struggles but at the same time the main vehicle for society's collective processing of experience and self-reflection (signified by the vertical double-headed arrow of the model). In all its complexity, public debate therefore functions as the main mediating factor between the level of conflict and the level of consensus. Public debate expresses, interprets, and processes collective experiences of conflict into suggestions of coherent meaning that condense the experiences and integrate them with the previous experience-based common sense of the political collective in question – either affirming, modifying, or transforming it. Hereafter, the result of this processing forms the new consensual frame of political practice – and so on.

The normativity of this understanding of the political process is, in other words, *immanent* by nature, based on historical experience. In this sense, when an ethic of universalism, democracy, and human rights is at the centre of the political culture of a given nation-state, it is not due to a transcendental morality but to historical courses of conflicts and associated processes of experience in which the societal forces that have fought for universally oriented reforms have gained the necessary position of power in order to realise and institutionalise them in the formation of compromises. Conversely, an established universalistic political culture can be rolled back, if particularistic currents gain power and submit society to chauvinistic and excluding experiences of conflict.

Although political culture constitutes an obligating normative orientation for society as a whole, it will always represent a *hegemonic* interpretation of the societal experiences of conflict and tend to play down or even marginalise social interests and issues that have not been able to manifest themselves in a sufficient position of strength in order to influence the formation of compromises. Correspondingly, social and political struggles leading to shifts in power relations also pave the way for changes in the politico-cultural hegemony of interpretation.

The understanding of democracy that the model above is based on differs fundamentally from the widespread economy-focused *rational choice* definition of the political process as a question of 'aggregation of special interests'.[9] The rational choice tradition, presently the prevailing understanding of the political process among professional politicians and administrators, views the political process in terms of competition between market agents. In other words, it reduces the democratic process to the level of conflict and thereby to bargaining between individual special interests.

The proposed model, on the contrary, has an obvious affinity with the current discussions on *deliberative democracy*.[10] Deliberative democracy integrates elements of the liberal concept of democracy focusing on the participation of the individual, and the republican tradition advocating common responsibility and the reciprocal obligation of citizens. In contrast to these classic positions, however, deliberative democracy does not regard political positions as fixed entities, but as in principle changeable in the deliberative process. Furthermore, deliberative democracy is understood as a combination of debating public

24   *Politics and Democracy*

opinion formation and decision-oriented parliamentary formation of compromises, i.e. legislation. The parliamentary channelling and further adaptation of the participatory opinion formation among citizens are, in other words, regarded as a necessity in complex modern society.

A major point in the deliberative conception of democracy is that an active citizenship in the shape of broad participation in an open public debate does not only in a quantitative sense expand democracy but contributes to *qualifying* political decisions, to creating a greater mutual understanding, and to furthering a higher degree of social inclusion. A solution-oriented reflection of common societal concerns constitutes the criterion of deliberative debate. To be sure, this does not imply an expectation of debate necessarily leading to general agreement, but the concept operates with the theoretical possibility that the debaters might change their minds during the process, because the debate has qualified their insight into the aspects of the matter in question. Correspondingly, it is a possibility that new disagreements emerge as a consequence of the deeper insight, or that the debaters stick to their original points of view – but now on a more qualified basis.

So, the presented model's understanding of public debate as the central mediator between the level of conflict and the level of consensus of the political process is in many respects parallel to the conception of deliberative democracy. This parallelism is further accentuated by the common emphasising of the dialogical nature of opinion formation, of the experience-based nature of common concerns, and of the reasoning reference to the common good ('arguing') as a necessary dimension of a democratic political process.

But the interpretation of deliberative democracy presented here does not assume that all agents and political positions have equal possibilities of gaining presence in the process of deliberation. As mentioned above, the democratic political process is characterised by hegemonic relations, and as historical experience has shown, marginalised interests and issues occasionally have to express themselves in activist forms, including civil disobedience, in order to achieve visibility and voice in the political distribution of resources, opportunities, and legitimacy. In this sense, social movements and activism form crucial developmental conditions of a functioning deliberative democracy.[11]

In the argument above, public debate was categorised as the main mediator between the level of conflict and the level of consensus of the political process. This calls for a more precise conceptualisation of the implications and perspectives of public debate than the established, quite heterogeneous discussion in the field seems to offer. For this purpose, the following argument will introduce a distinction between, on the one hand, 'public discourse' as a specific modality concept that holds a normative rationale related to the ideal of engaged democratic participation of citizens (the remaining part of Chapter 2); and on the other hand, 'public space' as a descriptive overall concept for the totality of generally accessible societal fields of practice (Chapter 3).

Public Discourse and Civic Engagement

The Public Sphere and Deliberative Democracy

An obvious point of departure for a reflection on public debate is Jürgen Habermas' classic analysis of the rise and decline of the bourgeois public sphere.[12] His thesis of decline which characterised the public sphere of established bourgeois society as no less than 'refeudalised', has been severely criticised throughout the years – even by the originator himself in the Foreword of the new edition[13] – and today should be regarded as merely of historical interest. But Habermas' conceptualisation of the basic idea of the bourgeois public sphere is still able to make a productive contribution to the discussion, namely, the notion that mediation between contending private interests and overall governmental regulation should take the shape of communicative, reason-based interaction between citizens in a specific, differentiated sphere of practice. Furthermore, in this differentiated sphere, neither economic nor social status should be deciding factors, but only the better argument with a convincing reference to the common good. This basic idea is still of interest, partly in its capacity as a precise and nuanced reconstruction of the revolutionary bourgeoisie's conceptualisation of the good society, which was destined to supersede absolutism; partly as the foundation of ideas on which the historical construction of the institutions of democracy actually took place, and which even today constitute the legitimacy of modern democratic society.

This rational core of both the conceptualisation and the institutionalisation of the notion of the public sphere is, in other words, still in a position to claim the status of reality as an immanent normative guideline of social practice, even although its practical impact on the societal regulation of conflicts and the distribution of resources may often seem marginal. However, Habermas does not limit his analysis to the historical reconstruction of a specific, class-bound self-conception and its hegemonic shaping of the principles of societal intercourse: he also refers to the public sphere and universal reasoning in a utopian-progressive sense as the necessary means to overcome the reifying systemic mechanisms of capitalism and bureaucracy, in their capacity as barriers to the realisation of a free, democratic society. In this sense, the malaise of modern society is due to the fact that the principle of the public sphere has not in practice obtained the status in the regulation of societal intercourse to which it should be entitled in its capacity as the principle of democratic societalisation par excellence – and the notion of social emancipation thus refers to the correction of this malaise.

In the course of Habermas' work there has been a development in his understanding of the nature and the potential of public debate. In the early works, it was a basic assumption that a non-coercive communication based solely on arguments of reason would be able to create consensus (in the sense of general agreement and common will). In his later works,[14] however, he stresses that conflicts of power and disagreement are basic conditions of social interaction, but that the

26 *Politics and Democracy*

specific form of interaction of the public sphere is characterised by a 'procedural consensus'. In this phase, consensus is understood as a basic agreement on the principles of handling conflicts and general criteria of validity of communicative action, in theory, facilitating – but not in practice guaranteeing – mutual under-standing and reflection of common concerns. Quite parallel, in other words, to the notion of the experience-based consensual nature of political culture sug-gested above.

The latter conceptualisation of the public sphere has inspired other central figures of the tradition of deliberative democracy such as James Fishkin[15] and John Dryzek.[16] They emphasise that, rather than creating consensus in the sense of rational agreement, public debate immediately tends to contribute to raising the awareness of problems and intensifying disagreements. The constructive effects of debate are not least to be found in long-term shifts in the politico-cultural spectrum of opinions, and its consensual qualities first of all concern the framework of debate that is characterised by a 'metaconsensus' (Dryzek) on the terms of processing disagreements. The normative assumption by the early Hab-ermas (and by the early, revolutionary bourgeoisie) of general agreement as the objective of public debate is, in other words, not considered a feasible ideal, but nevertheless, this ideal is granted a *heuristic* relevance (Bernhard Peters) as a normative basis for evaluating empirical public conversation.

In this interpretation, the principle of the public sphere always holds a major or minor *gradual* reality in the political process of democratic societies, and its normative dynamic depends on its rootedness in societal institutions, in the life-world's cultural orientations of action, and the citizens' reciprocal expectation patterns. As pointed out earlier in the presentation of the consensual level of the political process, critique of empirical public communication does not refer to an abstract ideal, but to an immanent experience-based normativity. Correspond-ingly, deliberation is not defined as per se oriented towards agreement, but as matter-of-fact-oriented, dialogically arguing dispute within a consensual under-standing of the existence of common concerns. This is the conception of the nature of public debate and deliberative democracy that the following argument is based on.

Modalities of Public Discourse

Since the early 1970s, Habermas' conception of the bourgeois public sphere as the adequate normative basis for general social emancipation in modern society has been confronted with various types of critique.[17] In this spectrum, Oskar Negt and Alexander Kluge's critical dialogue with Habermas' theory of the public sphere in 1972[18] still positions itself as the most thorough and fruitful cri-tique, since it both acknowledges the central relevance of Habermas' project and at the same time develops an alternative point of departure for the concept of the public sphere, considerably expanding its theoretical field of vision.

As mentioned above, in Habermas' theory, the concept of the public sphere refers to a specific, differentiated field of practice in which citizens interact

Politics and Democracy 27

dialogically on the basis of universal, critical reason and – via the institutions of parliamentary democracy – discursively mediate between the privately organised spheres of society and overall state regulation. Negt and Kluge confront this notion with an expanded concept of the public sphere, which in principle includes all socially relevant forms of experience. Their concept of the public sphere, in other words, transcends modernity's separated fields of practice and encompasses all types of collective formation of meaning.

The motivation for this expanded definition of the concept is that, according to Negt and Kluge, the conceptualisation of the public sphere by Habermas and the early bourgeoisie is characterised by highly exclusive features, and is therefore unsuited to serve as the claimed general frame for reflecting all relevant social experience. Their argument is not least that different backgrounds in terms of class, education, etc. equip individuals quite unequally with respect to the competence to master abstract, universal reasoning. Furthermore, Habermas' focus on the public sphere as a differentiated field of practice neglects those types of concrete experience and socially relevant formation of meaning that originate in the private spheres of social life. This includes partly the experience of individuals created by the process of socialisation in the family and the associated formation of gender roles and general expectations regarding human intercourse etc.; partly the variety of work-related experiences, including elements of heteronomy and social hierarchy in immediate cooperative relations, as well as the market's more anonymous mechanisms of compulsion and marginalisation. In the current perspective, we could add ethnic and sexual minorities' experiences of discrimination.

In addition, Negt and Kluge point to a specific, private type of experience of crucial importance to society, namely, the subjective everyday life experience of all individuals, with unorganised, sensuous-emotional impulses of resistance, compensating fantasies and daydreams of unspecific change which emerge in the process of wrestling with an everyday life that in large parts appears heteronomous. The main source of these impulses of resistance springs from the conflict between, on the one hand, the linear, quantitative structure of time that commands work life and the competitive relations of the market and from there tends to spread to society as a whole, and, on the other, the more qualitatively oriented, cyclic time rhythms that characterise human sensuous and emotional needs and the communicative processes of the life-world.

These fragmented subjective resources of resistance point critically to the unsatisfactory conditions that produce them, and they, therefore, in principle, hold an emancipatory potential for change. However, this potential does not automatically become reality – this would imply that the subjective resources of resistance are being processed and organised consciously in a collective context of practice. When this happens, the raw material of a qualitatively different type of public sphere emerges, the formation of a public sphere from below, which in contrast to the abstract, universal perspective of the bourgeoisie's classic idea of the public sphere takes its point of departure in the concrete and specific. In 1972, Negt and Kluge conceptualised this entity as the 'proletarian public

28   *Politics and Democracy*

sphere'. In spite of its obvious connotations, this term does not refer to a public sphere exclusively related to the working class. It represents a counter-concept to the bourgeois public sphere, based on *general* social experience and the multiplicity of concrete subjective resources marginalised by the concept of the bourgeois public sphere.[19]

In the following, these two contrasting perspectives on collective formation of experience will be updated and conceptualised as *discursive* entities: respectively, the 'universally reasoning public discourse' (the bourgeois public sphere) and the 'subjective experience-reflecting public discourse' (the proletarian public sphere). As opposed to the inevitable socio-spatial connotations that tend to make discussions on the 'public sphere' blurry, this distinction explicitly does not refer to separate *forums*, but to different *modalities* of experience formation, each of which holds both positive potentials and limitations in a perspective of deliberative democracy. Furthermore, 'public discourse' will be understood as a *meta-discourse* in relation to the variety of specific discourses of practice (scientific, economic, political, aesthetic, religious, etc.). Public discourse addresses these differentiated practices and associated experiences in an overall and integrative perspective, but the processing may operate in different modalities.

As suggested, the modality of subjective experience-reflecting public discourse is based on societally generated collective experiences and specific subjective resources that are being marginalised by the abstract, generalising modality of universally reasoning public discourse. When public forums emerge in everyday life contexts, they are propelled by these repressed subjective resources of resistance, and they can take the shape of processes of politicisation from below, the formation of subcultures, oppositional artistic movements, etc. The modality of subjective experience-reflecting public discourse, in other words, is closely related to the concept of 'the political' as defined earlier, since both concepts point to the life-worldly raw material that is being processed and shaped in the formation of political consciousness and voice among citizens.

If, conversely, the diffuse impulses of resistance of everyday life are *not* being processed collectively and discursively in the shape of subjective experience-reflecting public discourse, they remain private, unfocused, dynamic forces that are activated in compensatory fantasies, and not least in the individuals' imaginative exchange with the standardised models of wishful dreams offered by the industries of consciousness (commercial culture and media, advertising, etc.). In this connection, Negt and Kluge suggest yet another concept, the 'public spheres of production', to characterise the type of collective formation of meaning and shaping of social spaces of practice represented by the industries of consciousness. Whereas both the universally reasoning and the subjective experience-reflecting modality of public discourse following their distinct premises are characterised by a critical, dialogical basic principle of exchange, the discourse of public spheres of production addresses the recipient in a monological, instrumentalising manner in order to channel his/her private fantasies and longings into a prosaic act of buying and consuming. The latter modality will in the following be called 'consumerist public discourse'.

Politics and Democracy 29

In this terminology, the processing of collective experience in late modernity draws on contradictory principles for the formation of meaning in the shape of the modalities of universally reasoning, subjective experience-reflecting, and monological, consumerist public discourse. The crucial question, then, is in which ways and in which proportions these modalities are operational in actual social practice. We will often be dealing with social processes and forms of practice in which more than one of these modalities are active and involved in some kind of interaction, but the fundamental relationship of conflict between them endures, and their respective weight in society's organisation of experience is of vital importance for the developmental conditions of the democratic process.

The impulses of resistance that everyday life generates and that feed both subjective experience-reflecting and consumerist public discourse, are closely intertwined with the broader issue of late modern identity formation. This relationship will be elaborated in the following section.

Late Modern Identity Work and the Political

Predominant positions in the debate address the current conditions and developmental possibilities of democracy as increasingly intertwined with questions of individual and collective identities. The concept of identity, however, is defined and used in a multiplicity of ways in the various positions of the debate, and it is therefore difficult to establish a common point of reference when discussing the theoretical and practical implications – including, in particular, the democratic perspectives – in the interrelationship between political and identity-related issues. One point of reflection seems to be of significant importance to this discussion, namely, the relationship of tension between the notion of democratic equality of citizens and the notion of unique individual or group-based identity. In this relationship of tension, the basic conflict between universalising and particularising dynamics characterising the cultural and political processes of late modern society manifests itself in a very tangible way.

In this perspective, the most prominent cultural theories of the present have one limiting feature in common: they all regard identity solely as a concept for positioning in an ongoing symbolic power struggle. To this category of theories belongs the position of Pierre Bourdieu as well as the entire post-structuralist tradition in the wake of Foucault, including much of the Anglo-Saxon tradition of Cultural Studies and Identity Politics. Whether the analytical focus is on class relations, habitus groups, antagonistic discourses, ethnic lines of conflict, or the gender relationship, at the outset, these theories reduce the issue of identity to an at once collective and particularistic discourse of power.[20] Individuals' display of identity is in its totality viewed as embedded in power struggles between existing, collective discourses. The theories do not operate with a general, overall level of discourse where dialogical interaction and the formation of common experience across discursive borderlines could be a possibility, and therefore these symbolic positionings and struggles for hegemony are defined as monologic by nature: the individual display of identity is understood as inscribed

30 *Politics and Democracy*

in advance within the particularistic 'either–or' thinking of monologic, collectively binding discourses.

In this line of thinking, an ideal of 'universal equality' would represent a symbolic focus for particularistic power struggles (according to the question 'which position is able to conquer hegemony over the ideal of "universal equality" and define it authoritatively on the premises of its own particular discursive interests?') rather than a general perspective to further strengthen universal potentials in the ongoing development of culture and society. Likewise, the individual's pursuit of a unique identity would here be viewed as completely embedded in the struggles of collective discourses and thus devoid of any dynamics of its own and of individual potentialities of change.

In contrast to the positions characterised above, the proposal here is, in an overall perspective, to understand the issue of identity on a societal scale as permanently involved in the experience-based formation of society's political culture, as outlined above: as a characteristic of the political process of democratic societies, the struggle between special interests, particular forms of practice and divergent processes of experience unfolds in constant interaction with an overall, politico-cultural level of universal reflection in which, in principle, the possibility exists for dialogical exchange, learning processes, and identification of common concerns. In this scenario, the universalistic ideal of equality and the particularistic, individual, or group-based attempts to establish a unique identity represent actual, dynamic, and experiential factors in the development of culture and society which cannot be reduced to one another, but whose concrete, actual forms of interaction are of critical importance to which kind of cultural and social development will occur.

The following account should be understood as a critical theoretical illumination of the relationship between identity and the processes of politicisation, i.e. the constitution of 'the political' as outlined above.[21] On this basis, the attempt will furthermore be made to tentatively evaluate the democratic potentials and possible pitfalls in the current developments in the relationship between identity and the processes of politicisation in late modernity – not least the basic relationship of tension between universalistic and particularistic currents.

The present argument advocates a non-essentialist understanding of identity as a historically constructed and processually variable entity. From this basic point of departure, the argument corresponds with the long and heterogeneous line of tradition in sociology, psychology, philosophy, anthropology, and gender studies that conceptualises identity as an entity that is not fixed once and for all, but is permanently being 'negotiated'. According to this broad tradition, identities are, in other words, continuously being adapted to the conditions of social interaction, and the shape and content of identities are at any time defined by the concrete process of negotiation.

Despite this basic correspondence, the negotiation metaphor appears inadequate in order to understand the complexity of the present conditions of identity formation. My thesis is that the late modern issue of identity should be analysed as the interplay of two dimensions, of which the negotiation metaphor is only able to reflect one. It therefore provides a reductionist account of the processes and perspectives of the issue of identity, illuding that identity in its entirety is at the disposal of conscious, explicit positioning in a negotiation game. Instead of 'negotiation', the following uses terms like 'processing' and 'identity-seeking' as more open and indeterminate conceptualisations of the process of wrestling with the identity challenges of social interaction.

The suggestion is that we can benefit from operating with an analytical distinction between two dimensions: 'identity as dynamic' and 'identity as discursive practice'. The distinction is necessarily analytical because the dimension of dynamic only manifests itself in the staging of actual, specific practices rather than in a 'pure' form, but the thesis is that each given discursively organised (i.e. 'negotiated') practice feeds off a dynamic that holds a multiplicity of fundamental possibilities for realisation, an indeterminate potential for change, and therefore cannot be reduced to the discursive horizon and self-conception of this particular practice.

Initially, the dynamic of identity is reactive by nature. It represents a social psychological impulse towards re-balancing that is released in individuals and collectives when habitual conceptions of value, life-world structures and circuits of interhuman relations are destabilised or disintegrate.[22] Or, to use a different terminology: when established self-regulating balances in social exchange are displaced, a reaction of a 'balance economy'[23] is released. This dynamic identity work seeks to reorganise the individual's or the collective's existing resources of experience and adjust them to the new conditions of practice. Identity work is thus initially determined by crisis due to loss of orientation; it operates idiosyncratically, according to the principle of availability, and its activity is solely directed towards pragmatically re-establishing a fungible balance in the exchange relation to the surrounding world.

Balance-seeking identity work is furthermore *ambivalent* by nature:[24] it unfolds – and obtains its dynamic force – in the field of tension between the experience of loss and pain triggered by the end of life-historical certainties and the undetermined, loose opening of new challenges and life options that the same process brings about. In other words, the dynamic of identity is not in itself oriented in a specific direction or otherwise determined as regards content or discourse, and therefore it can, in principle, become the driving force in cultural and political processes of any kind. Political, cultural, and aesthetic narratives and actions serve as specific discursive practices that form, focus, and channel the dynamic as they develop. And as modern history has shown, the register of discursive possibilities includes regressive identification with a totalitarian mass movement as well as emancipatory, universalistic democratic engagement in the common good, and a self-sufficient individualistic or a particularistic subcultural self-definition.

But at the same time, conditions of practice will always apply that modify and condition the actual plasticity of the dynamic of identity: on the individual level, it is the particular individual's specific life history that constitutes the building blocks for identity work. Major differences remain concerning the

32   *Politics and Democracy*

resources that concrete individuals have at their disposal due to their social and cultural background – so, although all modern individuals are doing reflective identity work, they are not doing it on the same conditions. Correspondingly, political collectives, e.g. political movements or nation states, perform identity work on the basis of their specific historical experiences of internal and external conflicts.

In other words, modern identity formation is a process of construction, but it is an *experience-based* construction with its accompanying limitations and inertia, not an arbitrary construction with a smorgasbord of choices. Furthermore, as Chapter 3 will elaborate, the social space of practice in which an identity-seeking discursive practice attempts to realise itself, is at any time characterised by specific struggles, collective experiences, constellations of interests, and hegemonic discourses that mark the playing field that is available to identity-seeking discursive practice.

The present argument considers this complex notion of identity work to be the general condition of experience formation in late modernity, and it therefore also represents the central resource of the political and the necessary point of departure for a theoretical understanding of the perspectives and implications of processes of politicisation.

Culturalisation and Politicisation

The process of modernisation in general and the process of globalisation in particular are major distributors of the radical transformation of the structures and meanings of social life that trigger the ambivalent, balance-seeking dynamic of identity. This circumstance characterises the entire era of modernity, but the processes have accelerated considerably and have become more comprehensive since the 1960s.[25] The unbinding of a collective dynamic of identity and its organisation in shifting discursive practices – including the political – is thus not a historically new phenomenon. For instance, the struggles of the labour movements of the late nineteenth and early twentieth centuries also included a dimension of identity work, which, among other things, was discursively expressed in an autonomous cultural self-definition and its accompanying institutions (unions, political parties, cultural associations). But these historical movements were active in a space of practice that was nationally defined and characterised by clearly identifiable lines of conflict, class relations and associated collective life contexts, and life options, which equipped the balancing identity work with clear points of orientation, and thus channelled the unbound dynamic of identity into the discursive practice of the class struggle.

Today, however, we operate in a late modern, partly globalised space of practice with non-lucid relations and constellations of interests. Moreover, in the rich part of the world, we face extensive complications of the class structure and an even more far-reaching differentiation of the processes that create and recreate the social order and the processes that organise cultural meaning for individuals.[26] With the individual's increasing economic, legal, and cultural unbinding, processing and channelling the dynamic of identity-seeking become an urgent reflective project that each person continuously has to come to terms with. In this process, the traditional forms of community erode, as well as the associated collective patterns of identity work. Identity work is individualised, and the societal consequence of this spread of individual, dynamic, and ambivalent identity-seeking processes on a mass level is that social practice tends to become *culturalised*:[27] in societies of this type, subjectively meaningful cultural factors – input for identity work – seem to motivate individuals to act, rather than merely economic interests and class structures.

The present argument acknowledges a substantial rational core in the cultural sociology of Pierre Bourdieu,[28] but it contests the adequacy of some of his basic categories in respect to present society. In view of late modernity's extensive dissolution of class-specific life contexts and the associated individualisation of the challenges of identity work in a life-historical perspective, it no longer appears plausible to keep up the notion of the status of the childhood environment, the habitus group, as an overriding, life-long mark and a collectively binding frame of orientation for identity work. Under the current conditions, life-historical experience formation is necessarily of a more individualised and fragmented nature, and in this background, identity work cannot meaningfully be understood as strictly determined by the experiential resources stemming from the childhood environment. It appears to be a more reasonable assumption that these, evidently important and basic, resources are continuously being selected, processed, and reinterpreted in interplay with experiences from later phases of life – with the challenges of the current context of practice as the fulcrum.

Likewise, Bourdieu's reduction of the struggles of the social context to the continuous contention between given habitus groups – and his confinement of identity work to representing an element in collective positionings in the symbolic power struggle between upper class, middle class and working class – appears to be an unsatisfactory point of departure to understand the perspectives of the contemporary condition of identity work. According to later major empirical sociological investigations,[29] it is significant that cultural orientations and group formations in late modernity no longer appear to be organised in close affinity to the economic hierarchy of society. In contrast to Bourdieu's diagnosis (based on data from France in the 1960s) of a vertical distinction between habitus groups within a common societal frame of reference, cultural groupings today tend to develop on the basis of individualisation and appear in the shape of a plurality of horizontally positioned life-style environments. According to Schulze, each of these environments is further based on a specific aesthetic-cultural orientation of taste, and their criteria of prestige are therefore incommensurable. Hence, contemporary cultural prestige struggles tend to be internal matters of each life-style environment. The interrelationship between the life-style environments, on the other hand, is characterised by each environment's perception of its own orientation of taste as superior to that of the others, and the attention that the environments grant each other is limited to reciprocal indifference or aesthetic contempt. In other words, in late modernity, on the conditions

34 *Politics and Democracy*

of individualisation, cultural orientations seem to have widely autonomised themselves from the (evidently still existing) societal hierarchy of economic and political power.

Correspondingly, on the premises of culturalisation, the point of departure to establish political identity is not the collective defined by the social structure, but the experience formation of the individuals in question, characterised as it is by ambivalence, genuine uncertainty, and contingency. Political identity formation and political practice are on this basis far more fluid and unpredictable entities than was the case in earlier phases of modern society. This main tendency is reflected in the extensive collapse of the classic, interest-based patterns of voter identification with parties[30] as well as – in reaction to this – in politicians' attempts to create an almost intimate, personal appeal to the individual voter. The development of the dimension of citizens' political identity formation, that relates to the agents of institutional politics, is thus leaving the classic relationship of identification behind in favour of a more transient type of relationship that Fritz Breithaupt has termed 'siding based on empathy'.[31] As opposed to the lasting and comprehensive nature of identification, siding with an agent occurs in connection with a concrete, singular situation of conflict, and there is nothing to stop one from choosing to side with another agent in the next situation of conflict. According to Breithaupt, the decision to side with one or the other combatant on the stage of parliamentary politics is made spontaneously in the context of a specific situation; it can further be based on interests as well as desire and fascination and may occur consciously or unconsciously. In the identity work of the individual citizen, the decision is motivated by an empathy with the chosen party that emerges in the individual's narrative, coherence-seeking processing of the conflictual context in question; empathy can further be established and legitimised emotionally as well as rationally. Election campaigns are therefore to a high degree about the individual politicians' efforts to create a relationship of empathy with the voters that is strong enough to legitimise the voters' siding with them.

Evidently, social practice still entails a vast dimension of unequal distribution of resources and material life opportunities, and organised special interests are still struggling along the lines of class structures, thus contributing to the formation of basic, material conditions of society – but this dimension is decreasingly being reflected in the late modern issue of identity. Or rather: it is – like questions of ethnicity, gender, sexuality, etc. – reflected in the identity work of individuals when it manifests itself in a pivotal role in the discursive organisation of concrete processes of experience, i.e. when social practice attributes meaning to it. Under the conditions of individualisation and culturalisation, these collective frames of reference are, in other words, not to be regarded as a priori determining factors but as questions of concrete social practice and discursive experience formation. But it remains a crucial question for the developmental perspectives of late modern society how the evidently still existing interrelationship between identity issues and politico-economic structures can be made reflective, both in individual identity work and in political discourse, i.e. how diffuse, orientation-seeking impulses can be organised by subjective experience-reflecting public discourse.

The term 'culturalisation', in the present sense, should not be confused with an essentialistic, 'culturalist' understanding of identity and the political, as represented by, for example, Samuel P. Huntington.[32] On the contrary, the concept of culturalisation refers to the specific, late modern *conditions* of processes of identification and experience formation, not to a given substance or a specific discursive practice. The concept further offers an understanding of particularistic, culturalist essentialism as one type of late modern identity formation among others. The fact that this specific type of identity work has been able to achieve a relatively prominent position in contemporary theoretical and political debates at the expense of the reflection of universal rights and equal distribution is, in other words, not due to 'cultural destiny' but to specific, changeable historical conditions of experience formation and constellations of power.

It is further an important point that the process of individualisation and culturalisation does not necessarily lead to self-sufficient, particularistic individualism – the crucial question is what kind of discursive practice and meaning formation is created between the unbound individuals and society at large. In this perspective, individualisation should be understood as a structural condition that can form the basis of a conflictual plurality of discursive practices. Individualism in the selfish sense is one of these, universalistic civic engagement in society another. The decisive point is which principles of societal action and historical experience underlie the particular identity-seeking practice. In this respect, it is significant that late modernity has developed as part of the general globalisation process, which, without exaggerating, can be characterised as dominated by the market and thus as politically underdeveloped: so far, global integration has only to a very limited degree resulted in institutions and forums for discussion and public opinion formation on a global level that are able to match the market forces.[33] Although they should not be regarded as determining, these overriding circumstances tend to strengthen the incentives of the identity work of unbound individuals to orientate themselves towards the market relations' discursive horizon of self-sufficient special interests.

As outlined above, processes of politicisation always involve both individual and collective identity issues, but as is evident, differentiation is necessary: on the one hand, historically, as indicated above, and, on the other, in a current perspective in respect to the global imbalances in development and distribution produced and reproduced by the market-dominated process of globalisation.

Culturalisation of the political process – in the sense of the increasing charging of political discursive practice with unbound individuals' ambivalent, balance-seeking dynamic of identity – is a tendency that up until now has primarily unfolded in late modern democratic welfare societies. In the rest of the world, the situation is, roughly speaking, characterised by shifting combinations of economic scarcity, clear-cut political and economic power relations, profiled social struggles, manifest relations of mutual dependency between individuals in collective life contexts, as well as a more or less intact, mutually obligating

36 *Politics and Democracy*

context of tradition which serves as the meaning-constituting framework for social practice. Under these circumstances, the discursive practice of identity work is, in other words, intimately intertwined with established discourses of social power.

In late modern democratic welfare societies, the political process also includes both identity issues and conflicts over power and the politics of distribution, but they are rarely integrated in one and the same discursive practice. This circumstance is in part due to the extensive institutionalisation of conflict regulation in these societies, where reasonably well-functioning parliamentarian institutions, collective bargaining systems, and welfare-state redistribution mechanisms largely ensure that these quantitative political themes do not impose themselves on the everyday identity work of the ordinary citizen.

Concurrent with the increase in national income, the unbinding of the individual, and the tendency towards culturalisation following from this, new areas of politics of a more qualitative kind have crystallized (environment, ethnicity, gender, sexuality, minorities' conditions, global peace, global justice, etc.), and it is mainly in these areas that identity-seeking processes become integrated with a political discursive practice. In other words: the forms of practice that characterise the new social and cultural movements from the 1960s and onwards.[34]

But this tendency to focus identity-seeking political engagement on qualitative areas of politics stands or falls with late modern society's material wealth. In reality, this requires as a precondition that the rich countries of the West remain in a position to command the global flow of resources to their own benefit, as well as the actual functioning of the welfare state's institutionalised, quantitative distribution policy. If these terms are no longer guaranteed, an integrated relationship between social struggles of interests and identity-based orientation is liable to re-emerge in Western societies. In the social groups who are the losers in the process of globalisation (e.g. traditional industrial workers, the unemployed with a low educational background, but also increasingly educated citizens, whom the labour market downgrades to precarious, low-paid jobs), the rudiments of such integration are already visible: frustration over their marginalisation as regards the distribution of wealth and life opportunities is often politically dealt with in close connection with identity-motivated, particularistic efforts to marginalise the immediately visible symptoms of globalisation: immigrants from non-Western countries.[35]

Politicisation of unbound individuals' identity-seeking processes does not occur automatically. And when it does occur, there is no advance guarantee that the process of politicisation will have a universalistic, democratic character – it may just as well assume self-centred or fundamentalist, totalitarian forms. This is entirely dependent on the concrete circumstances in which the process of politicisation is inscribed – on its relationship with the prevailing constellations of interests, hegemonic discourses, and politico-cultural experiences, as well as with the character and adaptation of the experiences of conflict to which the politicised discursive practice of identity gives rise upon encountering the context.

Politics and Democracy 37

This culturalised politicisation process constitutes the dynamic of the political as outlined above. It is more unstable and fragile than other, more institutionalised types of political discursive practice because of the key role played by the ambivalent, directionless dynamic of identity in its formation. The concrete political visions of change are fused with existential and emotional identification issues of the participating individuals. These issues are basically diffuse but they take shape in the process of politicisation in dialectical interplay with the discursive practice in which they are involved and the associated formation of experience. In these processes, the question of political success or fiasco therefore assumes an intensified character: in principle, the unbound individuals' entire balance of identity with respect to the surrounding world, the very question of their social recognition,[36] is at play in their concrete struggles to have their demands met.

This intensification supplies the discursive practice with a high degree of engagement and, in favourable times, politicisation processes of this kind can be exceedingly productive and rewarding for the participating individuals as well as for political culture in general. But in times of adversity – if they encounter considerable opposition or are simply bureaucratically or violently marginalised by authorities or other political agents – their fragility becomes apparent as they tend to change into either total disillusion or fundamentalism. To suffer political defeat implies a totalising violation of one's identity that is dealt with either by retreating from the violating reality or by even fiercer practice of resistance in which one's self-conception is absolutised and the adversary's discourses are denied legitimacy. As we have seen in some of the consequences of the 1968 uprising, in the European 'autonomous' movement of the 1990s and in the worldwide movements against the capitalist version of globalisation around the turn of the century, for instance, these processes may result in totalitarian thinking and in a militant practice that may endanger democratic political culture as such.[37] In addition, this kind of politicisation process tends to promote a strictly collectivist discourse of identity that is not capable of reflecting the legitimate individual needs of the participants nor the concerns of society in general.

Political movements that are to a large extent motivated by identity work continuously provide society with new kinds of experiences of conflict. In the interest of further developing democracy so that it is on a par with developments in society, it is therefore crucial that these experiences are integrated with the historical experiences of conflict in society's universal, democratic political culture. In other words, these processes of politicisation should be treated as a valuable, yet fragile, societal resource. But, at the same time, one should be aware that these processes of politicisation seldom start off being equipped with a horizon of reflection that contains a subtle notion of the common good, and that marginalisation may easily cause them to radicalise unproductively.

Identity-motivated processes of politicisation are typically based on particular questions and single issues, and in order to further the democratic perspective of

38   *Politics and Democracy*

these processes, it seems vital that this particular starting point is gradually transcended. Such an approach provides the necessary scope, so that the concrete theme of struggle can be reflected on and weighed with respect to other legitimate social interests, as well as to the common good as a universal discursive framework for the democratic process. To this should be added learning processes in interaction with other political agents in the area, in which all parts learn how to recognise diversity and deal with conflict peacefully and with a view to compromise, and to accept that particular interests should always be able to legitimise themselves with respect to the universal perspective of the common good.

Notes

1 Max Weber, *Wissenschaft als Beruf/Politik als Beruf. Studienausgabe* (Tübingen: Mohr, 1994).
2 Talcott Parsons, *Politics and Social Structure* (New York: The Free Press, 1969).
3 Central positions in this debate are outlined in Thomas Bedorf and Kurt Röttgers (eds), *Das Politische und die Politik* (Frankfurt am Main: Suhrkamp, 2010). See also Anneka Esch-van Kan, Stephan Packard, and Philipp Schulte (eds), *Thinking – Resisting – Reading the Political* (Zürich: diaphanes, 2013).
4 Carl Schmitt, *Der Begriff des Politischen* (Berlin: Duncker und Humblot, 2002).
5 Ernesto Laclau and Chantal Mouffe, *Hegemony and Socialist Strategy* (London: Verso, 1985).
6 Hannah Arendt, *Was ist Politik?* (Zürich: Piper, 2003).
7 Oskar Negt and Alexander Kluge, *Maßverhältnisse des Politischen* (Frankfurt am Main: S. Fischer, 1992).
8 The basic line of thinking behind the model was developed in my habilitation (Henrik Kaare Nielsen, *Demokrati i bevægelse. Sammenlignende studier i politisk kultur og nye sociale bevægelser i Vesttyskland og Danmark*, Aarhus: Aarhus University Press, 1991) as a result of a major comparative analysis of the politico-cultural interplay between new social movements and the political establishment in West Germany and Denmark in the 1960s, 1970s and 1980s. It was later (in Henrik Kaare Nielsen, *Kultur og modernitet*, Aarhus: Aarhus University Press, 1993) elaborated and presented as a generalised thesis on the basic relations of the political process in modern, democratic societies.
9 Kristen Renwick Monroe (ed.), *The Economic Approach to Politics* (New York: HarperCollins, 1991).
10 Jürgen Habermas, *Faktizität und Geltung* (Frankfurt am Main: Suhrkamp, 1992) (English translation, *Between Facts and Norms*, Cambridge, MA: MIT Press, 1996); Jean L. Cohen and Andrew Arato, *Civil Society and Political Theory* (Cambridge, MA: MIT Press, 1992); James Fishkin, *The Voice of the People* (New Haven, CT: Yale University Press, 1995); John S. Dryzek, *Foundations and Frontiers of Deliberative Governance* (Oxford: Oxford University Press, 2010); Jørn Loftager, *Politisk offentlighed og demokrati i Danmark* (Aarhus: Aarhus University Press, 2004); Jane Mansbridge and John Parkinson (eds), *Deliberative Systems: Deliberative Democracy at the Large Scale* (Cambridge: Cambridge University Press, 2012); Hélène Landemore, *Democratic Reason* (Princeton, NJ: Princeton University Press, 2013); Christian Kock and Lisa S. Villadsen (eds), *Rhetorical Citizenship and Public Deliberation* (Philadelphia, PA: Pennsylvania State University Press, 2012); Mark E. Warren, 'Can We Make Public Spheres More Democratic through Institutional Innovation?' in Henrik Kaare Nielsen, Christina Fiig, Jorn Loftager, Thomas Olesen, Jan Lohmann

Politics and Democracy 39

Stephensen and Mads P. Sorensen (eds), *The Democratic Public Sphere: Current Challenges and Prospects* (Aarhus: Aarhus University Press, 2016).

11 Iris Marion Young, 'Activist Challenges to Deliberative Democracy', *Political Theory* 29(5) (2001).

12 Jürgen Habermas, *Strukturwandel der Öffentlichkeit* (Neuwied: Luchterhand, 1962) (English translation: *The Structural Transformation of the Public Sphere*, Cambridge: Polity, 1989).

13 Frankfurt am Main: Suhrkamp Verlag, 1990.

14 For example, *Fatizität und Geltung*, op. cit.

15 Fishkin, *Voice of the People*, op. cit.

16 Dryzek, *Foundations and Frontiers,* op. cit.

17 For example, Bernhard Peters, 'Der Sinn von Öffentlichkeit', in Friedhelm Neidhardt (ed.), *Öffentlichkeit, öffentliche Meinung, soziale Bewegungen* (Opladen: Westdeutscher Verlag, 1994); Craig Calhoun (ed.), *Habermas and the Public Sphere* (Cambridge, MA: MIT Press, 1992); special issue of *Social Text* 25/26 (1990).

18 Oskar Negt and Alexander Kluge, *Öffentlichkeit und Erfahrung* (Frankfurt am Main: Suhrkamp, 1972) (English translation: *Public Sphere and Experience*, Minneapolis: University of Minnesota Press, 1993).

19 Evidently, in concrete social practice the question of marginalised subjective resources will be interwoven with conditions of class, gender, ethnicity, etc., but it remains a crucial theoretical point that the experience of marginalised needs and subjective resources of resistance is a basic, general feature of the late modern life-world. The concrete forms of this experience and the ways of processing and reflecting it, however, vary according to individual and group-specific conditions.

20 Seyla Benhabib (ed.), *Democracy and Difference: Contesting the Boundaries of the Political* (Princeton, NJ: Princeton University Press, 2002); Henrik Kaare Nielsen, *Konsument eller samfundsborger. Kritiske Essays* (Aarhus: Klim, 2007).

21 Henrik Kaare Nielsen, *Kritisk teori og samtidsanalyse* (Aarhus: Aarhus University Press, 2001).

22 Of course, these are fundamentally different types of processes (mental processes at an individual level, social processes at a group level), but the dynamic and forms of processing can be regarded as analogous.

23 Oskar Negt and Alexander Kluge, *Geschichte und Eigensinn* (Frankfurt am Main: Zweitausendeins, 1981).

24 Thomas Ziehe, 'Modernity and Individualisation', in J. Fornäs and G. Bolin (eds), *Moves in Modernity* (Stockholm: Almqvist and Wiksell International, 1992).

25 Anthony Giddens, *Modernity and Self-Identity* (Stanford, CA: Stanford University Press, 1991).

26 Nielsen, *Konsument*, op. cit.

27 Henrik Nielsen, *Kultur og modernitet* (Aarhus: Aarhus University Press, 1993).

28 Pierre Bourdieu, *Distinction* (London: Routledge & Kegan Paul, 1984).

29 For example, Gerhard Schulze, *Die Erlebnisgesellschaft* (Frankfurt am Main: Campus, 1992).

30 Peter Mair, Wolfgang C. Müller, and Fritz Plasser (eds), *Political Parties and Electoral Change* (London: Sage, 2004); Anu Kantola, 'Loyalties in Flux: The Changing Politics of Citizenship', *European Journal of Cultural Studies*, 6: 203 (2003).

31 Fritz Breithaupt, *Kulturen der Empathie* (Frankfurt am Main: Suhrkamp, 2009).

32 Samuel P. Huntington, *The Clash of Civilizations and the Making of World Order* (New York: Simon & Schuster, 1996).

33 Dieter Gosewinkel, Dieter Rucht, Wolfgang van den Daele, and Jürgen Kocka (eds), *Zivilgesellschaft – national und transnational* (Berlin: WZB, 2004); David Held and Anthony McGrew, *Globalization/Anti-Globalization* (Cambridge: Cambridge

40   *Politics and Democracy*

University Press, 2007); David Held, *Democracy and the Global Order* (Cambridge: Cambridge University Press, 1995).

34 Political science conceptualises this tendency as a shift from 'materialistic' to 'post-materialistic' values, cf. Ronald Inglehart, *The Silent Revolution* (Princeton, NJ: Princeton University Press, 1977).

35 Zygmunt Bauman, *Globalization: The Human Consequences* (New York: Columbia University Press, 1988); Peter Glotz, *Die beschleunigte Gesellschaft* (München: Kindler Verlag, 1999).

36 Axel Honneth, *Kampf um Anerkennung* (Frankfurt am Main: Suhrkamp, 1992).

37 Dieter Rucht, 'Kapitalismuskritik im Namen der globalisierungskritischen Zivilgesellschaft – alter Wein in neuen Schläuchen?', in Gosewinkel *et al.*, *Zivilgesellschaft*, op. cit.; Nielsen, *Demokrati*, op. cit.

References

Arendt, Hannah (2003) *Was ist Politik?*, Zürich: Piper.

Bauman, Zygmunt (1998) *Globalization: The Human Consequences*, New York: Columbia University Press.

Bedorf, Thomas and Kurt Röttgers (eds) (2010) *Das Politische und die Politik*, Frankfurt am Main: Suhrkamp.

Benhabib, Seyla (ed.) (2002) *Democracy and Difference. Contesting the Boundaries of the Political*, Princeton, NJ: Princeton University Press.

Bourdieu, Pierre (1984) *Distinction*, London: Routledge and Kegan Paul.

Breithaupt, Fritz (2009) *Kulturen der Empathie*, Frankfurt am Main: Suhrkamp.

Calhoun, Craig (ed.) (1992) *Habermas and the Public Sphere*, Cambridge, MA: MIT Press.

Cohen, Jean L. and Andrew Arato (1992) *Civil Society and Political Theory*, Cambridge, MA: MIT Press.

Dryzek, John S. (2010) *Foundations and Frontiers of Deliberative Governance*, Oxford: Oxford University Press.

Esch-van Kan, Anneka, Stephan Packard, and Philipp Schulte (eds) (2013) *Thinking – Resisting – Reading the Political*, Zürich: diaphanes.

Fishkin, James (1995) *The Voice of the People*, New Haven, CT: Yale University Press.

Giddens, Anthony (1991) *Modernity and Self-Identity*, Stanford, CA: Stanford University Press.

Glotz, Peter (1999) *Die beschleunigte Gesellschaft*, München: Kindler Verlag.

Gosewinkel, Dieter, Dieter Rucht, Wolfgang van den Daele, and Jürgen Kocka (eds) (2004) *Zivilgesellschaft – national und transnational*, Berlin: WZB.

Habermas, Jürgen (1962) *Strukturwandel der Öffentlichkeit*, Neuwied: Luchterhand (English translation: *The Structural Transformation of the Public Sphere*, Cambridge: Polity, 1989).

Habermas, Jürgen (1992) *Faktizität und Geltung*, Frankfurt am Main: Suhrkamp (English translation: *Between Facts and Norms*, Cambridge, MA: MIT Press, 1996).

Held, David (1995) *Democracy and the Global Order*, Cambridge: Cambridge University Press.

Held, David and Anthony McGrew (2007) *Globalization/Anti-Globalization*, Cambridge: Cambridge University Press.

Honneth, Axel (1992) *Kampf um Anerkennung*, Frankfurt am Main: Suhrkamp.

Huntington, Samuel P. (1996) *The Clash of Civilizations and the Making of World Order*, New York: Simon & Schuster.

Politics and Democracy 41

Inglehart, Ronald (1977) *The Silent Revolution*, Princeton, NJ: Princeton University Press.

Kantola, Anu (2003) 'Loyalties in Flux: The Changing Politics of Citizenship', *European Journal of Cultural Studies*, 6: 203.

Kock, Christian and Lisa S. Villadsen (eds) (2012) *Rhetorical Citizenship and Public Deliberation*, Philadelphia, PA: Pennsylvania State University Press.

Laclau, Ernesto and Chantal Mouffe (1985) *Hegemony and Socialist Strategy*, London: Verso.

Landemore, Hélène (2013) *Democratic Reason*, Princeton, NJ: Princeton University Press.

Loftager, Jørn (2004) *Politisk offentlighed og demokrati i Danmark*, Aarhus: Aarhus University Press.

Mair, Peter, Wolfgang C. Müller, and Fritz Plasser (eds) (2004) *Political Parties and Electoral Change*, London: Sage.

Mansbridge, Jane and John Parkinson (eds) (2012) *Deliberative Systems: Deliberative Democracy at the Large Scale*, Cambridge: Cambridge University Press.

Negt, Oskar and Alexander Kluge (1972) *Öffentlichkeit und Erfahrung*, Frankfurt am Main: Suhrkamp (English translation: *Public Sphere and Experience*, Minneapolis, MN: University of Minnesota Press, 1993).

Negt, Oskar and Alexander Kluge (1981) *Geschichte und Eigensinn*, Frankfurt am Main: Zweitausendeins.

Negt, Oskar and Alexander Kluge (1992) *Maßverhältnisse des Politischen*, Frankfurt am Main: S. Fischer.

Nielsen, Henrik Kaare (1991) *Demokrati i bevægelse. Sammenlignende studier i politisk kultur og nye sociale bevægelser i Vesttyskland og Danmark*, Aarhus: Aarhus University Press.

Nielsen, Henrik Kaare (1993) *Kultur og modernitet*, Aarhus: Aarhus University Press.

Nielsen, Henrik Kaare (2001) *Kritisk teori og samtidsanalyse*, Aarhus: Aarhus University Press.

Nielsen, Henrik Kaare (2007) *Konsument eller samfundsborger. Kritiske essays*, Aarhus: Klim.

Parsons, Talcott (1969) *Politics and Social Structure*, New York: The Free Press.

Peters, Bernhard (1994) 'Der Sinn von Öffentlichkeit', in Friedhelm Neidhardt (ed.), *Öffentlichkeit, öffentliche Meinung, soziale Bewegungen*, Opladen: Westdeutscher Verlag.

Renwick Monroe, Kristen (ed.) (1991) *The Economic Approach to Politics*, New York: HarperCollins.

Rucht, Dieter (2004) 'Kapitalismuskritik im Namen der globalisierungskritischen Zivilgesellschaft – alter Wein in neuen Schläuchen?' in Dieter Gosewinkel, Dieter Rucht, Wolfgang van den Daele, and Jürgen Kocka (eds), *Zivilgesellschaft – national und transnational*, Berlin: WZB.

Schmitt, Carl (2002) *Der Begriff des Politischen*, Berlin: Duncker und Humblot.

Schulze, Gerhard (1992) *Die Erlebnisgesellschaft*, Frankfurt am Main: Campus.

Social Text 25/26, 1990, special issue.

Warren, Mark E. (2016) 'Can We Make Public Spheres More Democratic through Institutional Innovation?' in Henrik Kaare Nielsen, Christina Fiig, Jorn Loftager, Thomas Olesen, Jan Lohmann Stephensen, and Mads P. Sorensen (eds), *The Democratic Public Sphere: Current Challenges and Prospects*, Aarhus: Aarhus University Press.

42 Politics and Democracy

Weber, Max (1994) *Wissenschaft als Beruf/Politik als Beruf. Studienausgabe*, Tübingen: Mohr.

Young, Iris Marion (2001) 'Activist Challenges to Deliberative Democracy', *Political Theory* 29(5).

Ziehe, Thomas (1992) 'Modernity and Individualisation', in J. Fornäs and G. Bolin (eds), *Moves in Modernity*, Stockholm: Almqvist and Wiksell International.

3 Public Space and Late Modern Forms of Public Practice

This chapter characterises important, overall features and conditions of late modern public interaction. This characterisation will serve as a general frame of reference in the subsequent chapters on the specifics of aesthetic intervention in the political field of practice.

The Conflictual Nature of Public Space

Whereas the present argument uses *public discourse* as a specific, normative modality concept, it defines *public space* as a descriptive concept referring to the totality of society's generally accessible (physical, medial, virtual) fields of action. In this sense, public space represents an open arena in which a multiplicity of different interests and formations of meaning are interacting. In other words, public space is understood as a heterogeneous, conflictual context that in an overall perspective can be analysed on the basis of the concepts *market, state,* and *civil society.*

To be sure, these classic concepts are not used in the social geographic sense as referring to separate sectors of society (private business, public administration, and voluntary organisations), but as three distinct ideal-typical principles of institutionalising social interaction. Or to put it another way: market, state, and civil society represent different forms of societalisation. In this sense, most empirical practices will include a conflictual multiplicity of these principles of interaction, and in order to address the empirical practices analytically in a productive manner, we should therefore not be searching for 'pure' forms but, on the contrary, take our point of departure in mixed forms as a basic condition and from there investigate the reciprocal relationship of dominance between different forms of societalisation in the empirical practice in question.[1] In other words, the crucial issue is not *where* the action takes place (be it in a business enterprise, a state bureaucracy, or a grassroots movement) but *how* agents in a given practice reflect upon themselves and relate to society as a whole – whether their actions are dominated by, for example, monological special interests, formal legalism, or a dialogical self-conception.

In relation to the conceptualisation of public discourse developed above, this distinction can be understood as follows: the nature of civil society's form of

44 *Public Space and Forms of Public Practice*

societalisation is *communicative* in the dialogical sense of the term and draws on the modalities of both universally reasoning and subjective experience-reflecting public discourse, representing two distinct variants of communicative action. In contrast, the expansive, *money-mediated* societalisation of the market draws on the monological dynamics of special interests and the modality of consumerist public discourse; and the *power/legislation-mediated* societalisation principle of the state monologically submits social interaction to juridical formalisation and bureaucratic control.

Ideal-typically, a society in which the societalising principle of the market dominates will focus on individual self-interest while the perspective of the common good of society remains marginal; a society in which the mediation form of the state dominates will tend to regulate all social interaction by formal legislation and associated institutions and hence turn the population into passive clients; and in a society in which civil society dominates, the active, democratic participation of the citizens will be in focus.

In this definition, there is, in other words, a close affinity between civil society as a communicative principle of societalisation and the dialogical modality of democratic public discourse. Together they constitute a specific form of communicative-dialogical mediation of practice in public space in which they continuously engage in a conflict of hegemony with the mediation forms of the market and the state. The mediation forms of the market and the state are characterised by being not communicative but formal, and they have historically demonstrated an expansive nature: they have disseminated their respective formal regulatory mechanisms to increasingly larger areas of social life.[2]

As Habermas conceptualised it in his metaphor of *colonisation*: the formal mediating forms of the market and the state ('the system') have throughout the history of modern society tended towards expanding into the communicatively organised social structures ('the life-world'), thus altering them to money transactions or bureaucratic regulations – causing reification and dysfunction, but occasionally also communicatively organised resistance. To be sure, in Habermas' analysis, the point of a civil society-oriented critique of market and state is not that these formal principles for establishing societal relations are in themselves problematic and dispensable, but rather that historically they have spread to areas of social life where they do not belong, and where they therefore cause damage.[3] So, a civil society democratisation perspective does not aim at entirely replacing the market and the state with communicative interaction, but rather at limiting formal, systemic regulation to the areas where it functions constructively and where there would not be any democratic point in letting public debate do the regulating.

This standing conflict of hegemony between the mediation principles of the market, the state, and civil society permeates the public space of modernity, and the status of communicative public opinion formation in public space is therefore at any time a question of concrete democratic struggles and of power relations between different social interests and principles of organisation of practice.[4] In this public dealing with conflicting interests and opinions, civil society

Public Space and Forms of Public Practice 45

potentially represents a democratic counter-principle to the market's and the state's formal, expanding forms of societalisation. However, civil society action only becomes productive in a democratic perspective, if it is organised under the auspices of interests that are pushing for universalistic, comprehensively oriented, further development of democratic institutions and on this basis at the same time recognise the legitimacy and the societal value of cultural diversity. As argued above, political engagement propelled by identity issues is at the outset a delicate potential that is easily forced into particularistic or even chauvinistic politicisation processes if it is confronted with threats of social marginalisation or the loss of privileges.

This complex understanding of public space differs from other existing definitions of the concept. For instance, Hannah Arendt uses the term 'public space' in the modal sense of public discourse when she, in the tradition of classical Greek philosophy, defines public space as the space of engaged and obligating conversation, a realm of freedom in which citizens realise themselves as human beings.[5] In a modern context, this definition is parallel to the qualities of public interaction in the sense of civil society, but it remains blind to the market-mediated and state-mediated forms of interaction and formations of meaning that are increasingly dominating the generally accessible spaces of practice in late modern society and thus challenging the scope for free debate among citizens.

A similar limitation can be found in the theory of Chantal Mouffe in which 'public space' is likewise used as an equivalent of public opinion formation, i.e. the described civil society-oriented understanding of public discourse.[6] However, one of Mouffe's main points is that public opinion formation is not consensus-based but conflictual, and that public space should basically be regarded as a battlefield. Public opinion is therefore hegemonic by nature; it always marginalises and silences voices that have not been able to manifest themselves with sufficient strength in the debate. So far, Mouffe's argument seems plausible, but she totalises the conflictual dimension of public debate to the point that her theory becomes unable to even consider the possibility of a universal perspective of reflection as a capacity of public debate. As stated above, the present argument is based on the assumption of the existence of this possibility, the thesis being that a universal perspective of reflection is not guaranteed nor realised automatically, but that it can emerge in the process of conflictual interaction: in the shape of an experience-based knowledge of public interaction as simultaneously dealing with conflicts and common concerns.

In other words, although the positions of Arendt and Mouffe are in many respects congenial to the present argument, they suffer from unsatisfactory limitations. In the following, public space will be understood in the heterogeneous and conflictual sense to include the formal forms of interaction mediated by the market and the state; and the communicatively mediated forms of interaction of civil society will be understood as in themselves conflictual, but equipped with the potential to reflect the common good. Whether this potential is realised or not depends on the nature of the common experiences society makes in public debate and in the hegemonic struggles in public space in general.

46 *Public Space and Forms of Public Practice*

The existence of a public space of action is a necessary precondition for the unfolding of a democratic public discourse, but it does not represent a sufficient guarantee for such development. In the definition presented above, public space is characterised by permanent hegemonic struggles between the market's, the state's, and civil society's forms of interaction. The term 'democratic public discourse', on the contrary, is exclusively related to civil society and denotes specific dialogical-communicative forms of interaction that may develop in public space, but do not do so necessarily.

The intensification of the active, enlightened political participation of the population and thereby the strengthening of civil society's communicative mediation of social intercourse vis-à-vis the money-mediation of the market and the power-mediation of the state constitute the precondition for the further development of democracy in the deliberative sense of the term. However, it does not seem plausible that this process can be based solely on the Habermasian ideal of a rational, universally arguing discourse.[7] The process will have to include the reflection and integration of the multiplicity of subjective resources and sensuous-emotional needs and identity issues that constitute the dynamic of politicisation from below, but which, conversely, do not in themselves imply any overall, universal perspective. As outlined above, these resources represent the necessary raw material, but they need processing in order to qualify as political.

According to several empirical studies, the main contribution of civil society agents to the development of democracy does not stem from a balanced conduct of debate in the sense of universally reasoning public discourse, but, on the contrary, from their early, sensitive registration and reflection of specific societal problems related to subjective everyday life issues and their ability to attract public attention to their cause, e.g. by way of spectacular actions, including civil disobedience.[8] If the processing of these experiences of conflict by the political system and general public debate is inclusive and dialogical by nature, the horizon of reflection of civil society agents at the grassroots level may in the process transcend its particular point of departure and include common concerns of society, and their struggle may have a constructive impact on the further development of democratic political culture.

In other words, a deliberative perspective on democratic development has to conceptualise a productive, mutually enlightening and politicising interplay of elements of universally reasoning and subjective experience-reflecting public discourse. In a perspective of democratic civil society, these two types of public discourses are interdependent: the universally reasoning public discourse needs the subjective experience-reflecting public discourse as a driving force and as a diversifying, sensitising counterpart in the realisation of the principles of universal normativity. Correspondingly, the resources of the subjective experience-reflecting public discourse can only unfold democratically at the level of society as a whole if their dynamics and experiences of conflict are being processed within the discursive framework of the common good, and in a qualifying dialogue with the universally reasoning public discourse's aspiration for an overall ethical consensus.

Public Space and Forms of Public Practice   47

In this conceptualisation, evidently, it makes no sense to speak of 'the public sphere' in terms of one, unambiguously demarcated space. Parliament-oriented public debate, as it unfolds in socio-political discussions, in political journals and books, in the publicistic newspapers, and in public service media, operates in the mode of universally reasoning public discourse. But this type of debate coexists with – and engages in conflictual interplay with – a diverse multiplicity of partial publics and counterpublics in the shape of social movements and subcultures processing social experience and cultural issues in the mode of subjective experience-reflecting public discourse.

In the following, the term 'democratic public discourse' refers to this perspective of the modes of universally reasoning and subjective experience-reflecting public discourse interacting.

Types of Publics

In an influential article in 1992, Nancy Fraser presents a number of critical arguments against Habermas' classic theory of the public sphere.[9] These arguments correspond to a large degree with the critique by Negt and Kluge in terms of the theory's blindness to issues of crucial importance for the social framing conditions of public opinion formation (class, gender, experiences from private spheres of life, etc.).[10] Fraser further presents a typology of publics that is well suited as a basis for a more concrete differentiation of institutional dimensions of public exchange. Whereas the present argument up until now has focused on the relationship of conflict between a variety of modal principles of experience and meaning formation in public space, Fraser's typology brings us closer to the specific, more or less institutionalised, forms of practice characterising democratic politics and the different *scenarios* for public debate that they imply.

Fraser suggests a distinction between, on the one hand, a 'strong public' which she defines as the institutional parliamentary debate that is characterised by *will formation* leading towards formal decision-making, and, on the other, a 'weak public' understood as the non-institutional, extra-parliamentary debate characterised by a public *opinion formation* without decision-making authority. As it shows, this distinction has a close affinity with the duality of 'politics' and 'the political'.

The following argument will suggest a further differentiation of this distinction. Since the distinction is about concrete forms of practice, it does not follow the dividing lines of the modalities outlined above. For instance, Fraser's concept of a 'weak public' must be interpreted as including both *overall, universally oriented forums of debate* and *partial publics integrated in local everyday life* – in other words, two different types of civil society publics that are both characterised by the processing of life-world experiences, the dialogical struggle of positions, and the formation of political opinion. But the processing operates according to different modalities, depending on whether the overall or the grassroots level is at stake. Thus, the 'weak public' holds elements of both universally reasoning and subjective experience-reflecting public discourse.

48   *Public Space and Forms of Public Practice*

In an ideal-typical sense, it further represents the potential for communicative, reflective processing of society's conflict experience and thereby for a mediation between the conflict and consensus dimensions of the political process based on the arguing principle. In other words, this scenario implies the type of public interaction that the present argument defines as characteristic of deliberative democracy.[11]

As regards the 'strong public', we can likewise advantageously add a distinction between two dimensions: on the one hand, the will formation that expresses itself in formal decision-making – which we could call the 'output' side of the political system or the *governmental decision-maker public*. This public is heavily framed by the international conventions and treaties that the nation-state in question has acceded to, the consideration of the mechanisms and agents of the global market, international alliances and geopolitical interests of the state, existing institutionalised compromises, the technocratic design of decision proposals by the civil service, and the common interest of contending partners in keeping the negotiation process in the dark. The implicit scenario, in other words, is a type of public that does not invite deliberation ('arguing') but rests on a non-public negotiation game according to the 'bargaining' principle. The actual public aspect merely amounts to the monological presentation of decisions already made, and therefore, in this scenario, associations with the representative power-modality of the feudal public do not seem completely out of order.

On the other hand, the strong public includes the *public of parliament-oriented mass media*. This public does not in itself possess decision-making authority, but it is connected with the institutional decision-making process, since the predominant agents of this public are the same professional politicians who make the decisions in formal institutional forums. In this type of public, politicians, further, in interaction with journalists, play a mediating role by discursively legitimising decisions to the citizens and by participating in and reflecting on the opinion formation of civil society concerning the continuing decision-making process. In this context, politicians in principle act as civil society agents, and the media maintain their classic role as controllers of institutional power on behalf of civil society. This type of public constitutes the 'input' side of the political system, in as far as politicians here provide themselves with the necessary democratic legitimacy and support behind the formal institutional process of decision-making.

Thus, the interaction in the public of parliament-oriented mass media is in complex ways interconnected with the opinion formation that takes place in the universally oriented forums of civil society debate, and in this sense, it has scope to practise elements of the universally reasoning public discourse. If an opinion formation emerging from civil society is to influence the process of political decision-making, it further requires that it is able to position itself as hegemonic opinion in the public of parliament-oriented mass media.

However, the public of parliament-oriented mass media at the same time forms the arena for intense competition between special interests, including power struggles between the professional political agents who aspire to become

Public Space and Forms of Public Practice 49

or remain decision-makers. The deliberative arguing principle will therefore in this type of public be under permanent pressure from the monological discourses of power struggles and political marketing (in the modality of consumerist public discourse), which to a large degree narrow the scope for deliberative dialogue.

In precisely this context, Bernhard Peters' characterisation of public communication as *triadic* in structure appears plausible: the combatants are striving in order to convince an audience, not each other.[12] Further, the individual debater often acts as a representative of a *political camp* which additionally prompts the agent to cling to his/her point of view in order to preserve or improve his/her position in the internal hierarchy and prestige struggle of the camp. In other words, a deliberative endeavour to engage in a genuine dialogue and seek common solutions is a rare driving force in the interactions of the public of parliament-oriented mass media.

On these terms, the central battle between debaters internally and between debaters and the media often tends to be displaced from the political content to the metaphorical *framing* of the issue in question. According to George Lakoff, framing represents an extremely efficient tool for guiding and shaping public attention.[13] A successful framing addresses unconscious emotions and mental structures in the audience and channels them into a specific interpretative frame. Once this connection has been established, the audience will be close to immune to alternative framings – and correspondingly eager to engage in relations of empathy within the successful framing. Politics, so says Lakoff, is therefore about dominating the public framing of issues, and the road to this goal is via the persistent, monological launching of one's own idea of framing. If one, on the contrary, engages in a critical dialogue with the framing efforts of one's counterpart, one contributes to attracting increased public attention to the view of the opponent, thereby marginalising one's own position in the public of parliament-oriented mass media.

As it appears, Lakoff's analysis only reflects the conflict level of the political process, and its potential in a perspective of deliberative democracy is therefore limited, but it provides an excellent background characterisation of the predominant self-conception and practice among agents in the public of parliament-oriented mass media. In accordance with the experiences from the long tradition of political propaganda, the agents are well aware that words have a strong, directing impact on which issues conquer the attention of the public.[14]

This conception of political struggle manifests itself clearly in the phenomenon *spin*, in which professional politicians, media advisers, and commentators systematically strive to draw focus away from political content that is inconvenient to their respective positions in the struggle, instead placing the form aspect of debate at the centre. Politics is thereby reduced to a power struggle dominated by strategic communication and tactics, and debate appears a zero sum game with unequivocally distributed roles of winner and loser. As a part of this tendency, political agents are predominantly categorised and assessed as more or less cunning power players according to their ability to evade dealing substantially with unpleasant questions, as more or less forceful, more or less credible as

50   *Public Space and Forms of Public Practice*

persons, etc. – at the expense of political content and the reflection of associated, qualitative societal options.

Undoubtedly, this tendency towards shifting the focus onto questions of form and tactics and the underlying strategic motives of politics reflects a real condition of political struggle on the stage of the public of parliament-oriented mass media. In other words, the tendency represents a source of insight into the realities at the level of conflict in the political process, and as such it is processed and analysed in a variety of self-reflecting programmes in the media. But also as critical meta-reflection, this process-oriented angle on politics risks becoming self-reinforcing and thus contributing to the evaporation of the question of socio-political content of reason in the positions of politicians.[15]

Finally, the competition in the field of mass media adds fuel to the same fire, since the media in their struggle over public attention and market shares mainly use polarising and sensationalist staging of political debate and its agents.[16] Apart from the counter-productive nature of these tendencies from the perspective of deliberative democracy, they are, according to empirical investigations, creating distaste for politics in broad sections of the population. Citizens with both high and low levels of education express concern about the polarising and confrontational style of the mass media public and wish a genuine, matter-of-fact-oriented public dialogue where arguments are reason-based and agents let each other finish speaking.[17]

The implicit debate scenario of this type of public is, in other words, contradictory: it holds dialogical potential based on the universally reasoning public discourse, but the conditions to realise these potentials are permanently under pressure from the monological special interests of professional politicians and the professional media.

An important factor in public debate that has not been treated in the typology above, is the expert publics, whose knowledge and interpretations of factual matters in specific areas of society are eagerly used as arguments by decision-makers, political parties, journalists, and civil society agents when they support their respective agendas – and are being ignored or discredited when they don't. The reason for choosing not to include these expert publics is that their influence on general public debate and experience formation is not direct. They represent important substantial foundations of political debate, but their input is always mediated through the filters of the four presented types of publics.

In practice, the political process is of course not divided according to the suggested ideal-typical distinctions. On the contrary, it is characterised by mixed processes in which a disorganised multiplicity of interests and dynamics criss-cross. It nevertheless remains relevant to keep an analytical distinction between the four types of publics (the partial civil society public, the overall civil society public, the public of parliament-oriented mass media, and the governmental decision-maker public) and their respective scenarios, since they represent quite different conditions for a deliberative democratic process in which the question of scope for dialogical exchange and the reflection of universal concerns is crucial.[18]

Public Space and Forms of Public Practice 51

As has been argued above, first of all, the two civil society types of public have the potential of unfolding spaces for deliberative democratic processes. In this perspective, the reciprocal relationship of dominance and the concrete interplay between the types of publics in political practice will be decisive for the overall nature and developmental possibilities of the democratic political process.

Contemporary Conditions of Practice in Public Space

As a further, necessary elaboration of the theoretical frame of reference for the analysis of the interrelationship between aesthetic and political practice, the following sections provide a brief outline of basic contemporary conditions of public interaction, such as tendencies towards technocratisation and aestheticisation, and the specifics of physical, medial, and virtual spaces of practice.

Neoliberal Technocratisation

The general, conflictual interplay between the mediation forms of market, state, and civil society in public space has in later years increasingly been influenced by a development that radicalises the expansive dynamic of economic and bureaucratic rationalities. Since the early 1990s, critical political science has analysed this type of societal development as a consequence of the transformation of the classic nation-state into a 'national competitive state' due to its involvement in the emergence of increasingly globalised conditions of practice.[19] In the wake of the liberalisation of the terms of transnational movement of capital, the nation-state's classic political tools for controlling and regulating the economy have become obsolete. In the attempt to keep investments internally, on national ground – and, if possible, attracting investment from abroad – the states of the rich Western countries have adapted to the changed conditions and found their new role in optimising the national industry's competitive position in the world market. A central element of this effort is the attempt to make national society in its entirety functional in relation to the conditions of international business competition by way of market-strategic reforms and planning measures.

However, since the global market conditions are genuinely incalculable and constantly changing, nobody is able to predict with any certainty which measures and strategies will be successful. In this cognitive vacuum, a compact and powerful mainstream has been established among economists, politicians, and administrators of the rich countries and their cooperation organisations (e.g. the OECD and the European Commission) based on and affirming the mutual assumption that increasing international competition is necessary in order to ensure economic growth but at the same time represents an all-embracing challenge to national welfare institutions.

The mainstream diagnosis therefore prescribes that all available societal resources must be mobilised in order to secure the competitiveness of the national industry on the world market, and that all sectors of society must

52   *Public Space and Forms of Public Practice*

promptly be reorganised to the benefit of this overall purpose: technology development, work productivity, infrastructure, level of taxation, public health, education, research, culture, sport, etc. – everything has to be drilled and optimised according to the generalised international standards that this mainstream has authorised.

In this process, economic and bureaucratic mediations of societal practice are expanding in public space, reducing all other types of societal practice and experience to instrumental resources of market competition, marginalising the communicative mediation of civil society, and limiting the scope for democratic public discourse and democratic choices.

Furthermore, democratic public discourse is under pressure from the ongoing privatisation of increasingly larger areas of society's common knowledge and culture. The basic point of the development towards a post-Fordist 'knowledge society' is not that we as a society are necessarily becoming any wiser, but that knowledge is comprehensively being commodified and thus emphatically turned into private property. In the OECD countries, knowledge has been appointed the central strategic resource in global competition, and market agents are therefore eager to ensure as much knowledge as possible as their intellectual property.[20] At issue is not only knowledge that the market agents themselves have created or purchased, but all available knowledge that might possibly have a business potential and that is not already protected by intellectual property rights – be it indigenous people's knowledge of medicinal herbs that the medical industry is expropriating by patenting it, or the cultural industry's advancing appropriation of society's common cultural heritage.[21] Following the pattern of the historical 'primitive accumulation'[22] in which the commons were enclosed by force and appropriated by private interests, an expropriation of society's common resources of knowledge is currently taking place, and this expanding privatisation challenges free public access to knowledge and thereby erodes the basis of society's life-worldly creativity and its capacity to reflect common concerns.

In a political perspective, this overriding technocratic mainstream among economic, political, and administrative elites further commits the leading political parties to the same basic principles of 'the necessary policy', a policy that is supposedly 'without alternatives'. In other words, with regard to political content, the vast majority of the political spectrum is characterised by a high degree of consensus. Behind the polarising positioning in the public of parliament-oriented mass media, the influential parties' policies on central issues such as welfare and economic growth are close to identical. The appeal that is destined to make the voters choose one party over the other is therefore primarily established via the staging of individual politicians as particularly forceful and credible persons in the media, thus addressing the orientation-seeking identity work of citizens with offers of both aesthetic fascination and a guarantee of future welfare.

The growing populist counter-reaction to technocratic neoliberalism is displayed in the shape of a 'policy of values' as opposed to the neglect of the question of values by 'the necessary policy'. This position also draws on the tendency

Public Space and Forms of Public Practice   53

towards culturalisation: the rationale being that politicians profile themselves by creating a clear, emotion-based polarisation of positions in a political sub-field – often claiming that the values that they represent (religion, family, life, nation) incarnate a given, pre-political essence. They thereby offer potential voters a lucid point of orientation for identity work and thus a basis for empathy and for taking sides. But this type of profiling – effective as it often may be – takes place at the cost of the overall societal picture and politics' dimension of common concerns of society.

Overall Process of Aestheticisation

Another prominent condition of practice and formation of meaning in public space is the tendency towards aestheticisation. This tendency will be conceptualised more thoroughly in Chapter 4; in the present context, the concept merely points to the fact that the invitation to engage in an aesthetic type of exchange is spreading from the field of cultural artefacts and activities to becoming, in principle, all-embracing: there is practically no approach in contemporary public space that is not equipped with an intensified appeal to the senses and emotions of the recipient.[23] By way of thoroughly designed visual, acoustic, tactile, olfactory, and taste-related attributes, physical space, utility objects, commercial transactions, media communication, social relations, and the identity constructions of everyday life are raised above their prosaic functionality and endowed with an indeterminate, sensuous-emotional surplus meaning. The whole context of life thus increasingly appears as designed for aesthetic exchange.

On the side of the recipient, the dynamic of this process of aestheticisation stems from the generalised identity work and the associated culturalisation of social orientation described above. Identity work can assume a multiplicity of forms and operate according to cognitive, moral, and aesthetic discourses, but the aesthetically intensified appeal to senses and emotions obviously manifests itself as the most immediately accessible and efficient channelling of the culturalised orientation issues.

On the sender's side, we have a mixed choir of business and the advertising industry, the mass media, politicians, various organisations, social and cultural movements, and artists. These different types of agents all relate to the tendency towards aestheticisation as a general condition of competition with regard to achieving attention in public space, and they therefore in their own different ways adjust their forms of approach to this condition which is thereby permanently reinforced and becomes increasingly dominant. The fierce market competition and the associated struggle over the attention of the consumer form the primary incentive of this development, but due to the continuous expansion of market appeals in public space as a whole, they further tend to define all other agents' conditions of possibility in terms of making themselves visible and gaining voice in public space.

The consumption appeals of the market aim to endow both consumer goods and commercially relevant social spaces with a symbolic surplus value that

54   *Public Space and Forms of Public Practice*

activates the imagination of the recipient and promises an intensified sensation of life and a raised social prestige as implications of the recommended choice of consumption.[24] In other words, this is a dominating tendency towards monologically addressing the culturalised identity work of recipients in the modality of consumerist public discourse, thereby stimulating identity work in instrumentalising and restricted patterns.

Conditions of Physical Spaces of Practice

As pointed out above, the development of a democratic public discourse, capable of processing all relevant social experience, cannot be reduced to the abstract and overall form of reflection of the universally reasoning public discourse. It must also comprise conflictual social action in which agents with different interests and points of view interact in common spaces of practice, gain new experiences, challenge each other's preconceptions, and in this process develop a consciousness of common concerns and mutual obligations in spite of differences. Such spaces of practice, where informal encounters and processes of experience across partial publics take place, are increasingly scarce resources in late modern everyday life, and this fact constitutes a significant problem for the developmental perspectives of a democratic public discourse.[25]

The point of this characterisation is not to declare the physically and socially limited public space of ancient Athens, *the agora*, a relevant ideal of public space in far more complex late modern society. The point is to stress that different types of spaces of practice hold different potentials of experience formation, and that it is, first of all, in the type of communicative practice in which individuals in a physico-spatial sense impose themselves on each other and experience concrete mutual obligation that agents may develop their own means of production to constructively comprehend and process conflicts in the immediate context of everyday life, and, on this basis, also may develop a capacity to understand and act in relation to overall societal conflicts.

As indicated above, concerning the analytical distinction between public space and public discourse, there is no necessary link between, on the one hand, a common everyday experience of interacting with strangers in a civilised manner in urban space and, on the other, a genuinely political deliberation in which different opinions on specific societal issues interact dialogically and in mutual respect. But both in the shape of general cultural experience formation and specific political opinion formation, interaction with strangers in concrete physical spaces of practice holds a special potential for raising the consciousness and engagement of citizens as regards common concerns of society. This type of experience thus implies crucial perspectives for a democratic civil society and for a public interaction that is able to combine the recognition of differences and the reflection of the universal principles of the common good.

The increasing absence of such mixed spaces of practice and experience in late modern everyday life is partly due to prominent features of urban development, such as the tendency towards separating groups of the population with

Public Space and Forms of Public Practice   55

different social and cultural backgrounds[26] – and like the ongoing transformation of city spaces into zones of pure consumption at the expense of the physical and aesthetic facilitation of activities of civil society. Instead of encouraging encounters between strangers and the reflection of common concerns across differences, public spaces in late modernity increasingly appear as forums for the smooth, harmonising appeals of consumerist public discourse. Such functionalised urban spaces frame and condition a practice in which the individuals serve as arbitrary objects of projection for each other's diffuse daydreams and resentments and as stages for individuals to monologically present themselves through their life-styles. In addition, governmental surveillance activities are continuously spreading in urban space. The unfolding of civic engagement in physical space is thus under pressure from an expanding crossfire of market appeals and the panopticon.

But in spite of these restricting conditions, society's physical spaces of practice are still scenes of an interaction that primarily defines itself in relation to the communicative horizon of the life-world and that has potential regarding civil society-oriented identity formation and democratic public discourse. Examples are local, self-organised political, cultural, and artistic activities in urban space in the tradition of the grassroots movements of the 1960s and 1970s and interventions in urban space by different communities of contemporary participatory culture. A multiplicity of local participatory communities based on ideals of sustainability, sharing, and the creativity of everyday life are working by way of subjective experience-reflecting public discourse in the attempt to create social spaces on their own terms.[27] To be sure, these self-organised forms of participation are nevertheless to a lesser or greater degree interacting with other types of agents and discursive practices in public space, and although this may not be reflected by the participatory culture, this interaction is often characterised by unequal power relations.[28]

Conditions of Medial Spaces of Practice

Furthermore, the development of the spaces of practice and experience of everyday life is intertwined with the predominant role achieved by the mass media in social and cultural life as a whole. Due to globalisation's dramatic expansion and complication of economic, technological, and political interdependencies, the individual's space of relations reaches far beyond the horizon of everyday experience.[29] In this constellation, the mediation of experience by the mass media increasingly dominates the collective formation of meaning. The basic role of the media is to continuously provide a suggestion of an understanding of social reality, in which complexity is reduced to the point where the everyday consciousness of ordinary citizens is able to process it and gain orientation from it. On these premises, the media create the necessary basis for maintaining citizens' *trust* in the institutions of modernity – in spite of genuine risks and uncertainties as regards the globalised development of societal relations.

56 *Public Space and Forms of Public Practice*

It is, however, crucial for the perspective of public discourse, according to which principles this necessary reduction of complexity takes place: if the individual is addressed as an empowered, reflective citizen, who is expected to possess own resources in terms of intellect, emotions, and senses in order to process complex experiential material, we can speak of an *enlightened* invitation to trust the institutions. In this scenario, the institutions are staged as constructed and changeable entities that may not appear lucid in all dimensions, but which one can relate to, reflect on and attempt to influence.

If the reduction of complexity, on the contrary, neglects the appeal to reason and merely addresses senses and emotions, social reality is staged as a possibly fascinating, but basically inscrutable condition of destiny, the individual is addressed as an affirmation-oriented consumer or as a disempowered client, and the trust in institutions that this scenario invites remains *non-enlightened.*[30] As indicated above, due to the genuinely incalculable nature of contemporary societal relations, the media to a large extent tend to reduce complexity by aesthetic means: complex conflicts are reduced to trivial narratives of Good vs. Evil, politicians are staged as medial consumer goods and offered as icons of personal identification, rather than as representatives of political programmes, etc., thus inviting the recipients to engage in a non-enlightened relation of trust. All in all, this strengthens the appeal of public space to the individual as a consumer at the expense of his/her incentive to engage in public reflection as a citizen.

In addition, the mass media's progressively more marked status as competing market agents struggling for attention contributes to fragmenting public space, and their sensationalist profiling in the battle over market shares tends to marginalise the issues and agents of reflecting public debate.[31] In this market competition, mass media and politicians engage in a continuous conflict concerning who frames the public agenda and which time rhythms should have priority: the media are producing and competing on the terms of who comes first with the news, which makes their time horizon very short, whereas the political process operates on the slower rhythms of election periods and negotiation games and therefore within a longer time horizon. The medial representation of the political process always unfolds in a relationship of conflict between these opposite interests and priorities.[32]

It might further be interpreted as a consequence of this intensified relationship of conflict that political parties in their appeal to voters are increasingly attempting to communicate directly to the private interests and issues of potential voters, in the shape of marketing and approaches via social media, i.e. avoiding the channelling of the mass media, the journalists and the editorial process.[33] Donald Trump's unceasing stream of monologic statements on Twitter may serve as an extreme example. Considering the terms that the media are offering, this tendency may appear understandable, but at the same time, it represents a privatisation of the horizon of communication and thus a decay of public interaction. Just like the tendency towards letting opinion polls decide policy, the private, monologic voter appeal contributes to transforming political relations to market relations: politics becomes a commodity that is to be sold to private individuals, rather than a proposal of a public dialogue on the regulation of common concerns.

Furthermore, in the perspective of civil society, this development of the late modern space of relations necessitates the mediation of knowledge that does not originate from the individuals' immediate everyday life experience. Under these conditions, forming an opinion and acting as a citizen on a competent level not only depend on communicative interaction in concrete spaces of practice and experience. It also implies the ongoing acquisition of a large fund of knowledge on geographically remote conditions and non-lucid relations of exchange and interdependency between near and far. In the terminology of Negt and Kluge, this constellation requires an interplay between 'immediate experience' (understood as sensory-based knowledge which the individual has acquired in direct, bodily, and mental exchange with the physical world) and 'mediated experience' (knowledge acquired at second hand). Both types of experience are crucial preconditions for being able to orientate oneself in the modern space of relations, so the distinction between them is not aimed at granting immediate experience a monopoly on being 'real', but merely at pointing out a fundamental difference in respect to the 'quality of reality' which implies perspectives for the conditions of possibility for democratic processes of empowerment.

As Dieter Hoffmann-Axthelm has argued, it is the basic principle of human formation of experience that we acquaint ourselves with the world through our senses, and by analogy to the immediate, sensory-based experience of our previous life history.[34] Concurrent with the development and differentiation of this primary foundation of experience, the ability to practise an increasingly abstracting formation of analogy emerges and allows us to integrate mediated experience; but the sensory-based patterns of immediate experience remain the fulcrum, also for the acquisition of mediated experience.

With respect to the potential of the late modern space of relations to develop a democratic public discourse with a productive interplay between the subjective experience-reflecting public discourse, based on the formation of concrete, diverse experiences, and the overall reflection of the universally reasoning public discourse, the interesting question is thus whether the dominance of the media and mediated experience still allows the process of analogical acquisition sufficient scope to function, and thus enables individuals to develop a competent identity as citizens. Or whether the sensory-based potential and the ability to form experience-integrating analogies in reality are being exhausted under the present conditions, with a common lack of orientation and judgement as a consequence – which would leave the diffuse resources of resistance of everyday experience to the instrumentalising processing of consumerist public discourse.

This issue is further related to the question as to which conditions of possibility for democracy are inherent in the general tendency towards accelerating social processes. The unlimited global financial transactions, technological development, the comprehensive interlacing of national economies, and the global networks of communication are all, by way of their constantly increasing velocity and their creation of global simultaneity, contributing to establishing

58 *Public Space and Forms of Public Practice*

new terms for the political process. These accelerated conditions tend to collide with the qualitative, experience-reflecting time rhythms that a deliberative democratic opinion formation requires in order to unfold productively. The basic democratic principle of the enlightened, dialogic exchange between empowered citizens is, in other words, under pressure from global framing conditions that accelerate the political process and constantly confront it with complex, solution-demanding problems that in respect to the dynamics of time, scope, and implications reach beyond the capacity of general democratic debate.[35]

In recent decades, the mass media have undergone a strong organisational and business-oriented professionalisation as market forces have increasingly gained ground in the field. In this process, the fierce competition over readers/viewers/listeners and advertisers has become the main, urgent condition of all institutional agents in the medial space of practice. Not least the challenge posed by the Internet in general and social media in particular in terms of attracting both users and advertisers plays a huge role in this development. The media products' appeal to the immediate inclinations of a broad audience has in this process advanced to being the superior focus of the mass media, whereas classic journalistic, scientific, artistic, and cultural criteria of relevance and quality have been pushed into the background. In other words, the tendency is that the public in the overall media landscape has been transformed into clients and consumers, no longer being addressed as citizens engaged in a public exchange over common concerns.

In the attempt to attract as large an audience as possible, the media intensify the aestheticising measures: the spectacular, the scandalous, intriguing revelations from the intimate lives of celebrities, personal showdowns between top politicians, the non-reflective, sensationalist spreading of the very newest news – all are ingredients of a contemporary media landscape that rather presents itself as a branch of the entertainment industry than as playing the classic role of guarantor of enlightenment, critical debate, and control of established power holders. For public service media and publicistic media, the classic role of the mass media still holds a prominent position in their self-conception, but in practice they are competing for attention against the agents of the media market, and their concrete handling of the classic role is increasingly marked by the conditions of competition defined by the commercial media.

The charging of the entire output of the media with aesthetic appeals to senses and emotions implies challenges to discursive borders, for example, between private and public matters. However, these challenges do not necessarily result in the disappearance of discursive distinctions, but merely imply that contents like e.g. domestic violence or the moral habitus of politicians are no longer matters of privacy. The power of fascination that sensationalist media and the advertising industry continuously derive from the challenging of the borders of privacy, stems from the fact that the discursive border is still functioning although concrete contents are occasionally shifting sides.

As a main tendency, the medial space of practice is characterised by a multiplicity of mixed forms in which enlightenment, debate, and entertainment on floating and opaque premises are integrated into the same media product.[36] This type of product, also known as 'infotainment', is obviously the main representative of what the mass media are capable of accomplishing on the current terms of competition.[37] The strength of this is the ability of the aestheticised media products to gain the attention of a broad audience, also concerning political, economic, and scientific topics; the weakness is the meagre or totally absent dimension of critical reflection and dialogic processing of the topics in their capacity as common concerns of society. This weakness contributes actively to marginalising the perspective of public discourse from public space.

Conditions of Virtual Spaces of Practice

The Internet with its specific medial characteristics is inscribed in this overall picture of the public space of late modernity. The virtual space of practice, to which the interface of the World Wide Web grants access, is correspondingly permeated by conflicts between the principles of universally reasoning, subjective experience-reflecting and consumerist public discourses and the associated, conflicting formations of experience and meaning. In respect to quality of experience, the Internet further represents an ambiguity: on the one hand, it contributes to the increasingly predominant status of mediated experience in society; on the other, by way of the interactive potential of the Net interface, it must at the same time be regarded as an aspect of the current condition of acquiring immediate experience.

In this context, it is a central question regarding the potential of Internet use in relation to the democratic public, according to which discursive principles the concrete interface has been constructed. Which possibilities of control and interaction does it open and close? Which implicit intentionality (commercial, artistic, political, technocratic, or repressive in terms of surveillance) frames the interaction and formation of experience facilitated by the interface, and to what extent does it make a genuine, dialogical exchange possible? These features of the interface condition practices in the virtual space of action, but without determining them in a strict sense – in other words, the concrete use of the media still implies scope for critical reflection and alternative, autonomous practice.

Ever since the 1990s, we have been witnessing a continuous production of wishful thinking around the issue of the democratic potentials of the Internet. There are, however, a number of central issues that are still left in the dark by these cheerful interpretations of the potentials of the Net. For instance, it constitutes a crucial difference whether the individual in his/her practice on the Net is acting in the role of committed, participating citizen, as monologically acting market agent, as bureaucratically framed user of the services of the public sector, or as object of governmental or commercial surveillance. Only the first mentioned of these roles has democratic relevance, and even in this category not all Net practice can be classified as democratic in a dialogic, critically reflecting sense of the term: as demonstrated lucidly by the 2016 campaigns for Brexit and to elect Donald Trump as US president, allegedly democratic agents and

60 *Public Space and Forms of Public Practice*

organisations do not hesitate to spread lies in order to strengthen their position and discredit the opposite side – thus contributing to push society further towards a state of 'post-factuality'.[38] And to complete the picture, overtly anti-democratic elements, including terrorist organisations, are also active on the Net, and seek to disseminate their misinformation disguised as arguments.

Furthermore, the role of the citizen as such is under pressure on the Internet which since 1993 and 1994 has been the target of an immense process of colonisation by market forces.[39] The commercialisation of access to the Net, the orientation of Internet regulations towards facilitating trade transactions, the increasing advertisement financing of all sorts of Net activities, the massive and expansive presence of private companies, etc., have to a large extent submitted Internet interaction to consumerist public discourse, thus using advanced communication technology in a targeted manner and beyond any critical dialogue in order to establish a direct link between the economic interests of business and the private desires and inclinations of the individual consumer. This practice is evidently generally considered legitimate, but it has absolutely nothing to do with democracy, if we thereby understand the reflective, dialogical, political organisation of common concerns of society.

In the light of this process of commercialisation, Jodi Dean denies the Internet any democratic relevance. According to Dean, critical civil society activity will also inevitably be absorbed by the prevailing 'communicative capitalism' on the Net.[40] This analysis seems, however, to be too deterministic, considering that the Internet still functions as a field of practice for a multiplicity of non-commercial agents, networks, and institutions who use the Net on their own terms. In spite of their discursive autonomy, these activities are nevertheless conditioned and restricted by the dominance of the market, in the sense that the market-defined competition in the virtual space of practice makes it considerably more difficult for autonomous civil society initiatives (whether they are political, social, or artistic) to attract attention and establish themselves on the Net.

It will be a basic assumption in the following that if the Internet deserves particular attention in the perspective of democratic public discourse, it must be on the basis of its own, unique, medial properties, and not just as an expanded and accelerated version of the traditional media. The expansion, the acceleration, and immediate availability of gigantic amounts of information are, of course, in a quantitative sense, important new features of the Internet, but its qualitative innovation consists in its facilitation of horizontal two-way communication, i.e. its 'many to many capability'.[41] Apart from the interactive potential, the Internet also grants the individual an immediate opportunity to publish directly to a global public. So, in principle, the Internet constitutes a vast field of opportunity from the perspective of both the universally reasoning and the subjective experience-reflecting public discourse.

However, the actual use of the Net exploits the new medial possibilities of the interface only to a limited degree. The Internet is to a large extent used as an ordinary mass media: public authorities, political parties, and agents of the market address their recipients via the Net in the same one-way mode of communication that they have traditionally used in printed material and TV spots. Apart from this, the Internet is first of all used for private e-mail correspondence, entertainment, and the search for information, whereas politics plays a marginal role in activity on the Net as a whole. Dialogic Internet communication that orientates itself towards universally reasoning public discourse, so far remains of peripheral importance in comparison with the proportions of consumerist public discourse and private communication on the Net.

In this quantitative sense, it looks only slightly better for the elements of subjective experience-reflecting public discourse on the Internet, since they also stand quite in the shadow of commercial and private Net use. But in qualitative respect, the Net represents a crucial resource for the communication and the collective processing of experience of autonomous civil society initiatives. A diverse multiplicity of social, cultural, and artistic movements, subcultures, participatory communities, etc. use the Net for internal communication, public presentations, campaigning, organising demonstrations, putting pressure on politicians and media, etc.; and the immediacy of Net communication tends to intensify activists' expectations of being able to have an immediate impact on societal issues, to be directly connected and to be participating in real time in events that take place far away in terms of physical space. The capacity of networked communities to spread information immediately and potentially 'go viral', constitutes an immense mobilising resource for civil society initiatives, but the very same capacity enables the uncontrollable, self-reinforcing, viral spread of lies and disinformation, including 'shitstorms' that channel collective aggression beyond any reason – so it remains an ambivalent feature of Net communication.

As the development in a number of North African and Middle Eastern societies in 2010–2011 showed (the Arab Spring), the Net and not least the social media further have the capacity to play the role of channels of communication and coordination for the mobilisation of popular resistance by democratic forces against dictatorial regimes.[42] Similarly, the Occupy Wall Street movement that originated in New York in September 2011 and quickly spread to countries all over the world, both internally and externally made extensive use of Internet communication.[43]

In order to assess the potentials of the Internet in terms of democratic public discourse, however, it is crucial to be aware that these currents represent civil society practice which operates in both physical and virtual space at the same time: their activity originates in experiences and relations in 'real life' and in a common effort to bring about concrete changes, whereas virtual space is integrated as a supplementary frame for a common, inward formation of identity, and as a public platform for outward communication. At the end of the day, it was the persistent, bodily occupation of the physical urban space of Cairo by large crowds of people and the military's abstaining from dissolving the crowds by way of physical violence that brought about the fall of the Mubarak regime, not the associated communication in virtual space. Likewise, the decline of Occupy Wall Street in reality already started as the police in November 2011 violently ended the physical occupation of Zuccotti Park in New York's financial district.

62 Public Space and Forms of Public Practice

In the long run, virtual communication alone was unable to sustain the engagement of the activists.

Apart from its possible role in such specific civil society practices, virtual space may in general contribute to compensate for the above-mentioned increasing scarcity of physical, urban spaces designed to facilitate public, communicative interaction between citizens. In addition, virtual space offers the opportunity of creating communicative circuits and relations of practice that transcend the limits of physical space and thus open the perspective of a global civil society. Those movements and subcultures (i.e. partial civil society publics) using the Internet in this way in order to create critical, public reflection in an interplay with 'real-life' practice in the shape of horizontally communicating forms of politics, are productively exploiting the uniquely new medial potentials of the Internet.

The strength of these forms of political participation, in contrast to the traditional hierarchical forms of party politics, is that they offer the individual the opportunity of immediately and directly becoming a valid and active participant. Their weakness in the perspective of a democratic public discourse, on the other hand, is partly that they lack a democratically legitimising formal mandate, and partly that they tend to fragment public, communicative interaction, and marginalise the obligation of the agents in respect to reflecting society as a community of historical experience, including common politico-cultural values and standards of public interaction. Inwardly, these autonomous networks may function as highly productive publics based on the mode of subjective experience-reflecting public discourse, thus developing both a strong, common identity and nuancing learning processes in relation to their respective topics. But, as pointed out in the previous section, outwardly, this very combination of identity work and political commitment will often make them appear as monological partial publics with an exclusive focus on their own themes and interests.[44] Partial publics developing into echo chambers primarily serving the mutual affirmation of the participants constitutes a widespread phenomenon.

As pointed out earlier, this reflects a general limitation of the immediate horizon of experience of partial publics which it is essential to overcome in an overall perspective of late modern democracy. In other words, if the Internet is to be developed further as a space of practice of civil society, and thus gain relevance in an overall perspective of democratic public discourse, it implies that partial publics transcend their particularistic self-presentation and create forums for common, transverse discussion. The aim of this would be the emergence of a new political culture on the Internet which would integrate universalistic reflection and recognition of difference – and thus be able to operate within the discursive framework of the common good without invalidating particular network identities.

So far, however, partial publics have primarily appropriated the Internet as a media for their individual issues, not as a media for universal public reasoning. The explanation for this may evidently be that a need for overall public forums on the Net has hitherto not manifested itself with sufficient urgency for partial

Public Space and Forms of Public Practice 63

publics to foster the necessary initiatives. Needs emerging from social practice will always be the decisive factors as to whether a media is brought into play in relation to political issues.[45] At the same time, each media form is characterised by distinct medial properties that facilitate and condition specific forms of realisation of the practice needs in question – and in this perspective, the interface of digital media carries features that in principle may contribute to weakening the developmental conditions of overall public forums on the Internet.

Until now, general experience indicates that 'pure' Net communication, i.e. without the interplay with 'real-life' practice, does not provide optimal conditions for establishing democratic dialogue between citizens. Numerous analyses of political debates on the Internet show concurrently that a hyperactive minority typically conquers the scene and primarily uses the public space of the Net for monological proclamations of their allegedly indisputable opinions.[46] Corresponding tendencies occur in other, purely virtual forums: in spite of the medial potential of the weblog and the general image of blogging as a media of interactivity and dialogue,[47] a closer view reveals the 'blogosphere' as dominated by the monological self-presentation of individuals and by the formation of groups that confirm unity inwardly, but do not engage in outward dialogue.[48]

In recent years, the virtual communities that are unfolding on social media platforms like Facebook, Twitter, YouTube, Instagram, etc. have increasingly included elements of political postings and debate. On these platforms, individual identity work is performed in interaction with continuous streams of postings and comments that may address – and be addressed by – the participating individuals in both cognitive, moral, and aesthetic discourses and within private as well as public horizons of feeling and reasoning. For the participants, these streams play the role of narrative structures[49] that they can relate to and contribute to, gain orientation from, and that may challenge or affirm their ongoing identity formation both emotionally and intellectually. To the extent that political interventions in the streams take place, they become part of the material that identity work processes – or neglects.

However, according to a recent, major survey on politics and social media use in the USA,[50] political communication is far from predominant. Only 9 per cent of social media users are frequently engaged in political debates, and although political interventions increasingly occur in streams on Facebook and Twitter, only 20 per cent of the users like to be confronted with them – the rest either don't care, try to ignore them, or are worn out by their expansion and frustrated over the hostile tone and the polarising content. Further, most of those who engage in political debates on social media make an attempt to stay clear of debaters with whom they disagree strongly – thus intensifying the tendency towards creating echo chambers that establish internal consensus by blocking out parts of reality.

The vast majority of social media interactions primarily seem to serve the purpose of individual self-presentation, identity profiling (e.g. in the shape of staging oneself as an absolute success on Facebook and Instagram or demonstrating superior wit by throwing flashy one-liners on Twitter), letting off steam,

64 *Public Space and Forms of Public Practice*

and mutually affirming communication within a particular, private horizon, rather than the facilitation of an overall reflecting, democratic dialogue.[51] Undoubtedly, these forums, operating in the mode of what we might term 'monological public self-presentation', fulfil a need in individual identity work, but they represent a use of the Internet media which neither in the universally reasoning nor the subjective experience-reflecting sense has anything to do with a democratic public discourse.

In other words, Net communication that is not involved in an interplay with 'real-life' practice primarily seems to appeal to the individual as a self-centred consumer, i.e. to his/her private needs and special interests, rather than to his/her capacity as a citizen orientated towards dialogue and the common good. The background for this tendency is complex, but involves as a crucial element some characteristics of the interface of the World Wide Web and the virtual space of practice. As mentioned above, due to the medial possibility of interactivity, virtual space implies an element of the formation of immediate experience, but at the same time it must be noted that this type of experience has a restricted quality.

Whereas face-to-face interaction implies a broad spectrum sensory relation in which the agents offer each other a complex response, adding a variety of nuances to the verbally communicated content and thus throwing it into relief, the virtual encounter is characterised by a restricted, almost frictionless, sensory quality. As pointed out earlier in relation to the concepts of immediate and mediated experience formation, this distinction is not aiming at granting one type of interaction a monopoly on being 'real', but merely at distinguishing between different qualities of reality with different characteristics and potentials. Both face-to-face communication and virtual communication are absolutely necessary in the late modern space of relations, but due to their respective interactive sensory qualities, they imply different degrees of involvement and mutual obligation between the agents.

In face-to-face interaction, we offer our bodily integrity as a pledge to our commitment and credibility, and at the same time we demonstrate a degree of trust and recognition of the counterpart that we would not be able to communicate virtually – no matter what bandwidth the interface may reach.[52] In addition, face-to-face communication is the form of experience in which we, in the perspective of our individual life-histories, have developed our basic social competences and to which also, in later phases of life, essential dimensions of our judgement and ability to make qualified distinctions remain connected.[53]

The fact that important political and economic negotiations and the settling of major agreements still necessarily imply face-to-face meetings – even although matters might technically very well be dealt with in virtual space – is a strong indication that this qualitative difference is actually operative in social practice. When complicated and important questions are at stake in economic and political relations (or in love relations, for that matter), and the highest possible degree of mutual trust is necessary, virtual communication is, in other words, insufficient – on such occasions the presence of the body and the sincerity of the face and eye contact are required as guarantors. Furthermore, the participants of

Public Space and Forms of Public Practice 65

more informal virtual communities typically develop a need for also getting together in 'real life' every now and then, since this quality of interaction is experienced as more binding and thus more consolidating for the community than the purely virtual relation.[54]

In other words, when purely virtual political debating forums seem to encourage agents to participate in a discourse of special interests rather than commit themselves to reflecting on the common good, an obvious explanatory factor could be the restricted, almost frictionless, sensory quality of the interface and virtual communication, which to a higher degree appeals to the expansive projection of one's own needs, wishes, and immediate, private opinions than to the complex reflection of both one's own and the counterpart's points of view in relation to the discursive framework of the common good.

Another way of putting this is that the agents of virtual communication, neither in a physico-spatial, a bodily, nor a social sense are dependent on one another: the communication is not associated with any common or mutual responsibility which might connect the agents in binding relations. Moreover, on this background, pure Net communication will typically not encourage the development of a practical readiness among the participants to recognise each other's points of view and basic legitimacy to the extent that they are willing to seek agreement, make compromises, and commit themselves to reflecting the common good – in other words: act as democratic citizens in public interaction.[55]

In the terminology developed above: in order for identity work in general and everyday life's diffuse impulses of resistance in particular to become the driving force of action on the basis of subjective experience-reflecting public discourse, a social context of obligating relationships and dialogic, reciprocal counter-play is required. Otherwise, the identity-seeking and the impulses of resistance will instead tend to take the form of diffuse anger, private prejudice, and monologic aggression – as is well known from the widespread trolling, harassing practices, and shitstorms on the Internet.

As pointed out above, the Internet today represents an invaluable resource for partial publics and counter-publics operating in the mode of subjective experience-reflecting public discourse, and thereby for a horizontal many-to-many communication which connects interaction in virtual space with relations and committed activity in 'real life'. In this sense, the Internet forms an important framing condition for the possible current development of an increased democratic participation in the shape of civil society interaction. But, as we have also seen, partial publics so far exhibit considerable limitations in the perspective of an overall democratic public discourse, due to their tendency to form closed circuits and to neglect transversal dialogue within the discursive framework of the common good. In other words: on the Internet, subjective experience-reflecting public discourse holds a relatively strong position, whereas the position of universally reasoning public discourse so far has remained weak.

If the communicative practice of partial publics is to be able to contribute to a productive interplay between subjective experience-reflecting and universally reasoning public discourses and thereby to the development of a participation-based,

66 *Public Space and Forms of Public Practice*

democratic civil society, which is also competent in an overall, socio-political perspective, learning processes are necessary, in which the diverse, autonomous communities of practice challenge each other dialogically and open their respective particular horizons towards a universal public discourse. The Internet would still not be able to replace the classic mass media and parliamentary forums in respect to the overall processing and interpretation of the conflict experience of society, but the Net might play an important role as the channel through which partial publics combining 'real life' and Net activity intervene in common public debate.

But these positive potentials of the Internet in a perspective of democratic public discourse are at the same time accompanied by a number of risks. As we have seen, consumerist public discourse has established itself in an extraordinarily strong position in the public space of the Internet and has shaped its predominant formations of meaning in the monological forms of private fantasies of consumption. In an interplay with the liberalist mainstream of political life, the agents of cultural industry thus both in 'real life' and in virtual space contribute actively to the positioning of special interests and immediate private preferences as the fulcrum of social practice – at the expense of the perspective of reflecting the common good. The discursive hegemony of consumerist public discourse further implies that the predominant formation of meaning concerning the Internet focuses on precisely those medial properties that aim at facilitating the user as a self-centred consumer, who expects his/her own urges and needs to be satisfied immediately and without friction. The appeal of this promise of the Net as an infrastructure for the realisation of private, monological, wishful thinking is strong, and so far tends to marginalise alternative formations of meaning with regard to the Net as a possible forum for engaged dialogical exchange between citizens. The private, self-presenting individual pressing the Facebook 'like' button has nothing to do with the deliberation of common concerns.[56]

Finally, we should consider the risks to a democratic civil society public that emanate from the increasing, comprehensive, governmental surveillance activity on the Internet, and from the action-conditioning forms of control that are always implied in the very construction of the interface. It would in this respect be crucial for the developmental possibilities of a democratic public discourse that these forms of control be based on the communicative, critically reflecting principles of civil society, and not on the formal principles of the market or the state. The potentials of the Internet in respect to a democratic public discourse are, in other words, closely connected to the question of the development of social and political relations of power – in virtual space as well as in 'real life'.

Notes

1 At the agent level, 'civil society' refers to the multiplicity of individual and collective agents who contribute actively to society's democratic participation and political opinion formation: social movements, citizens' initiatives, political parties, debaters, etc. See Jean L. Cohen and Andrew Arato, *Civil Society and Political Theory*

Public Space and Forms of Public Practice   67

(Cambridge, MA: MIT Press, 1992). But as pointed out, the concrete practices of these agents typically include elements of market and/or state societalisation as well.

2 Jürgen Habermas, *Theorie des kommunikativen Handelns*, vols 1–2 (Frankfurt am Main: Suhrkamp, 1981) (English translation: *Theory of Communicative Action*, vols 1–2, Boston: Beacon Press, 1984).

3 For example, the demotivating consequences among professionally committed employees of the accelerating, neoliberal control regime in public organisations; the increasing industrialisation of public child care and care for elderly people marginalising the element of non-instrumental interhuman communication; and the submission of education, research, art, and culture to criteria of economic usefulness, whereby the inherent potential of non-directed learning processes and making completely new experiences suffers.

4 When Nancy Fraser and Kate Nash (2014) argue that today the public sphere can only be addressed as a transnational entity, they are right in respect to the relations and conflicts of *public space*. But *public discourse* as a specific dialogical-communicative principle of mediation has so far only achieved a fairly solid institutionalisation within (certain) democratic nation-states, and since the focus in this context is the contemporary challenges and prospects of this specific principle of mediation, the democratic nation-state will form the horizon of the argument. For the transnational/global perspective, see Nancy Fraser and Kate Nash, *Transnationalizing the Public Sphere* (Cambridge: Polity Press, 2014), and Ingrid Volkmer, *The Global Public Sphere* (Cambridge: Polity Press, 2014).

5 Hannah Arendt, *The Human Condition* (Chicago: University of Chicago Press, 1958).

6 Chantal Mouffe, *The Return of the Political* (London: Verso, 1993).

7 Gunnar Schmidt, 'Zivile Gesellschaft und öffentlicher Raum', *Leviathan* 4 (1995).

8 Jürgen Gerhards. 'Diskursive versus liberale Öffentlichkeit', *Kölner Zeitschrift für Soziologie und Sozialpsychologie*, 1 (1997): 49; Michael Schudson, 'Why Conversation Is Not the Soul of Democracy', *Critical Studies in Mass Communication*, 14(4) (1997).

9 Nancy Fraser, 'Rethinking the Public Sphere', in Craig Calhoun (ed.), *Habermas and the Public Sphere* (Cambridge, MA: MIT Press, 1992).

10 See also Christina Fiig, 'A Powerful, Opinion-Forming Public? Rethinking the Habermasian Public Sphere in a Perspective of Feminist Theory and Citizenship', *Distinktion: Scandinavian Journal of Social Theory*, 12(3) (2011).

11 Evidently, conflicts and power struggles also occur in civil society forums at both grassroots and overall levels, just as civil society organisations often act as representatives of special interests – see the analyses in Donatella della Porta and Dieter Rucht (eds), *Meeting Democracy. Power and Deliberation in Global Justice Movements* (Cambridge: Cambridge University Press, 2013). But the scenario that defines the self-conception of these forums explicitly focuses on life-world interests and dialogical ideals, which differs from the scenarios of the other types of publics that are of a more composed nature. Thus, while overt power struggle and discursive prioritisation of systemic interests count as normal elements of parliamentary party politics, they will basically be perceived as problematic foreign bodies when they appear in civil society forums.

12 Bernhard Peters, *Der Sinn von Öffentlichkeit* (Frankfurt am Main: Suhrkamp, 2007).

13 George Lakoff, *Don't Think of an Elephant!* (White River Junction, VT: Chelsea Green Publishing, 2004).

14 Nicholas Jackson O'Shaughnessy, *Politics and Propaganda* (Manchester: Manchester University Press, 2004).

15 Anker Brink Lund, 'Mediedebat som politisk mantra', in Henrik Kaare Nielsen and Finn Horn (eds), *Kritik som deltagelse* (Aarhus: Klim, 2006).

16 Nick Davies, *Flat Earth News* (London: Random House, 2008).

68   Public Space and Forms of Public Practice

17 Louise Phillips and Kim Schrøder, *Sådan taler medier og borgere om politik* (Aarhus: Aarhus University Press, 2004), p. 147.
18 See also Nick Couldry, *Why Voice Matters* (London: Sage, 2010).
19 Joachim Hirsch, *Vom Sicherheitsstaat zum nationalen Wettbewerbsstaat* (Berlin: ID Verlag, 1998).
20 Joachim Hirsch, 'Wissen und Nichtwissen: Anmerkungen zur "Wissensgesellschaft"', in Oliver Brüchert and Christine Resch (eds), *Zwischen Herrschaft und Befreiung* (Münster: Westfälisches Dampfboot, 2002).
21 Lawrence Lessig, *Free Culture* (New York: Penguin Press, 2004); Henrik Kaare Nielsen and Søren Pold, 'Kulturkamp.com – mellem åbne værker og intellektuel ejendomsret', in Søren Pold and Lone Koefoed Hansen (eds), *Interface – digital kunst and kultur* (Aarhus: Aarhus University Press, 2007).
22 Karl Marx, *Capital*, vol. 1 (Harmondsworth: Penguin, 1976 [1867]), Chapter 24.
23 Wolfgang Welsch, *Ästhetisches Denken* (Stuttgart: Reclam, 1990); Martin Seel, *Ästhetik des Erscheinens* (Frankfurt am Main: Suhrkamp, 2003) (English translation: *Aesthetics of Appearing*, Stanford, CA: Stanford University Press, 2005); Wolfgang Welsch (ed.), *Die Aktualität des Ästhetischen* (München: Wilhelm Fink Verlag, 1993); Ulrik Bisgaard and Carsten Friberg (eds), *Det æstetiskes aktualitet* (Copenhagen: Multivers, 2006); Morten Kyndrup, *Den æstetiske relation* (Copenhagen: Gyldendal, 2008); Birgit Eriksson, Henrik Kaare Nielsen, and Jacob Lund, *Æstetisering* (Aarhus: Klim, 2012); Henrik Kaare Nielsen, *Æstetik og politisk offentlighed* (Aarhus: Klim, 2014).
24 Wolfgang Ullrich, *Habenwollen. Wie funktioniert die Konsumkultur?* (Frankfurt am Main: Fischer Taschenbuch Wissenschaft, 2008).
25 Richard Sennett, *Uses of Disorder: Personal Identity and City Life* (London: Faber and Faber, 1996).
26 Hartmut Häußermann, Dieter Läpple, and Walter Siebe, *Stadtpolitik* (Frankfurt am Main: Suhrkamp, 2008).
27 Henry Jenkins, Mizuko Ito, and danah boyd, *Participatory Culture in a Networked Era* (Cambridge: Polity Press, 2016).
28 Christian Fuchs, *Social Media* (London: Sage, 2014); Nico Carpentier, *Media and Participation. A Site of Ideological-Democratic Struggle* (Bristol: Intellect, 2011); Steven Griggs, A. Norval, and H. Wagenaar (eds), *Practices of Freedom: Decentred Governance, Conflict and Democratic Participation* (Cambridge: Cambridge University Press, 2014); Patrizia Nanz and Claus Leggewie, *Die Konsultative. Mehr Demokratie durch Bürgerbeteiligung* (Berlin: Wagenbach, 2016); Alex Demirovic (ed.), *Transformation der Demokratie – demokratische Transformation* (Münster: Westfälisches Dampfboot, 2016); John Keane, 'Monitory Democracy?' in Sonia Alonso, John Keane, and Wolfgang Merkel (eds), *The Future of Representative Democracy* (Cambridge: Cambridge University Press, 2011).
29 Anthony Giddens, *Modernity and Self-Identity* (Stanford, CA: Stanford University Press, 1991).
30 Henrik Kaare Nielsen, *Kritisk teori og samtidsanalyse* (Aarhus: Aarhus University Press, 2001).
31 Joseph N. Capella and Kathleen Hall Jamieson, *Spiral of Cynicism: The Press and the Public Good* (Oxford: Oxford University Press, 1997).
32 Daniel Fetzner and Stefan Selke (eds) *Selling Politics* (Furtwangen: Hochschule Furtwangen, 2005).
33 Sigge Winther Nielsen (ed.), *Politisk Marketing* (Copenhagen: Karnov Group, 2011).
34 Dieter Hoffmann-Axthelm, *Sinnesarbeit* (Frankfurt am Main: Campus, 1984).
35 Hartmut Rosa, *Weltbeziehungen im Zeitalter der Beschleunigung* (Frankfurt am Main: Suhrkamp, 2012).
36 Peter Dahlgren, *Media and Political Engagement* (New York: Cambridge University Press, 2009).

Public Space and Forms of Public Practice 69

37 Nick Davies, *Flat Earth News* (London: Random House, 2008). Although Donald Trump's 2016 presidential campaign heavily criticised the established media, these characteristics of the mass media public were the very element in which his success was formed: by constantly and with overt fascination focusing on Trump's outrageous conduct and statements, the media framed him as the most interesting candidate in the race and thus provided him with an aestheticised attention that contributed to his victory.

38 Farhad Manjoo, *True Enough: Learning to Live in a Post-Fact Society* (Hoboken, NJ: John Wiley and Sons, Inc., 2008); Ari Rabin-Havt, *Media Matters, Lies, Incorporated. The World of Post-Truth Politics* (New York: Anchor Books, 2016).

39 Henrik Kaare Nielsen, *Konsument eller samfundsborger? Kritiske essays* (Aarhus: Klim, 2007).

40 Jodi Dean, *Publicity's Secret: How Technoculture Capitalizes on Democracy* (Ithaca, NY: Cornell University Press, 2002).

41 Howard Rheingold, *The Virtual Community* (New York: Addison-Wesley Publishing Company, 1993); Peter Dahlgren, *The Political Web* (Basingstoke: Palgrave Macmillan, 2013); Niels Ole Finnemann, 'The Internet and the Public Space', *Nordic Media Trends*, 9(1) (2006).

42 In connection with these events, however, a problematic tendency has developed towards exaggerating the role of the Internet and the social media. Concrete investigations point out that communication via social media was in reality limited to a narrow, well-educated elite and that the role of this communication was more complex and ambivalent than initially assumed, since it unintentionally also provided the governmental apparatus of surveillance and repression with useful information. Further, the 'hype' around social media tends to play down the central role that the classic mass media played in the process: partly as the actual information channels of the masses, partly as the producers and distributors of the titillating hype about the social media as revolutionary agents per se. Cf. Jon Alterman, 'The Revolution Will Not Be Tweeted', *Washington Quarterly* 34 (2011); Evgeny Mozorov, *The Net Delusion* (London: Allen Lane, 2011).

43 Manuel Castells, *Networks of Outrage and Hope* (Cambridge: Polity Press, 2012).

44 Wim van de Donk, Brian D. Loader, Paul G. Nixon and Dieter Rucht, *Cyberprotest: New Media, Citizens and Social Movements* (London: Routledge, 2004); Cas R. Sunstein, *Republic.com 2.0* (Princeton, NJ: Princeton University Press, 2007); Nielsen, *Kritisk teori ...*, op. cit.

45 Nick Couldry, *Media, Society, World* (Cambridge: Polity Press, 2012).

46 Rheingold, *Virtual Community*, op. cit.; Barry N. Hague and Brian D. Loader (eds), *Digital Democracy* (London: Routledge, 1999); Jakob Linaa Jensen, *Den digitale demokratiske dialog* (Aarhus: Aarhus University Press, 2003); Lars Torpe, Jeppe Agger Nielsen, and Jens Ulrich, *Demokrati på nettet* (Aalborg: Aalborg University Press, 2005); Klaus Bruhn Jensen (ed.), *Interface://Culture* (Frederiksberg: Samfundslitteratur, 2005).

47 Jan Schmidt, *Weblogs. Eine kommunikationssoziologische Studie* (Konstanz: UVK Verlag, 2006).

48 Geert Lovink, *Zero Comments: Blogging and Critical Internet Culture* (London: Routledge, 2007).

49 Zizi Papacharissi, *Affective Publics: Sentiment, Technology, and Politics* (Oxford: Oxford University Press, 2014).

50 Pew Research Center (25 October 2016) *The Political Environment on Social Media*, available at: www.pewinternet.org (accessed 21 November 2016).

51 Geert Lovink, *Networks without a Cause: A Critique of Social Media* (Cambridge: Polity Press, 2012); Jakob Linaa Jensen and Jesper Tække (eds), *Facebook – fra socialt netværk til metamedie* (Copenhagen: Samfundslitteratur, 2013).

70 *Public Space and Forms of Public Practice*

52 Gernot Böhme, 'Leibliche Anwesenheit im Raum', *Ästhetik und Kommunikation* 108 (2000); Howard Rheingold even ascribes a basic element of 'ontological untrustworthiness' to virtual communication. According to Rheingold, the transmission of images via webcams would not change this feature of virtual communication, since the transmission would not be able to represent the 'life force' or the 'breath' of the agents (Rheingold, *Virtual Community*, op. cit., p. 172).
53 Bernd Guggenberger, *Das digitale Nirwana* (Reinbek: Rowohlt, 1999).
54 Rheingold, *Virtual Community*, op. cit.; Bettina Heintz and Christoph Müller (1999) Fallstudie: 'Die Sozialwelt des Internet', available at: http://paedpsych.jku.at:4711/LEHRTEXTE/HeintzMueller99.html (accessed 3 November 2016).
55 Mark Poster, *Cyber Democracy: Internet and the Public Sphere* (Irvine, CA: University of California, 1995).
56 Claus Leggewie, 'Den Laptop auch mal zuklappen', in Christoph Bieber and Claus Leggewie (eds), *Unter Piraten* (Bielefeld: transcript Verlag, 2012).

References

Alterman, Jon (2011) 'The Revolution Will Not Be Tweeted', *Washington Quarterly* 34.

Arendt, Hannah (1958) *The Human Condition*, Chicago: Chicago University Press.

Bisgaard, Ulrik and Carsten Friberg (eds) (2006) *Det æstetiskes aktualitet*, Copenhagen: Multivers.

Böhme, Gernot (2000) 'Leibliche Anwesenheit im Raum', *Ästhetik und Kommunikation* 108.

Brink Lund, Anker (2006) 'Mediedebat som politisk mantra', in Henrik Kaare Nielsen and Finn Horn (eds) *Kritik som deltagelse*, Aarhus: Klim.

Bruhn Jensen, Klaus (ed.) (2005) *Interface://Culture*, Frederiksberg: Samfundslitteratur.

Capella, Joseph N. and Kathleen Hall Jamieson (1997) *Spiral of Cynicism: The Press and the Public Good*, Oxford: Oxford University Press.

Carpentier, Nico (2011) *Media and Participation: A Site of Ideological-Democratic Struggle*, Bristol: Intellect.

Castells, Manuel (2012) *Networks of Outrage and Hope*, Cambridge: Polity Press.

Cohen, Jean L. and Andrew Arato (1992) *Civil Society and Political Theory*, Cambridge, MA: MIT Press.

Couldry, Nick (2010) *Why Voice Matters*, London: Sage.

Couldry, Nick (2012) *Media, Society, World*, Cambridge: Polity Press.

Dahlgren, Peter (2009) *Media and Political Engagement*, New York: Cambridge University Press.

Dahlgren, Peter (2013) *The Political Web*, Basingstoke: Palgrave Macmillan.

Davies, Nick (2008) *Flat Earth News*, London: Random House.

Dean, Jodi (2002) *Publicity's Secret: How Technoculture Capitalizes on Democracy*, Ithaca, NY: Cornell University Press.

Della Porta, Donatella and Dieter Rucht (eds) (2013) *Meeting Democracy: Power and Deliberation in Global Justice Movements*, Cambridge: Cambridge University Press.

Demirovic, Alex (ed.) (2016) *Transformation der Demokratie – demokratische Transformation*, Münster: Westfälisches Dampfboot.

Eriksson, Birgit, Birgit Eriksson, Henrik K. Nielsen, and Jakob Lund (2012) *Æstetisering*, Aarhus: Klim.

Fetzner, Daniel and Stefan Selke (eds) (2005) *Selling Politics*, Furtwangen: Hochschule Furtwangen.

Public Space and Forms of Public Practice 71

Fiig, Christina (2011) 'A Powerful, Opinion-Forming Public? Rethinking the Habermasian Public Sphere in a Perspective of Feminist Theory and Citizenship', *Distinktion: Scandinavian Journal of Social Theory* 12(3).

Finnemann, Niels Ole (2006) 'The Internet and the Public Space', *Nordic Media Trends* 9(1).

Fraser, Nancy (1992) 'Rethinking the Public Sphere', in Craig Calhoun (ed.) *Habermas and the Public Sphere*, Cambridge, MA: MIT Press.

Fraser, Nancy and Kate Nash (2014) *Transnationalizing the Public Sphere*, Cambridge: Polity Press.

Fuchs, Christian (2014) *Social Media*, London: SAGE.

Gerhards, Jürgen (1997) 'Diskursive versus liberale Öffentlichkeit', *Kölner Zeitschrift für Soziologie und Sozialpsychologie* 1(49).

Giddens, Anthony (1991) *Modernity and Self-Identity*, Stanford, CA: Stanford University Press.

Griggs, Steven, A. Norval, and H. Wagenaar (eds) (2014) *Practices of Freedom. Decentred Governance, Conflict and Democratic Participation*, Cambridge: Cambridge University Press.

Guggenberger, Bernd (1999) *Das digitale Nirwana*, Reinbek: Rowohlt.

Habermas, Jürgen (1981) *Theorie des kommunikativen Handelns*, vols 1–2, Frankfurt am Main: Suhrkamp (English translation: *Theory of Communicative Action*, vols 1–2, Boston: Beacon Press 1984).

Hague, Barry N. and Brian D. Loader (eds) (1999) *Digital Democracy*, London: Routledge.

Häußermann, Hartmut, Dieter Läpple, and Walter Siebe (2008) *Stadtpolitik*, Frankfurt am Main: Suhrkamp.

Heintz, Bettina and Christoph Müller (1999) Fallstudie: 'Die Sozialwelt des Internet', available at: http://paedpsych.jku.at:4711/LEHRTEXTE/HeintzMueller99.html (accessed 3 November 2016).

Hirsch, Joachim (1998) *Vom Sicherheitsstaat zum nationalen Wettbewerbsstaat*, Berlin: ID Verlag.

Hirsch, Joachim (2002) 'Wissen und Nichtwissen: Anmerkungen zur "Wissensgesellschaft"', in Oliver Brüchert and Christine Resch (eds), *Zwischen Herrschaft und Befreiung*, Münster: Westfälisches Dampfboot.

Hoffmann-Axthelm, Dieter (1984) *Sinnesarbeit*, Frankfurt am Main: Campus.

Jackson O'Shaughnessy, Nicholas (2004) *Politics and Propaganda*, Manchester: Manchester University Press.

Jenkins, Henry, Mizuko Ito, and danah boyd (2016) *Participatory Culture in a Networked Era*, Cambridge: Polity Press.

Keane, John (2011) 'Monitory Democracy?' in Sonia Alonso, John Keane, and Wolfgang Merkel (eds), *The Future of Representative Democracy*, Cambridge: Cambridge University Press.

Kyndrup, Morten (2008) *Den æstetiske relation*, Copenhagen: Gyldendal.

Lakoff, George (2004) *Don't Think of an Elephant!* White River Junction, VT: Chelsea Green Publishing.

Leggewie, Claus (2012) 'Den Laptop auch mal zuklappen', in Christoph Bieber and Claus Leggewie (eds), *Unter Piraten*, Bielefeld: transcript Verlag.

Lessig, Lawrence (2004) *Free Culture*, New York: Penguin Press.

Linaa Jensen, Jakob (2003) *Den digitale demokratiske dialog*, Aarhus: Aarhus University Press.

72 Public Space and Forms of Public Practice

Linaa Jensen, Jakob and Jesper Tække (eds) (2013) *Facebook – fra socialt netværk til metamedie*, Copenhagen: Samfundslitteratur.

Lovink, Geert (2007) *Zero Comments: Blogging and Critical Internet Culture*, London: Routledge.

Lovink, Geert (2012) *Networks without a Cause: A Critique of Social Media*, Cambridge: Polity Press.

Manjoo, Farhad (2008) *True Enough: Learning to Live in a Post-Fact Society*, Hoboken, NJ: John Wiley and Sons Inc.

Marx, Karl (1976 [1867]) *Capital*, vol. 1, Harmondsworth: Penguin.

Mouffe, Chantal (1993) *The Return of the Political*, London: Verso.

Mozorov, Evgeny (2011) *The Net Delusion*, London: Allen Lane.

Nanz, Patrizia and Claus Leggewie (2016) *Die Konsultative. Mehr Demokratie durch Bürgerbeteiligung*, Berlin: Wagenbach.

Nielsen, Henrik Kaare (2001) *Kritisk teori og samtidsanalyse*, Aarhus: Aarhus University Press.

Nielsen, Henrik Kaare (2007) *Konsument eller samfundsborger? Kritiske essays*, Aarhus: Klim.

Nielsen, Henrik Kaare (2014) *Æstetik og politisk offentlighed*, Aarhus: Klim.

Nielsen, Henrik Kaare and Søren Pold (2007) 'Kulturkamp.com – mellem åbne værker og intellektuel ejendomsret', in Søren Pold and Lone Koefoed Hansen (eds), *Interface – digital kunst and kultur*, Aarhus: Aarhus University Press.

Papacharissi, Zizi (2014) *Affective Publics: Sentiment, Technology, and Politics*, Oxford: Oxford University Press.

Peters, Bernhard (2007) *Der Sinn von Öffentlichkeit*, Frankfurt am Main: Suhrkamp.

Pew Research Center (25 October 2016) *The Political Environment on Social Media*, available at: www.pewinternet.org (accessed 21 November 2016).

Phillips, Louise and Kim Schrøder (2004) *Sådan taler medier og borgere om politik*, Aarhus: Aarhus University Press.

Poster, Mark (1995) *Cyber Democracy: Internet and the Public Sphere*, Irvine, CA: University of California Press.

Rabin-Havt, Ari (2016) *Media Matters, Lies, Incorporated. The World of Post-Truth Politics*, New York: Anchor Books.

Rheingold, Howard (1993) *The Virtual Community*, New York: Addison-Wesley.

Rosa, Hartmut (2012) *Weltbeziehungen im Zeitalter der Beschleunigung*, Frankfurt am Main: Suhrkamp.

Schmidt, Gunnar (1995) 'Zivile Gesellschaft und öffentlicher Raum', *Leviathan* 4.

Schmidt, Jan (2006) *Weblogs. Eine kommunikationssoziologische Studie*, Konstanz: UVK Verlag.

Schudson, Michael (1997) 'Why Conversation Is Not the Soul of Democracy', *Critical Studies in Mass Communication* 14(4).

Seel, Martin (2003) *Ästhetik des Erscheinens*, Frankfurt am Main: Suhrkamp (English translation: *Aesthetics of Appearing*, Stanford, CA: Stanford University Press, 2006).

Sennett, Richard (1996) *Uses of Disorder: Personal Identity and City Life*, London: Faber and Faber.

Sunstein, Cas R. (2007) *Republic.com 2.0*, Princeton, NJ: Princeton University Press.

Torpe, Lars, Jeppe Agger Nielsen, and Jens Ulrich (2005) *Demokrati på nettet*, Aalborg: Aalborg University Press.

Ullrich, Wolfgang (2008) *Habenwollen. Wie funktioniert die Konsumkultur?*, Frankfurt am Main: Fischer Taschenbuch Wissenschaft.

van de Donk, Wim, Brian D. Loader, Paul G. Nixon, and Dieter Rucht (2004) *Cyberprotest: New Media, Citizens and Social Movements*, London: Routledge.

Volkmer, Ingrid (2014) *The Global Public Sphere*, Cambridge: Polity Press.

Welsch, Wolfgang (1990) *Ästhetisches Denken*, Stuttgart: Reclam.

Welsch, Wolfgang (ed.) (1993) *Die Aktualität des Ästhetischen*, München: Wilhelm Fink Verlag.

Winther Nielsen, Sigge (ed.) (2011) *Politisk Marketing*, Copenhagen: Karnov Group.

4 Political and Aesthetic Discursive Practice

As demonstrated above in the general conceptualisation of late modern public discourse, there is a point in distinguishing analytically between basic modal principles, on the one hand, and more mixed, concrete forms of practice, on the other. It will be the main argument in the following that in the more specific conceptualisation of the current development in the relationship between aesthetic and political practice, it is correspondingly fruitful to distinguish between a level of basic discursive principles and the more composed nature of the reality of social practice.

Aesthetic Discourse and Aesthetic Experience

It is widespread in current debate that late modern community formation is conceptualised as a matter of *taste*. In other words, social practice in general is regarded from the perspective of aesthetic discourse – not in the sense of art, but broadly understood as a sensuously and emotionally based principle for acting and creating meaning.

Thus, according to Pierre Bourdieu, habitually rooted preferences of taste orchestrate the positioning of the individual in social space and determine his/her orientation towards specific types of community.[1] In Gerhard Schulze's analysis of the 'experience society', the aesthetic orientation of taste has, due to the increasing level of general wealth, advanced to an overall societal condition which implies that a 'psycho-physical semantics' and the associated search of the individuals for 'positively charged psycho-physical states of feeling' have become predominant in the collective space of meaning. Communities accordingly take the shape of taste-based lifestyle groups.[2] Michel Maffesoli's analysis of late modern community formation as a new, aestheticised version of tribal society is likewise an exponent of the tendency towards generalising a specific, monologic understanding of taste and thus a specific variant of aesthetic discourse as the universal principle of social practice and meaning formation.[3] Furthermore, contemporary applications of this type of theory in lifestyle analysis and marketing strategies have the spotting and the co-creation of communities of taste as their main focus.

The intention is not to question the general thesis that aesthetic discourse plays a large – and increasing – role in late modernity, but merely to challenge

Political and Aesthetic Discursive Practice 75

these tendencies towards totalising a specific understanding of taste – and thereby a reduced version of aesthetic discourse – as the common denominator of contemporary communities by definition. With the aim of conceptualising the potentials and limitations of aesthetic discourse in relation to political community formation, the following suggests a more differentiated and dynamic frame of reflection which elaborates on inspirations from sociological theory, not least from the tradition of critical theory and especially Jürgen Habermas' theory of modernity.[4]

According to Habermas, modernity as a societal formation is not reducible to one totalising principle. In his sociological interpretation of Kant's philosophical thesis on the differentiation of reason (into understanding, practical reason and judgement), Habermas distinguishes between a cognitive-instrumental, a moral-practical and an aesthetic-expressive discourse (in Habermas' terminology 'rationality of action') that are working and generating meaning on their own specific terms – and corresponding discursive domains of practice dominated by the discourse in question. Habermas' own work does not offer an elaborated account of the relationship between aesthetic and political discourse, but primarily stresses the discursive differentiation and points out problematic implications in tendencies towards dedifferentiation such as the seductive reduction of political opinion formation to a matter of aesthetic fascination or the dogmatic reduction of aesthetic expression to political propaganda.

Habermas is not the only contemporary theorist who regards it as a general feature of the process of modernisation that a differentiation of a multiplicity of discourses and related, more or less institutionalised, fields of action has taken place. Regardless of substantial disagreements and terminological differences, leading sociologists, such as Niklas Luhmann, Pierre Bourdieu, Ernesto Laclau, and Chantal Mouffe coincide in conceptualising modernity as a discursively differentiated entity.[5]

In the development of modernity's institutions and general practices of everyday life, it has, in other words, been a basic principle to distinguish between the discursive domains of, e.g. economy, politics, science, art, and religion and to keep them apart in social practice. *Science* is an example of a strongly institutionalised field of practice which derives its legitimacy and its criteria of validity and relevance from a specific type of discourse and which solely answers to the cognitive rationality of action and the related, uncompromising and, in principle, open-ended search for truth.

Likewise, aesthetics and politics represent distinct discursive practices. As described above, the field of *political* practice comprises both formally and informally institutionalised forums and types of agents (from the governmental decision-maker public through the public of parliament-oriented mass media to the civil society publics at the grassroots and overall levels). No matter whether the agents in each concrete case draw on universally reasoning, subjective experience-reflecting, or consumerist public meta-discourse, they all operate according to the basic rationale of the political field of practice: the struggle for power in respect to the allocation of societal resources in the broadest sense and

76   *Political and Aesthetic Discursive Practice*

thereby to the social distribution of life opportunities. Within the normative framework of democratic political culture, political discourse is about conquering the definition of power over society's common concerns, and, as part of this process, about the contending political agents' struggle to close and determine the social formation of meaning on their own rules (see Chapter 2). The discourse is, in other words, to a high degree intrinsically goal-orientated.

The field of *aesthetic* practice is of a correspondingly composite nature: it also draws on both universally reasoning, subjective experience-reflecting, and consumerist public discourse, and it comprises both the highly institutionalised expert culture of art, the non-established, more or less sub-cultural art scene, the heterogeneous, more or less commercialised field of popular culture, various informal aesthetic activities of everyday life, and – emanating from the specific field into the general context of social practice – late modernity's overall process of aestheticisation, which tends to equip the whole life-world of modern individuals with experiential appeals to senses and emotions. Contrary to the orientation of political discourse towards determining definite, universal, and goal-orientated principles for the development of society, aesthetic discourse is characterised by its non-directed nature. The purpose of aesthetic practice is the practice itself. When it unfolds on its own premises, however, it continuously engages in dialogue with established formations of meaning, but without prescribing edifying alternatives to the meaning proposals of other discourses. Aesthetic discourse, in other words, opens the social formation of meaning in an indeterminate way, thereby encouraging the agents of aesthetic practice to perform the unceasing, autonomous, and pleasure-motivated seeking process that characterises the process of aesthetic experience.[6]

Furthermore, the potential of aesthetic experience has a close affinity with a key concept of German philosophical tradition: *Bildung*.[7] A relevant contemporary definition of this concept would liberate it from its historical subjugation to bourgeois elite culture and revitalise its universal rational core: the emphatic demand that the unbound, modern individual should transcend himself/ herself and develop towards empowerment by way of reflecting his/her self-realisation in obligation to the common good of society. In other words, a process of self-realisation that remains confined to the horizon of individual self-sufficiency does not qualify as *Bildung*.

The contemporary challenge of *Bildung* addresses all individuals, but it necessarily assumes different forms according to the social and cultural background resources of the concrete individuals in question. In other words, *Bildung* should, on late modern terms, be regarded as an overall concept with a plurality of concrete forms of realisation. The basic common denominator of late modern processes of *Bildung* is that they always involve challenge and reflective reshaping of established self-conceptions and meaning formations. In this sense, they represent a specific type of self-transcending human growth that integrates the development of individuals' sensuous, emotional, and intellectual potentials and makes them capable of reflecting on themselves in terms of their committing embeddedness in the overall socio-cultural context.[8]

Political and Aesthetic Discursive Practice   77

Aesthetic experience holds the potential for facilitating processes of *Bildung*, due to its indeterminately challenging nature and in as far as it, more broadly than a purely cognitive learning process, has a sensibilising effect and opens individuals' horizon for a complex (sensuous, emotional and intellectual) processing of the conflicts and ambivalences of late modern life-world. But there is no guarantee that this potential is realised in concrete processes of experience.

In the present context, the role of aesthetic practice in the general experience formation of society is in focus, and this relationship first of all takes shape in the public sharing of individuals' processing of reception experiences with aesthetic artefacts and aesthetic approaches in general. The research tradition of reception aesthetics has provided valuable concepts for the elaboration of these exchange processes: according to reception aesthetics, an aesthetic approach always relates in a specific way to the multiplicity of existing conventions of genre, and it is organised around an *implicit recipient* with specific characteristics that offer the empirical recipient means of orientation.[9] In this way, the artefact's invitation to reception plays a central – although not in a strict sense determining – role in the process of reception.

Within the framing of the formations of meaning created throughout the history of art and the public debate on aesthetics, including genre conventions and the associated institutionalised patterns of experiential expectation, the process of reception unfolds as a *projecting dialogue* between the life-historical experience of the recipient and the artefact in question.[10] The recipient projects a generally motivated expectation of meaning onto the artefact that 'answers' with its specific aesthetic characteristics, which causes the recipient to revise his/her expectation of meaning and project a renewed expectation onto the artefact that answers again, etc. In other words, aesthetic meaning formation should neither be understood as established beforehand by the artefact nor as the result of the recipient's arbitrary projection of a desired meaning onto a blameless object. On the contrary, aesthetic meaning formation unfolds as a *meeting* between an artefact with a multiplicity of characteristics and potentials of meaning and a recipient who brings his/her multifaceted life-historical experience in general and his/her present receptive motivation in particular into dialogic exchange with the artefact.

This dialogue operates on the basis of aesthetic discourse, and as pointed out above, it is in principle capable of activating intellectual, emotional, and sensuous forms of experience in the recipient. Due to this potentially integrating movement which furthermore is able to draw on both universally reasoning and subjective experience-reflecting public discourse, the process of aesthetic experience represents a comprehensive resource for *Bildung*, but, as mentioned, there is no guarantee of the emergence of this interplay between intellect, emotions, and senses. It depends entirely on the concrete interaction that takes place within the general cultural horizon of meaning between the artefact's invitation to dialogue, i.e. the aesthetic features of the object, and the recipient's subjective, experience-based, and situational capacity to accept the invitation.

The dialogic exchange between recipient and artefact may, in other words, remain confined to the sensuous-emotional dimension of experience and thus not

78   *Political and Aesthetic Discursive Practice*

include the potential dimension of reflective formation of experience and empowerment. In this context, Dieter Prokop points out a comprehensive, autonomised complex of powerful agents in the field of popular culture (the cultural industry, the media industry, advertising, etc.), who for market-strategic purposes are working, targeted on separating the recipient's emotions from his/her intellect and eliminating the possibility of an interplay between them. Instead, the emotional appeal is singled out and intensified, and the emotions are not addressed dialogically in their capacity as specific, personal forms of experience with individual potentials of development and empowerment. On the contrary, the aroused emotions are addressed monologically on the basis of consumerist public discourse, and due to the forms of approach of the standardised industrial products, emotions are channelled into a frame of unspecific, collective *moods* that appear determined by destiny. These generalised moods define the consumer groups of the cultural market and are designed in order to keep the recipients in a disempowered and disoriented state of emotional excitement.[11]

In addition, late modernity's general tendency towards aestheticisation, that was characterised in Chapter 3 in this volume, conditions social practice in general by expanding the invitation to engage in aesthetic exchanges from the relationship to specific artefacts to the context of life as a whole. As described, the forms of everyday life in the rich Western countries are increasingly designed with an emphasis on appeals to senses and emotions, and the individuals are thereby invited to dwell delightfully on the forms that are endowed with an intensified, but indeterminate notion of meaning. Hereby, a vast projection space is opened to aesthetic practice.

Late modern consumer culture's version of aestheticisation addresses and processes the dynamic of culturalised identity work in the modality of consumerist public discourse. Although this version is predominant, the general tendency towards aestheticisation, just like aesthetic artefacts, holds a multiplicity of genre options. In this sense, aestheticisation also leaves its mark on the design of a variety of fields of practice that are not as such part of consumer culture and thus submitted to consumerist public discourse. These fields of practice are in principle open to formations of meaning on the basis of universally reasoning and subjective experience-reflecting public discourse: the architectonic design of urban space, the processing and mediation of social experience by the media and – as will be elaborated in the following – the communication and self-presentation of political agents.

Differentiation and Conflictual Interplay of Discourses

The distinction between these fields of practice and types of discourse has been a crucial foundation for the development of both the institutions and the everyday life practice of modernity. But it is important to be aware that this fundamental and thorough process of differentiation does not imply that the numerous fields of action and associated discourses remain unaffected by one another. They are continuously involved in a complex, reciprocal interplay in which they engage in

Political and Aesthetic Discursive Practice 79

more or less conflictual relations with one another, and in which genuine issues of hegemony may occasionally arise.

In other words, rather than being regarded as reducible to one discursive principle (e.g. 'taste'), the collective formation of meaning should at all times be analysed as a specific and changeable relation of dominance between a plurality of discourses which process a broad and heterogeneous spectrum of social structures and types of experience. Depending on which discursive constellations are predominant at a given time, we may be dealing with quite different types of meaning formation with correspondingly different perspectives for the development of communities and of society and culture in general.

This conflictual interplay forms a basic condition of social practice, and if it takes place in ways that allow the maintenance of the involved discursive domains to the extent that they remain capable of creating meaning on their own premises, it may productively stimulate the fields of practice in question. But if the balance is disturbed, and one form of discourse colonises the other, problematic, dedifferentiating consequences may arise that make society as a whole poorer in terms of variety of types of knowledge and reflection, and thus reduce its ability to make qualitative distinctions and reflect nuanced, alternative possibilities of development.

In this sense, for instance, the field of scientific practice is currently involved in a hegemonic struggle, in which agents of the political and economic fields of practice are attempting to install their own goal-orientated utilitarian discourses in the field of scientific practice through legislation, resource incitements, and public pressure – at the same time marginalising non-utilitarian, qualitative, and critical research traditions as irrelevant forms of knowledge. As mentioned, the crucial question is not whether this kind of intervention exists – it continuously does – but whether it takes shape in ways in which the discourse of science still has enough scope to unfold on the premises of an uncompromising search for truth, or whether the external pressure for immediately applicable research results is becoming so strong that scientific discourse will no longer be able to create meaning on its own terms and will therefore break down and be replaced by a mercantile discourse.

In the following, the current interrelationship between aesthetic and political practice will be investigated in the light of this issue of discursive interplay and dominance. Specifically, aesthetic discourse's interventions in political practice will be the focus, including how aesthetic discourse is strategically integrated in the political process on the premises of political discourse. In terms of the model of the political process presented above, a prominent principle of aesthetic discursive intervention in the political process consists in political agents' use of aesthetic effects to establish themselves in a position of strength in the struggle of interests and the formation of compromises at the level of conflict.

The articulation of interests and the positioning in political power play always entail an aesthetic/performative dimension (in the shape of rhetorical style, visual staging, etc.),[12] and occasionally this dimension – in interplay with political and economic factors – can be decisive for the balance of power in political

80 *Political and Aesthetic Discursive Practice*

struggle. With respect to the fundamental relationship between aesthetic and political discourse, however, the crucial question appears to be on which premises and with which type of appeal the relationship is established – and which conditions of societal experience formation and development of democratic political culture are offered by these premises: is it a dialogic, challenging appeal, which allows the process of aesthetic experience to unfold? Or, on the contrary, a monologic, tranquilising approach that only appeals to regressive fascination?

Aesthetic Discourse and Political Community

In the following, the potentials and limitations of *aesthetic* discourse with respect to the formation of *political* communities will be discussed. Consistent with the argument above, it will be a basic assumption that a political community will always be based on a social interest and a common will to optimise the position of this interest in societal practice at large. The thesis is further that in a modern democracy, competent and sustainable political communities must be able to reflect beyond their own narrow horizon and attend to their interests in obligation to the common good as a discursive frame and correspondingly handle conflicts of interests in peaceful, dialogical forms.

If an aesthetic discursive intervention in political community formation contributes to enhancing the ability of the community in question to attend to its interests on these terms, we are dealing with a constructive discursive balance which strengthens and qualifies the political community. If, on the contrary, the intervention is of a nature that deprives the community of the means to develop its ability to reflect its interests dialogically and in obligation to the common good, we are dealing with a depoliticising de-qualification of the community in question. We may in this connection benefit from the aesthetics of Immanuel Kant[13] in distinguishing between three different categories of aesthetic discursive practice:

First, the monologic, hedonistic pleasure of satisfying immediate, sensuous inclinations and desires – individually or in communities, but always within a private, self-centred horizon. Kant characterises this type of discursive practice as orientated towards 'the agreeable' and as limited to the horizon of private interest and the immediate emotions and desires that it satisfies.

In the terminology of the previous chapters: the subjective dynamic that is channelled by the modalities of both consumerist and subjective experience-reflecting public discourse stems from the inclination to satisfy immediate sensuous urges of everyday life, and it is therefore initially oriented towards the aesthetics of the agreeable. However, whereas the formative work of subjective experience-reflecting public discourse transcends this restricted point of departure reflectively and dialogically, the formations of meaning generated by consumerist public discourse remain limited to the non-reflective, monological affirmation of immediate desires.

As will be shown in the following, this type of aesthetic discursive practice is an essential – although not all-encompassing – element in the heterogeneous

Political and Aesthetic Discursive Practice   81

tendency towards the aestheticisation of politics in late modernity. It is, for instance, significant for political agents' marketing of themselves with the political substance fading away behind spectacular staging and seductive forms that appeal exclusively to senses and emotions. The aim of this type of aesthetic practice is merely to be agreeable, and due to its suspension of critical reflection, it bears a danger of the political process degenerating into demagogic manipulation.

The judgement associated with this type of aesthetic practice is idiosyncratic by nature, based as it is on the private sensuous preference of taste, and Kant refers to it as 'private judgement'. In a political context, it further mobilises special interests by affirming the immediate aesthetic fascinations of the public and channelling them into the formation of political sympathies and antipathies – and thereby into the development of the imagination of belonging to particular political communities. In the perspective of the present argument, this type of discursive practice represents an aesthetic de-qualification of political community in so far as the private, monological interest is not being challenged towards self-reflexivity, nor is it brought into reflective exchange with the discursive frame of the common good.

Second, the discursive practice which Kant calls 'the aesthetic judgement of taste'. Contrary to private judgement, the aesthetic judgement of taste involves a universalising, reflective mediation between sensuous perception and concept. The judgement of taste refers to an aesthetic delight that is characterised by 'disinterested pleasure' in that the judgement rises above private interests and desires and paves the way for a contemplative, qualitatively estimating pleasure with regard to beautiful forms as such – also entitled 'the aesthetics of the beautiful'. Although it is based on the subjective feeling of pleasure or displeasure, the judgement of taste is by way of its disinterested nature characterised by an element of reflective distance from its object. In this discursive practice, beauty is released from the private sensuous interests and desires of the subject and addressed as a general quality of the object.

The judgement of taste further claims universal validity: it is proposed as a dialogical offer to the general public – as a suggestion how everybody might reasonably estimate the forms of the object in question. The judgement of taste operates on the basis of the assumption of an *a priori sensus communis* which makes it possible to communicate the disinterested feeling of pleasure or displeasure universally without making the detour via abstract concepts. The notion of *sensus communis* to which the judgement of taste refers can further be understood as a community-orientated ability to perform aesthetic estimation. In correspondence with the assumption of a *sensus communis*, the aesthetic formation of experience to which the judgement of taste gives rise, works within the horizon of established form-tradition in which order and formal harmony constitute the perception of beauty.

Furthermore, the beautiful is in Kant's philosophy a symbol of the good, in as far as the aesthetics of the beautiful implies a certain degree of cultivation and *Bildung*, in order to transcend merely sensuous desire and associated special

82   *Political and Aesthetic Discursive Practice*

interests, and in as far as the judgement of taste in its reference to the notion of *sensus communis* unfolds within a universal idea of morality and related ideals for politics.[14] In other words, Kant installs an affinity between, on the one hand, the form-estimating aesthetic judgement and its *sensus communis*, and, on the other, an *ethical* judgement and an associated ethical *sensus communis*.

Consequently, the judgement of taste bears essential, constructive potentials for the formation and qualification of political communities due to its discursive emancipation from the narrow horizon of special interests, its dialogical, public nature, its foundation in the notion of an aesthetic *sensus communis* and its possible exchange relation to an ethical *sensus communis*. Yet, in itself it seems to be an insufficient basis for the creation and development of competent and sustainable political communities. Partly due to its restriction to a non-conceptual, feeling-based estimation of forms, partly due to its emphasised disinterestedness and the associated lack of capacity to reflect conflicts of interests as a fundamental feature of society as an overall political community.

In a perspective of public discourse, the theory of aesthetic judgement further privileges universally reasoning public discourse while marginalising subjective experience-reflecting public discourse and the aesthetic and ethical types of experience that it processes. This points to the basic limitation in Kant that he conceptualises *sensus communis* as a universal, anthropological characteristic of humankind. More plausibly, we could regard a common ability to perform aesthetic assessment as a societalised sense of form, structure, composition, etc., i.e. as the result of historically and socio-culturally specific experiences and associated formation of the sensory apparatus, the forms of perception, and the reflective capacity. This point of departure would draw attention to the fact that, in practice, qualified participation in *sensus communis* and universal public reasoning implies that one acquires specific types of knowledge and experience and that the present societal conditions primarily equip individuals with a privileged, well-educated background with these qualifications. Individuals with a different background will have to laboriously acquire these competences at a later age – or remain excluded from the 'common sense'.

In this respect, Pierre Bourdieu has a point in his critical discussion of Kant's definition of the judgement of taste as 'disinterested' and *sensus communis* as a universal consensual frame.[15] It seems fair to say that this definition in historical practice has tended to generalise the elite's particular, refined orientation of taste as the universally valid and solely legitimate one – and correspondingly to marginalise more 'popular' orientations of taste as illegitimate and vulgar. On this background, Bourdieu emphasises that an aspect of interest is always inherent in the judgement of taste.

However, Bourdieu's analysis totalises this point of permanent power struggle and thereby neglects the rational core of the concept of the judgement of taste and *sensus communis*, namely, that the social reality of ongoing power struggle is interwoven with the emergence of a consciousness of common societal concerns and an experience-based political culture that transcends the horizon of special interests. In this respect, modern democracies, conflictual as they may

Political and Aesthetic Discursive Practice 83

be, have developed universal forms of reflection which in principle offer the possibility of establishing a community of citizens that reasons in obligation to the discursive frame of the common good.[16]

In other words, whereas Kant's theory on the judgement of taste can be criticised for unjustifiably universalising a specific orientation of taste, Bourdieu's critique of Kant marginalises the perspective of universality as such and thereby the associated potentials for the development of democracy. This limitation implies that Bourdieu's analysis of the political process remains confined to the horizon of agents struggling for special interests, whereas the universally reflecting horizon of citizens is non-existent, or rather, it is by definition regarded as a blind for the power strategies of the upper class. In other words, Bourdieu's analysis does not entail a perspective of possibility in which the processing of experiences with differences and conflicts might result in the perception and reflection of common concerns.

Correspondingly, Bourdieu does not address politics as a duality of struggle of interests and reflective, civic regulation of common societal concerns, but instead as a 'field of consumption' in which each agent acts, orientates, and positions himself/herself in the power struggle on the basis of his/her 'political taste'. As outlined above, this taste is understood as rooted in the lifelong, class-specific formation of embodied sensory, emotional, moral, and cognitive dispositions which Bourdieu conceptualises as 'habitus'. As the pivotal point of the practice of the individual, this habitually shaped taste further contributes to reproducing the same symbolic distinction and social division of class from which it originates.

As stated above, the present argument – along with that of Fraser, Negt and Kluge, and others – agrees that different social backgrounds equip individuals with quite diverse resources, e.g. in terms of qualifications for engaging in universal public discourse. But instead of Bourdieu's deterministic conceptualisation of this basic fact in the term of habitus, the suggestion is to regard these background resources as elements of a dynamic, ongoing process of experience in which learning processes and self-transcending political formation, i.e. *Bildung*, are possible perspectives. This processual perspective further points beyond Bourdieu's concept of taste which remains confined to the horizon of the aesthetics of the agreeable and the idiosyncrasy of private judgement. Hereby, the field is opened for transversal public dialogue on both taste and politics – and to realise that although taste in the restricted sense of Bourdieu often appears to be a factor in political processes,[17] politics as such cannot reasonably be reduced to the conduct of taste, just as political communities cannot be understood satisfactorily as mere communities of taste.

But the fact remains that a Kantian analysis based on the aesthetic judgement of taste in a perspective of public discourse will tend to sort out the dimensions of identity work that are not immediately universalisable as not publicly relevant – and thus to ignore them. The present argument suggests that instead of beforehand marginalising the drafts of meaning that are articulated in the discursive practices of the aesthetics of the agreeable and private judgement as worthless,

84   *Political and Aesthetic Discursive Practice*

they should be challenged dialogically and brought into interaction with a universal perspective of reflection. In other words, these dimensions of identity work should be regarded as potential raw material for the development of subjective experience-reflecting public discourse.

Third, is the type of aesthetic discourse which Kant refers to as the 'aesthetics of the sublime'. The point of departure for this type of aesthetic experience is the sublime feeling that is triggered when the individual is suddenly and unexpectedly deprived of control over the situation. In Kant, the sublime feeling arises in the confrontation with superior forces of nature, but it may also occur in relation to works of art or social events that punctually disrupt the customary frames and experiential forms of normality. The associated process of aesthetic experience unfolds in the modality of reflective judgement (cf. the next section on political judgement) as a re-establishing of control on new premises in which the individual, by means of reason, processes the experience of rupture, attempts to give it a lucid form, and redefines himself/herself in relation to it.

Here, we are dealing with an aesthetic experience which 'pleases immediately by reason of its opposition to the interest of sense'.[18] The delight of the sublime feeling is, in other words, highly ambivalent, a joy mixed with terror, the intensity of which can be so overwhelming that it momentarily suspends the experiential and communicative horizon of normality and manifests itself as an 'isolated moment of ruthless and contextless attention', as Martin Seel has put it.[19]

The sublime feeling, thus, is emphatically exceptional by nature. It emerges in the individual experience of rupture and loss of control, and it can therefore hardly be conceived as an edifying resource for the formation of politico-cultural communities. But in the individual's accompanying discursive restoration work in the shape of reason-based processing of the experience of sublimity, the displacements of patterns of experience and reflection which it has caused, may encourage processes of *Bildung* that may also have implications for the understanding of political communities in terms of, for example, expanding the reflective horizon of the participants and relativising self-interest. However, there is no guarantee of such opening and expanding developments: for instance, the experience of sublimity that the 9/11 terrorist attack on the Twin Towers in the USA triggered in the political public of the Western countries rather seems to have resulted in the emergence of a community of fear that closes in on itself and attempts to keep the surrounding world at a distance by military and bureaucratic means.

Furthermore, in the processes of social revolution, the periodic presence of sublime feelings may occur in the formation of political community. In such cases, we are dealing with a state of collective ecstasy which is nourished by the rapid flux of events and the all-encompassing and fundamentally incalculable character of the revolutionary changes. This type of aesthetic discourse, however, is both chaotic and transient and therefore not an adequate basis for the formation of sustainable politico-cultural communities. According to historical experience, the sublime feeling will be superseded by the more pragmatic and prosaic discourses of power and interest struggles and the gradual formation of an experience-based political culture, as the revolutionary process develops into more transparent and institutionalised forms. If we, on the contrary, imagine the politicised discourse of the sublime perpetuated, it would lead to totalitarian consequences in the shape of collectivistic pressure towards unity and identification, resulting in denial of conflicts and difference.[20]

This understanding of the aesthetic dimension of revolutionary processes bears some resemblance to Jacques Rancière's notion of the both politically and aesthetically breaking 'event' in which society's established, unequal, and basically unjust system of distribution of the sensible, 'police', is interrupted by 'the political', i.e. the intervention by the voices of the marginalised, thus making their arguments and demands audible and alternatives to the social order of 'police' visible.[21] By way of its aesthetic/performative dimension, the event accentuates the radically egalitarian nature of the political and thereby challenges not only the established distribution of resources, but society's whole organisation of the common space of meaning, including which perceptions, voices and visions are valid and legitimate.

However, Rancière's analysis appears to be devoid of any concrete, experiential perspective of process. Interest struggles and the associated processes of experience of the agents involved do not count as genuinely political, since they by definition refer to discourses based on inequality. The 'event', on the other hand, seems to be of an almost mythical nature: an apparently privileged, uninfected representative of a superior common good, i.e. the marginalised, somehow breaks through the aesthetic and political order of 'police' and paves the way for a true and altogether different society based on equality. Questions of judgement, aesthetic experience, the associated learning processes of individual agents and concrete potentials for political community formation have no place in this abstract dichotomy.

Political Judgement as a Composed Entity

It appears to be an uncontroversial assumption that a well-functioning democratic political community presupposes empowered citizens whose political judgement is qualified. However, as we have seen, the mentioned types of aesthetic discursive practice only to a limited extent equip the individual with this quality of judgement. But aesthetic discourse does not hold a monopoly on constituting judgement. If we conceive of judgement in the sense of the broad tradition from Aristotle's concept of *phronesis* via Kant's *Critique of Judgement* to Hannah Arendt's[22] and recently Oskar Negt's[23] and Christoph Menke's[24] interpretations of the concept, it becomes evident that judgement is not limited to aesthetic practice, but must be conceptualised as integral to the faculty of knowledge in general. It is further developed and cultivated in specific forms depending on the individual's practical life experience and the associated formative processes.

Judgement basically performs the mediation between the specific and the universal, between sensory object and theoretical *understanding*. But it differs from

86 *Political and Aesthetic Discursive Practice*

the logical-conceptual rationality of understanding by drawing on imagination, intuition, and emotions in its mediating activity. In this sense, judgement is an ability that cannot be formalised and reduced to general cognitive laws, but in concrete practice it nevertheless plays a central role in the establishment of general orientation. Judgement enables the individual to estimate whether a phenomenon is covered by an existing universal concept or not, and it equips the individual with an intuitive feeling of what is the general aspect of concrete situations and what is therefore suitable and relevant.

Kant further distinguishes between two modalities in the work of judgement: the *determinative* mode in which the movement of mediation takes its point of departure on the general level and subsumes the specific under an existing universal concept; and the *reflective* mode which departs from the specific and grants its unique qualities precedence over existing universal concepts. Therefore, reflective judgement dwells on the specific: it unfolds as an unceasing movement of investigation between an object that cannot be fully determined and a universal concept that cannot be found.[25] Both modalities play an important role for the orientation ability of the individual; but in a pointed turn of phrase, we could say that in the scenario of determinative judgement we only confirm what we already believe we know, whereas in the scenario of reflective judgement, we potentially gain new insight into the nature of the world.

Aesthetic judgement, as represented by the judgement of taste, operates in the reflective mode and establishes orientation on the basis of a disinterested and non-conceptual, subjective feeling of pleasure or displeasure in regard to forms – with a universalising reference to the aesthetic *sensus communis*.[26] Its investigative function may, by the mediating work of imagination, be brought into interaction with theoretical understanding as well as reason and the ethical *sensus communis*, but this interaction is not established automatically and may as well not materialise.

The judgement that unfolds in *political practice* in general, including public debate, in late modern democratic societies should be regarded as a composed entity. Like aesthetic judgement, it operates in the reflective mode in its investigation of a plurality of possible mediations between, on the one hand, a concrete political case or a special interest and, on the other, the consideration of the common good. This operation implies reflecting the multiplicity of possible, legitimate viewpoints on the subject in question, the ability to understand, respect, and engage in dialogue with other positions, and to argue one's own views in the light of this larger picture.

In this context, the condition of practice is always complex and genuinely difficult to estimate, and logical argumentation is generally at the most able to establish some degree of certainty as to what is true, just, and right.[27] But in contrast to aesthetic practice, political practice at some point implies that decisions are made. So, alongside ongoing power struggles, political judgement oscillates between reflective and determinative modalities and makes its assessments of political issues in continuous dialogue with reason and with reference to the notion of a political *sensus communis*.

Political and Aesthetic Discursive Practice   87

Ethical and aesthetic questions as to the personal credibility and rhetorical power of persuasion of political agents therefore often play a central role in the political process as guarantors of the certainty that a factually orientated political discourse is not fully able to provide. With contextually shifting weight, it is fair to assume that the operative judgement of political practice draws on cognitive, ethical, and aesthetic rationalities of action in its movement of investigation between the specific and the universal. In other words, it is not a question of either/or, but of mixed processes and a standing issue of discursive balance. In terms of rhetoric: political communication in principle always includes elements of logos, ethos, and pathos, but the balance between these elements is of crucial importance to the quality of communication, and, in the context of the present argument, it is necessary to distinguish between a multiplicity of forms of pathos that entail quite different perspectives for the political process.

But if the ideal is a democratic political community based on the public opinion formation of empowered citizens, it seems equally fair to say that relevant political judgement is first of all constituted by a rationally and factually qualified ability of estimation in respect to the *content dimension* of political matters, including the reflection of both conflicts of interests and common concerns. In this perspective, the judgement of taste's non-conceptual and disinterested communication of a subjective feeling of pleasure or displeasure in regard to forms appears in itself to be an insufficient basis for democratic political community formation.

To this end, we may find inspiration in the other main type of judgement which Kant presents in *The Critique of Judgement:* the teleological judgement. This type of judgement also operates in the reflective mode, but departing from the a priori assumption of a basic *purposiveness*, according to which the phenomenon in question is reflectively investigated by means of the overall, meaning-seeking, speculative movement of reason. This reason-based activity of imagination is further engaged in a close relationship of exchange with the ethical *sensus communis* which we in the political context might suitably define as society's experience-based politico-cultural community of values (i.e. the level of consensus in the model presented above), which is continuously shaped and reshaped as a dialectical effect of the positioning struggle of special interests and their attempts to define the common good on their own terms.

In other words, a qualified democratic political community relies on a judgement which primarily performs its mediation between the specific and the universal in dialogue with concepts and arguments of reason, and which is capable of reflecting conflicts of interests and of processing them towards the perspective of the common good. A political judgement that meets the challenges of late modern social reality has, in other words, to be able to work on the complex terms that interest struggles are a basic fact of society but that the collective experience of the process of struggle at the same time continuously generates the common good as a discursive frame, a political *sensus communis*, which we as a societal political community obligate ourselves to reflect in legitimising our actions.[28]

88 *Political and Aesthetic Discursive Practice*

Aesthetic judgement may, due to its very way of functioning, contribute to strengthening the universal perspective, the ability to establish a reflective distance to immediate, private inclinations and interests, which is necessary for the development of a democratic community, and the ability to imagine alternatives to the status quo. But its own means of production – the non-conceptual, disinterested, feeling-based estimation of forms and the fundamental rejection of reflecting the conflictual content dimension of social practice – makes it insufficient as the main principle for the formation of political communities. Instead, a reason-based political judgement should be granted precedence.

In the context of democratic public discourse, a qualified political discursive practice should, in other words, be able to present a convincing and vision-led analysis of the development of society that appears factually well founded, reflects the experience-based political culture of society in a plausible way, invokes trust due to its representatives' demonstration of moral integrity – and appeals in a universalising manner to senses and emotions. However, as we saw in Chapter 3, in this sense, the current main challenge for democracy is posed by the fact that the prevailing technocratic consensus in the economic, political, and administrative system is increasingly sorting out politics' content dimension as determined by non-negotiable necessities, and thus tends to reduce public political discourse to a contentless struggle about appearing personally sympathetic and aesthetically appealing. Or to a content-based populist discourse devoid of political judgement.

Potentials and Limitations of Aesthetic Experience

From the perspective of citizenship, aesthetic experience could be regarded as a potential resource to create the complex identity work necessary for a democratic, inclusive handling of experiences of conflict. As opposed to the intrinsic, power-orientated determinativeness of political discourse, which will frequently tend to support a particularistic orientation of identity work, aesthetic discourse in the Kantian sense is, as we have seen, characterised by its indeterminate interventions and open seeking processes. Furthermore, aesthetic practice represents a more nuanced and wide-ranging potential for identity work than a purely political discourse could accomplish. A successful process of aesthetic experience expands our sensuous, emotional, and intellectual capacities and thereby unbinds an emancipatory potential; but in correspondence with the specificity of the process of experience, we are dealing with a specific perspective of emancipation. As Rüdiger Bubner puts it, it is characteristic of the process of aesthetic experience that it 'sets us free without determining what for'.[29]

Whereas the conception of *taste* that characterises influential positions in the analysis of contemporary society (Bourdieu, Schulze, Maffesoli, *et al.*) represents an unchallenged, static, and monologic preference that does not reflect beyond itself (i.e. operates according to the aesthetics of the agreeable and private judgement), the process of aesthetic experience (based on the aesthetic judgement of taste or the aesthetics of the sublime) is by definition challenging

Political and Aesthetic Discursive Practice 89

the patterns of orientation of everyday experience. It offers new perspectives on established values and forms of practice, but does not prescribe any alternative organisation of meanings and relations. Aesthetic experience places us in an indeterminate, reflective relationship with the status quo and equally indeterminately unbinds us from being unreflectively subsumed under it.

In other words, aesthetic experience encourages late modern identity work to reflect beyond the boundaries of immediate individual preferences and to open itself up to a more complex and dialogic exchange with the world. The common, public sharing of aesthetic experiences thus forms a more open and potentially inclusive basis of social interaction than explicit, antagonistic conflicts of interest, and this type of experience could in this sense be a valuable contribution to the further development of a universal frame of reflection in society. Within this frame, the discourse of the common good might gain weight at the expense of particularistic special interests. In other words, aesthetic experience has the potential to transcend the narrow horizons of consumerism and self-sufficient ethnocentrism or nationalism and thereby strengthen the universal perspective of citizenship, and, in this sense, it represents a comprehensive resource to create engaged public interaction and to enhance the process of democratisation.

Aesthetic practice can, in other words, contribute considerably to society's general formation of experience and thus to the further development of democratic political culture. However, due to its basic indeterminateness, aesthetic experience does not in itself guarantee universality and democracy – this depends on its dialectical inscription into overall social practice, i.e. on the concrete, hegemonic interplay, which, at any given time, is established between aesthetic processes of experience and the historical and present conflict experiences reflected by political discourse. In other words, the concrete discursive horizon of the narrative adaptation of experience remains crucial for the democratic perspectives of identity work.

Notes

1 Pierre Bourdieu, *Distinction* (London: Routledge and Kegan Paul, 1984).
2 Gerhard Schulze, *Die Erlebnisgesellschaft* (Frankfurt am Main: Campus, 1992).
3 Michel Maffesoli, *The Time of the Tribes* (London: Sage, 1995).
4 Jürgen Habermas, *Theorie des kommunikativen Handelns*, vols 1–2 (Frankfurt am Main: Suhrkamp, 1981) (English translation: *Theory of Communicative Action*, vols 1–2, Boston: Beacon Press, 1984).
5 For example, Niklas Luhmann, *Soziale Systeme* (Frankfurt am Main: Suhrkamp, 1984); Pierre Bourdieu, *The Field of Cultural Production* (New York: Columbia University Press, 1993); Ernesto Laclau and Chantal Mouffe, *Hegemony and Socialist Strategy* (London: Verso, 1985).
6 To be elaborated later.
7 For example, Friedrich Schiller, *Über die ästhetische Erziehung des Menschen* (Stuttgart: Reclam, 1975 [1795]). An adequate English translation of the term *Bildung* does not exist.
8 Henrik Kaare Nielsen, *Kulturel offentlighed og kvalitet* (Aarhus: Klim, 2015).
9 Wolfgang Iser, *Der Akt des Lesens* (München: Wilhelm Fink Verlag, 1976).
10 Nielsen, *Kulturel offentlighed ...*, op. cit.

90 *Political and Aesthetic Discursive Practice*

11 Dieter Prokop, *Der kulturindustrielle Machtkomplex* (Köln: Herbert von Halem Verlag, 2005).

12 Detlef Georgia Schulze, Sabine Berghahn, and Frieder O. Wolf, *Politisierung und Ent-Politisierung als performative Praxis* (Münster: Westfälisches Dampfboot, 2006).

13 Immanuel Kant, *Kritik der Urteilskraft* (Stuttgart: Reclam 1963 [1790]) (English translation: *The Critique of Judgement*, Oxford: Oxford University Press, 1952). See also Paul Guyer, *Kant and the Claims of Taste* (Cambridge: Cambridge University Press, 1979); Howard Caygill, *Art of Judgment* (Oxford: Basil Blackwell, 1989); Martin Seel, *Ästhetik des Erscheinens* (Frankfurt am Main: Suhrkamp, 2003) (English translation: *Aesthetics of Appearing*, Stanford, CA: Stanford University Press 2005); Jørn Erslev Andersen, *Sansning og erkendelse* (Aarhus: Aarhus University Press, 2012).

14 Cf. Guyer, *Kant and the Claims of Taste*, op. cit., p. 312ff.

15 Bourdieu, *Distinction*, op. cit.

16 As outlined above, the discursive framework of the common good is experience-based and may be rolled back as a consequence of radical changes of its experiential foundation. But as long as the conditions of functioning modern democratic institutions and a general public debate are given, a universal ethical consensus should be regarded as a dimension of political reality.

17 For example, in the shape of the spontaneous, monological sympathy with which citizens often meet political proposals from 'their' party leader, while the same proposal from the camp of political opponents is met with an equally spontaneous, non-rationally founded antipathy. It is presumably a crucial point that this is an example of a type of opinion formation that is rooted in a specific form of political engagement, namely, the engagement of the passive spectator. Active forms of participation will to a higher degree involve the participants in a dialogic practice and challenge the agents to reflect and nuance their arguments.

18 Kant, *Kritik der Urteilskraft*, op. cit., p. 118

19 Martin Seel, 'Zur ästhetischen Praxis der Kunst', in Wolfgang Welsch (ed.) *Die Aktualität des Ästhetischen* (München: Wilhelm Fink Verlag, 1993), p. 407 (my translation).

20 Cf. Charles Taylor, 'Wieviel Gemeinschaft braucht die Demokratie?' *Transit* 5 (1992).

21 Jacques Rancière, *The Politics of Aesthetics* (London: Continuum, 2004).

22 Hannah Arendt, *Das Urteilen. Texte zu Kants politischer Philosophie* (München: Piper, 1985).

23 Oskar Negt, *Der politische Mensch* (Göttingen: Steidl, 2010).

24 Christoph Menke, 'The Aesthetic Critique of Judgment', in Daniel Birnbaum and Isabelle Graw (eds), *The Power of Judgment: A Debate on Aesthetic Critique* (Frankfurt am Main: Sternberg Press, 2010).

25 Cf. Rüdiger Bubner, *Ästhetische Erfahrung* (Frankfurt am Main: Suhrkamp, 1989).

26 See also Menke, 'Aesthetic Critique of Judgment', op. cit.

27 Negt, *Der politische Mensch*, op. cit.

28 Nielsen, *Konsument ...*, op. cit.

29 Bubner, *Ästhetische Erfahrung*, op. cit, p. 92 (my translation).

References

Andersen, Jørn Erslev (2012) *Sansning og erkendelse*, Aarhus: Aarhus University Press.

Arendt, Hannah (1985) *Das Urteilen. Texte zu Kants politischer Philosophie*, München: Piper.

Bourdieu, Pierre (1984) *Distinction*, London: Routledge and Kegan Paul.

Bourdieu, Pierre (1993) *The Field of Cultural Production*, New York: Columbia University Press.

Political and Aesthetic Discursive Practice   91

Bubner, Rüdiger (1989) *Ästhetische Erfahrung*, Frankfurt am Main: Suhrkamp.

Caygill, Howard (1989) *Art of Judgment*, Oxford: Basil Blackwell Publishers.

Guyer, Paul (1979) *Kant and the Claims of Taste*, Cambridge: Cambridge University Press.

Habermas, Jürgen (1981) *Theorie des kommunikativen Handelns*, vols 1–2, Frankfurt am Main: Suhrkamp (English translation: *Theory of Communicative Action*, vols 1–2, Boston: Beacon Press, 1984).

Iser, Wolfgang (1976) *Der Akt des Lesens*, München: Wilhelm Fink Verlag.

Kant, Immanuel (1963 [1790]) *Kritik der Urteilskraft*, Stuttgart: Reclam (English translation: *The Critique of Judgement*, Oxford: Oxford University Press, 1952).

Laclau, Ernesto and Chantal Mouffe (1985) *Hegemony and Socialist Strategy*, London: Verso.

Luhmann, Niklas (1984) *Soziale Systeme*, Frankfurt am Main: Suhrkamp.

Maffesoli, Michel (1995) *The Time of the Tribes*, London: Sage.

Menke, Christoph (2010) 'The Aesthetic Critique of Judgment', in Daniel Birnbaum and Isabelle Graw (eds), *The Power of Judgment: A Debate on Aesthetic Critique*, Frankfurt am Main: Sternberg Press.

Negt, Oskar (2010) *Der politische Mensch*, Göttingen: Steidl.

Nielsen, Henrik Kaare (2015) *Kulturel offentlighed og kvalitet*, Aarhus: Klim.

Prokop, Dieter (2005) *Der kulturindustrielle Machtkomplex*, Köln: Herbert von Halem Verlag.

Rancière, Jacques (2004) *The Politics of Aesthetics*, London: Continuum.

Schiller, Friedrich (1975 [1795]) *Über die ästhetische Erziehung des Menschen*, Stuttgart: Reclam.

Schulze, Detlef Georgia, Sabine Berghahn, and Frieder O. Wolf (2006) *Politisierung und Ent-Politisierung als performative Praxis*, Münster: Westfälisches Dampfboot.

Schulze, Gerhard (1992) *Die Erlebnisgesellschaft*, Frankfurt am Main: Campus.

Seel, Martin (1993) 'Zur ästhetischen Praxis der Kunst', in Wolfgang Welsch (ed.), *Die Aktualität des Ästhetischen*, München: Wilhelm Fink Verlag.

Seel, Martin (2003) *Ästhetik des Erscheinens*, Frankfurt am Main: Suhrkamp (English translation: *Aesthetics of Appearing*, Stanford, CA: Stanford University Press 2005).

Taylor, Charles (1992) 'Wieviel Gemeinschaft braucht die Demokratie?' *Transit 5*.

5   Power-Oriented Aesthetic Interventions in Politics

As exemplified earlier, designing political practice aesthetically is not an exclusively late modern phenomenon. But aesthetic staging has in late modernity advanced to a general condition of practice that political agents are bound to relate to in order to gain visibility. Politics is involved in a permanent competition with a multiplicity of other appeals to senses and emotions: physical spaces and objects of everyday life are insistently pointing to themselves in their capacity as designed entities; individual identities and social relations are understood and practised as constructed and malleable; media and advertising industries are struggling for our attention by targeting our senses and emotions in various spectacular ways; politicians are consciously staging themselves and boosting their aesthetic appeal in order to gain our attention and strive to persuade us to support them by radiating an aura of empathy and personal credibility.

Aesthetic interventions, in other words, hold a prominent position in public space and everyday life in general. As indicated above, this should not necessarily in itself be regarded as a problem; the decisive question is on which discursive premises this position is established and held: are we dealing with a productive interplay between e.g. aesthetic and political discourse in which they throw each other into relief, challenge and stimulate each other, and open a more nuanced understanding of a political issue? Or is the aesthetic discourse marginalising the political, obstructing its ability to create meaning on political terms, thus reducing political opinion formation to a matter of sympathy or antipathy on the basis of unreflective emotional inclinations and immediate preferences of taste?

As pointed out in Chapter 1, the interesting question is not 'aesthetic staging or not?', but 'aesthetic staging how?'. It is crucial for the perspective of aesthetic intervention whether it in practice leaves space for a mutually qualifying interaction between sensuous/emotional appeal and reason, or whether it exclusively targets the immediate pleasing of senses and emotions. In the former case, aesthetic intervention dynamises politics and may have an empowering, democratising potential; in the latter, it represents dedifferentiation, depoliticises the issue in question, and makes us less qualified in our reflective capabilities on both individual and societal levels.

Following this line of thinking, the ambition will be to establish distinctions between a plurality of specific types of appeals to senses and emotions and their

Power-Oriented Aesthetic Interventions 93

respective compatibility with processes of reflection, thus proposing an elaborate foundation to analyse what sort of impact different types of aesthetic intervention are liable to have on society's public opinion formation and political culture. As a primary distinction, 'aesthetic intervention' will be used as an overall concept for all kinds of aesthetic intertwinement with politics, whereas the term 'aestheticisation' conceptualises the specific categories of interplay where the discursive balance tips and aesthetic discourse dominates or even marginalises the political. Furthermore, a distinction between 'power-oriented' and 'artistic' types of aesthetic intervention will be introduced.

The analysis will primarily address these issues within the frame of reflection offered by reception aesthetics.[1] As pointed out earlier, this implies focusing on political communication in its capacity as a designed invitation to reception, i.e. as a communicative approach with a built-in model of reception. This implicit model of reception represents a condition that all empirical processes of reception relate to, but the relation should not be regarded as one of strict determination. The individual, empirical recipient's response to the invitation may go its own way and result in formations of meaning that bend and twist the proposal of the invitation in other directions: the recipient may not possess the knowledge that the implicit model of reception presupposes and therefore gains a different meaning – or none whatsoever – from the invitation. Or the recipient may consciously choose to respond contrarily, critically, or ironically to the approach. In other words, although the empirical process of reception works on the conditions of the implicit model of reception, the results of the former cannot be deduced from the latter.

In this chapter, the focus will be on the interventions by aesthetic discourse in political practice, including the ways in which aesthetic discourse is being integrated into the political process on the discursive premises of the latter. As pointed out earlier, it is a widespread principle of aesthetic intervention in the political process (cf. the model presented above) that aesthetic effects are used by political agents in order to establish themselves in a position of power in the struggle of interests and the formation of compromises. However, as outlined in Chapter 4, aesthetic practice holds a multiplicity of discursive possibilities, and aesthetic intervention in political practice can therefore mean a variety of things and imply correspondingly different perspectives for the development of culture and society.

Aesthetic Characteristics of the Four Types of Publics

Chapter 3 suggested an ideal-typical distinction between four types of publics (the governmental decision-maker public, the public of parliament-oriented mass media, and civil society publics at both overall and grassroots levels). The overall late modern tendency towards aestheticisation forms the context conditions of all of them, but in different ways and with different weightings. In the following, these differences will be characterised briefly, and subsequently a more elaborate outline of the specific conditions of meaning-formation of the public of parliament-oriented mass media will be presented.

94 Power-Oriented Aesthetic Interventions

In the context of the present argument, *the governmental decision-maker public* is of low complexity, in as far as it is an exponent of a ritualised aesthetic of representative statesmanship whose forms are clearly determined by their function of supporting governmental authority, the legitimacy of decisions made, and general trust and obedience towards the institutions. In other words, this type of aesthetic approach is monologic by nature, and its implicit recipient is *the citizen as a subject to the state*. This aesthetic genre is strongly defined by conventions. Outwardly, addressing the subjects, it aims to present alternating politicians as the presently incontestable incarnation of societal power. The monumentalising staging of the statesman (male or female) is designed in order to inspire the recipient with awe and vouch for the authoritative and competent handling of common concerns (Figure 5.1). Further, internally among decision-makers, this community of style strengthens their mutual trust in the complicated process of struggle for national interests, negotiation, and formation of compromises: the restrained, conventionalised aesthetic neutralises differences, signals sincerity and calculability, and affirms the mutual obligation of the involved agents.

The individual politician's scope for putting his/her personal stylistic mark on the staging is quite narrow: it is limited to a minor margin of freedom – for men with respect to the choice of tie, and for women with respect to cut and colour of suit and blouse. Further, you can profile yourself as a power figure by virtue of your choice of artworks for your representative rooms.[2] Apart from this, the crucial question is whether the institutional role is performed convincingly and with dignity. If this is not the case, it may cause severe damage to the image of the politician in question and ultimately to the legitimacy of the institution.

At the other end of the spectrum, the *partial civil society publics* offer a multiplicity of aesthetic profiles of resistance – be it a citizen initiative for keeping the local school, protests against cuts in the care for children or the elderly, grassroots initiatives in areas like animal rights, the environment, and climate, subcultural groups of political artists, etc. (Figure 5.2). As conceptualised above, these phenomena represent partial publics that initially draw on subjective

Figure 5.1 Meeting in the European Council, 18–19 December 2014.
Source: photo © The European Union.

Figure 5.2 Activists at International Women's Day, 8 March 2015 in Toronto.
Source: Shutterstock.

experience-reflecting public discourse. Internally, they process subjective needs, mutual disagreements and power issues, and societal experiences of conflict dialogically, but externally, they often tend to stage themselves and the specific case they are fighting for monologically with *the already agreeing sympathiser* as implicit recipient. The aesthetic approach is closely intertwined with the formation of political identity and will typically be dichotomous by nature, so that the appeal by way of idiosyncratic judgement invites a strong emotional identification internally and a strong demarcation outwardly, often in the form of creating decidedly hostile images of 'the others'.

As pointed out above, this type of grassroots politicisation in principle holds the potential for nuancing learning processes and development of a universal perspective on the struggles. But, on the other hand, such opening of the partial publics towards a dialogic, deliberative exchange in a broader democratic public is not a given matter. Monologic or even violent group formations on the extreme right and left and among radical Islamists are part of the political scene, and they are basically drawing on the same dynamic of identity work and impulses of resistance that, in a different context, treated in the modality of subjective experience-reflecting public discourse, may constitute a valuable democratising potential. However, these extreme groups are not processing the dynamic in democratic, dialogical forms, on the contrary, they are channelling it into a scenario of a brutalised power struggle. They intervene in public space with the aim of undermining democratic public discourse. In other words, partial

96 Power-Oriented Aesthetic Interventions

civil society publics should be regarded as ambiguous entities: as important democratic potentials and as possible counter-productive factors.

In practice, the two remaining types of publics are difficult to keep clearly apart – not least because they are both operating on the overall, socio-political level, to a large part are addressing the same issues, and are using the same media – although in different ways. Furthermore, professional politicians are active in both types of publics.

Overall civil society publics unfold in the general, open debate in public service media, in the publicistic newspapers and magazines, in parts of the blogosphere and the social media, in the debates of universally oriented social movements and NGOs, at socio-political debate meetings, and in the multiplicity of universally oriented discussions among engaged citizens in various forums of everyday life in workplaces, associations, neighbourhoods, families, and circles of friends.

Obviously, universally oriented civil society agents are also staging their protests and demands in order to arouse the interest of the media and thereby gain support among the population and be able to put pressure on parliamentary politics. But in the process of establishing this extra-parliamentary pressure, the aesthetic dimension of the discursive practice is generally subordinated to the matter-of-fact-oriented dimension of political content. The approach is dialogical by nature, departing from the assumption of a *sensus communis*, and the implicit recipient is *the engaged, universally reasoning citizen*. The example below is characterised by addressing the recipient dialogically and referring to a universalistic political ethic (Figure 5.3).

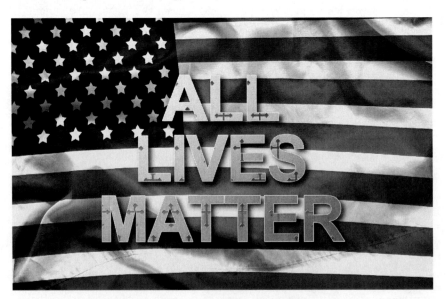

Figure 5.3 All Lives Matter Slogan on American Flag Background.
Source: Shutterstock.

The public of parliament-oriented mass media is dominated by the interplay between professional politicians and professional media. On the one hand, politicians represent a socio-political engagement and participate in public debate with concrete political ideas and proposals; on the other hand, each of them has a private interest in ensuring visibility, support, and re-election for themselves and their party. Correspondingly, on the one hand, public service media and publicistic media in general share the basic aim of contributing to creating a substantial and well-functioning socio-political debate, and on the other hand, they are engaged in an intense competition with each other and with purely commercial media to attract the attention of readers/listeners/viewers and thereby secure for themselves subscribers/customers, advertisers and/or public funding. In this double field of tension in the public of parliament-oriented mass media, a dynamic interplay unfolds between political and aesthetic discursive practice, and the implicit recipient of the approaches varies from *the universally reasoning citizen* to *the self-centred consumer*. These practices will be discussed further in the following section.

Aesthetic Intervention in the Public of Parliament-Oriented Mass Media

When we speak in general terms about the tendencies towards aestheticisation of the political process in late modernity, i.e. the tendencies towards intensifying the aspect of form and the appeal to senses and emotions while marginalising substance and the appeal to reason, we are mostly referring to phenomena in the public of parliament-oriented mass media. In the media's capacity as an arena for politicians' personal profiling and power tactics, and for media organisations' competition over market shares, this type of public implies strong incentives to attract attention by means of arousing senses and emotions rather than addressing the recipient as a critically reflective citizen.[3]

The possible consequences of the tendency towards aestheticisation for the collective formation of experience and society's political culture as a whole depend on the interplay and the relationship of dominance between all four types of publics. But in this overall constellation, the public of parliament-oriented mass media plays a pivotal role – partly due to its foundation in the media and professional politics which grants it more institutional weight and permanence than the more loosely organised and often transient civil society publics; partly because it represents an important framing condition of any process of civil society opinion formation: the latter will only be able to obtain decisive influence on the political decision-making process and society's collective experience formation, if it succeeds in establishing itself as a powerful position in the public of parliament-oriented mass media. Therefore, this type of public will be investigated further in the following.

Aesthetic intervention in the political process as it manifests itself in the public of parliament-oriented mass media, unfolds on two connected levels:

98   *Power-Oriented Aesthetic Interventions*

a level where the intervention concerns the design of specific artefacts, and an 'atmospheric' level that is related to the tendency towards equipping the late modern life-world as a whole with aesthetic appeals. The following will deal with examples of the most prominent forms of power-oriented aesthetic intervention in this type of public – first, at the artefact level, then at the atmospheric level. Subsequently, Chapter 6 will investigate aesthetic interventions that use artistic forms of expression and reflection.

The Artefact Level

In the interplay between the politician and the media, the politician is first of all staged as an aesthetic artefact that invites one to a projecting dialogue, i.e. the continuing dialogical movement of the reception process between the recipient's projection of an expected meaning and the artefact's 'answer' that modifies and nuances the meaning formation. In this type of public, it is always the politician as a person who is at the centre of the appeal and constitutes the object of aesthetic intervention, but, depending on the context, the main focus in the design of the artefact may be the politician's private characteristics and relations, the political power play he/she is engaged in, or the political content that he/she represents.

As pointed out earlier, the nature of the experience and meaning formation that is developed in the course of the projecting dialogue depends on the interplay between, on the one hand, the aesthetic design of the approach, i.e. its formal characteristics, genre features, and implicit recipient, and, on the other, the empirical recipient's experiential qualifications and readiness to engage in the dialogue. It is, in other words, a complex process, the result of which cannot be predicted in general terms. But, in all circumstances, the nature of the artefact's invitation plays a crucial conditioning role as to the scope and developmental perspectives of the projecting dialogue.

For instance, according to reception aesthetics, the degree to which an aesthetic approach is *open* or *closed* is of great importance to the quality of the dialogue it invites: a predominantly closed approach (in which the aesthetic expression is thoroughly oriented towards determining the political meaning of the invitation and presenting a nuanced picture of the wider political context) frames and channels the projection of meaning robustly and incites endorsement or objection on clear premises of substance. A predominantly open approach, on the contrary, will to a high degree leave the formation of meaning to the projections by the recipient within a vaguely defined frame of content. The greater the degree of openness, the larger and freer the scope of the recipient's meaning projections, but also the less qualified and nuancing the dialogue in the process. Ultimately, the open approach opens the floodgates to arbitrary, monologic projections of unprocessed private wishes or resentments.

An example of the use of open appeals that was successful in terms of power politics, was Barack Obama's presidential election campaign in 2008, in which predominantly unspecific visions of 'Hope' and 'Change' seem to have been

Power-Oriented Aesthetic Interventions 99

crucial factors in the mobilisation of voters. Likewise, Donald Trump's success-ful campaign in 2016 was to a large extent based on open approaches, such as the nostalgic, but relatively unspecific main promise to 'Make America great again'. Although this unprecedented campaign also contained a number of very specific political proposals (building a border wall and letting Mexico pay for it; withdrawal from international trade agreements, etc.), its appeal as a whole must be characterised as wide open, since the candidate throughout the process remained totally inscrutable and permanently changed his positions, seemingly according to his shifting moods.

The point is that in a perspective of democratic public discourse, an open appeal is unqualified if it is left to stand alone. As is also well known from popu-list propaganda in general, open appeals can mobilise and channel all sorts of diffuse frustrations and disorientated hopes of change – i.e. everyday life's mul-tiplicity of impulses of resistance – and may thus occasionally become a strong source of power in political struggle. But in such processes we are not dealing with democratic opinion formation, but, on the contrary, with the creation of volatile and unspecific moods on a mass scale. If an open appeal is to work con-structively in a perspective of democratic public discourse, it should, in other words, be combined with other forms of approaches that nuance and concretise the content matter of the appeal.

The present analysis regards it as crucial whether the appeals to senses and emotions in the mass media public take the shape of a one-dimensional confirm-ation of potential voters'/customers' immediate feelings and preferences of taste, i.e. they operate merely on the basis of the aesthetics of the agreeable and private judgement. Or whether the projection of meaning also meets a qualifying response that challenges the recipient's political judgement by addressing the dimension of conflicting social interests and is invited to process the challenge in the medium of universally reflecting reason. The latter would represent an appeal to political judgement as defined in Chapter 4.

However, it is the first precondition for catalysing political judgement among citizens that politicians and media who are designing the approaches wish to engage in this kind of exchange – and that rarely seems to be the case.[4] On the contrary, the approaches in the public of parliament-oriented mass media are to an overriding extent characterised by either a *polarising* or a *harmonising* form of aesthetic intervention, both of which invite restricted formations of meaning.

A *polarising* staging of politics is the preference of the mass media. Political debates are generally orchestrated in order to immediately confront any point of view with its absolute opposite in the spectrum of opinions. Rather than creating space for complexity, matter-of-fact reflection, and nuanced unfolding of argu-ments, this staging of debate contributes to reducing politics to a zero-sum game and politicians to quarrelling hotspurs in the arena of the entertainment industry. This tendency stems from the above-mentioned situation of increasingly intensi-fied competition for both the media and the politicians, and both sides see their interests served by the polarising staging. The media strive to attract the atten-tion of the public by presenting political content as sensational, dynamic, and entertaining; and politicians fight for victory in the debates, thereby strengthening themselves and their parties in the overall power struggle (Figure 5.4).[5]

Among politicians, in other words, polarising aesthetic intervention in a political dispute often serves as a calculated discourse of power. If you can get away with designing your opponent as a representative of Evil itself, as a traitor, a sympathiser of terrorism, a crypto-communist, a Nazi, an anti-Semite, or other sorts of irreparable folly, you deprive your counterpart of the status of partner in democratic dialogue. In correspondence with the dichotomous universe of B-movies, you hereby claim to have a monopoly on the virtues of democratic reason and accordingly position yourself advantageously in the political power play.

This shaping of political exchange stimulates neither a fact-oriented, arguing dialogue on disagreements nor a consensual understanding of common concerns of society. Rather, it cultivates a triadic structure of communication in which the contending parties are in reality speaking neither to each other nor to the general public, but to their own separate audiences.[6] The audience is addressed as already divided into factions with specific sympathies and antipathies that are consolidated by the performance of the hotspurs. This approach makes an aesthetic appeal to private judgement: the horizon of special interests remains unchallenged, and the audience is invited to delight in having its prejudice affirmed. In this sense, the model recipient of the mass media's staging of political debate is not the empowered, participating citizen but the self-centred, entertainment-seeking and affirmation-seeking consumer. This type of appeal

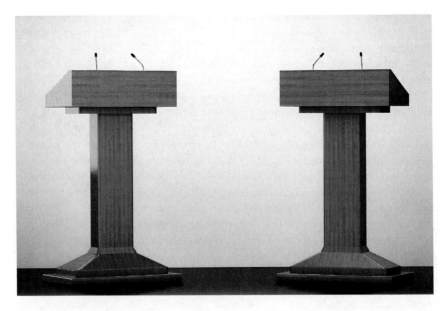

Figure 5.4 Debate Podium.
Source: Shutterstock.

Power-Oriented Aesthetic Interventions 101

is liable to leave a restricting mark on society's politico-cultural process of experience.

To be sure, not only dialogical, deliberative dispute generates political culture. Also monologic positionings may have long-term politico-cultural consequences, in as far as effect-straining rhetoric – if it is successful in framing debate – can gradually displace the general ethical lines of orientation. In recent years, this has been the case in many European countries in the field of immigration policy. Right-wing populist parties and related civil society organisations have persistently addressed foreigners as a problem to society, thereby gradually leaving their mark on the consensual ethical framework of politics and paving the way for a broad political acceptance of legislative restrictions in the field of immigration policy that would have been unthinkable in the 1990s.

However, the fact that political debate in the public of parliament-oriented mass media to a large extent carries these barren, polarised features, does not mean that the political process in late modern democracies no longer relates to arguments of reason and works out compromises that aim to weigh and balance special interests in consideration of the common good of society. However, this effort is increasingly not taking place in public forums but in bargaining processes that unfold in closed negotiations and governance networks. Consequently, it is not the process *towards* decision-making that invites reflective formation of experience and opinions in the general public, but at best the subsequent wrestling with the consequences of decisions already made.

Polarisation is a classic effect in political struggle and in the media's staging of politics, but since the start of the 2000s, it has obtained a particularly prominent status. The media public has in this period been thematically dominated by the strong polarisation of the conditions of politics which, emanating from the fields of foreign policy and security policy, has left its mark on the political public on both the national and the international level since the terrorist attack on the United States on 9/11, 2001.

This polarisation has a solid core of power politics concerning both geopolitical and economic interests, including the question of controlling 'the terms of trade' in the Middle East and not least maintaining access to the oil wells of the region. The constellation of interests surrounding these questions of power politics is of a highly complex nature in both the Middle East and in the West, but after 9/11 the multiplicity of interests and political positions in the field was forced into a reductionist, dichotomous scenario.

This simplified picture furthermore corresponded with the fact that, in safeguarding their interests, both sides legitimised their bloodshed by claiming to be defending sublime values. In this way, the political conflict was discursively transformed into a pure conflict of cultures, where, for instance, Samuel Huntington's thesis on the 'Clash of Civilizations'[7] served as a convenient legitimising ideology for reductionism; and on this background, polarisation developed a dynamic of its own in public consciousness by way of a stylising, aesthetic discourse. In other words, a complex political conflict was aesthetically intensified, and from the start we were operating in a scenario where a political process

102 *Power-Oriented Aesthetic Interventions*

based on reason, dialogue, and compromise-orientated interaction had no scope whatsoever.

The Al-Qaeda terrorists performed their self-appointed role as safeguards of Middle Eastern interests against 'infidel' Western interference in the shape of an uncompromising, violence-based monologue of power. As is the case with all terrorism, this type of practice is rooted in a condition of political and military powerlessness which terrorists seek to transform into a position of strength by incalculably spreading death and mutilation among innocent civilians and thus creating a climate of horror in order to undermine the social and political stability of society.

In other words, the destruction of the basic conditions of democracy is a central element in the strategy of terrorism in general, but contemporary Islamic terrorism adds a calculated aesthetic dimension: the attacks are carried out as spectacular, orchestrated acts of violence. The horrifying experience of the collapse of the Twin Towers disrupted the established patterns of imagination as to what a destructive, misanthropic will is able to accomplish. Accompanied by the many hours of indeterminacy that ensued, during which time the international public had no idea as to who was responsible and what was the background, this act paved the way for a general aesthetic experience of sublimity in the Kantian sense of the word, i.e. a horror-stricken fascination in the encounter with an unknown, incalculable, and dangerous superior force. On a lower scale, the same effect applies to the recent truck-massacres carried out by ISIS supporters in European cities and the public beheadings of Western hostages on social media.

This represents an extremely effective type of aesthetic intervention in politics which charges the political process with a conflictual but indeterminate sensuous-emotional intensity able to suspend the reason-based judgement of public debate and ultimately to cause the dissolution of democratic political culture from within. In full accordance with the intentions of its strategists, this type of aesthetic intervention has served to strengthen their position in the political power play in the sense that terrorism has become a factor that permanently occupies a huge amount of attention in international politics.

At the same time, it has destabilised the political process in its capacity for handling conflicts of interest in a civilised manner, and the perspective of this type of aesthetic intervention in politics is therefore the replacement of politics by barbarism and the rule of violence. This development has been carried further by the continued terrorist activities of radical Islamists, but also by de-civilising counter-measures by democratic countries: increased surveillance and confinement of civil rights, the establishment of spaces devoid of civil rights such as the Guantanamo camp, the use of drones for liquidating suspects without a trial (and the collateral damage to blameless civilians) on foreign territory.

In other words, the Western counterpart in this dichotomous scenario has conducted a parallel aesthetic staging of politics: in a semi-religious setting, a complex, global constellation has been stylised to the conflict between Democracy and 'the axis of Evil', between freedom and terrorism. As a simple reflex of the fundamentalist worldview of the terrorists, Western leaders have formed a

Power-Oriented Aesthetic Interventions   103

political space of meaning which is modelled in accordance with classic stereo-types: 'You're either with us or you're with the terrorists.' The scenario is a per-manent state of emergency with apocalypse lurking around the corner, and, consequently, where there is no scope for discussion and disagreement on the inner lines.[8] Instead of attempting to realise the reflective potential of the experi-ence of sublimity and on this basis submit the established practices of world pol-itics to a reason-based critical revision, the processing of experience has, in other words, remained confined to idiosyncratic judgement's highly reduced version of aesthetic discourse, which in this context has been used to simplify and close down the public space of reflection.

This aesthetic reduction of complexity and the related positioning of Western state leaders as firm, energetic, and uncompromising guarantors of democracy and peace against attacks from the powers of darkness have strengthened these leaders in the power struggles at the national level and granted them an extended freedom of action on the international scene. But as a consequence, the same aesthetically profiled, uncompromising approach to politics is threatening the democratic process that the discourse claims to protect; this occurs in the form of authoritarian conduct, including throwing suspicion on and intimidating crit-ical voices in public debate, and in the shape of exponentially growing surveil-lance activities that threaten to undermine civil liberties. The politico-cultural formation of experience, which is caused by this polarising aesthetic intervention in politics internally in democratic societies, is thus characterised by a narrowing of the horizon of reflection and a disempowered orientation towards conformity with the politicians in power.

Harmonising staging on the basis of the aesthetics of the agreeable is prom-inent in the public approaches by politicians themselves. In the effort to appeal effectively to the identity work of citizens, politicians tend to present their respective visions of the good society as non-conflictual communities of experi-ence or value. This staging is established by means of generally pleasing sensu-ous appeals and monological, emotion-based marketing of the politician in question as a confidence-inspiring person: smiling, sympathetic, well-dressed, authoritative – therefore trustworthy.[9] This type of approach is predominant when politicians and parties present themselves on their own terms in the public of parliament-oriented mass media and in election propaganda. In accordance with Lakoff's points in his theory of *framing*, critical demarcations against opponents typically only implicitly form the context of the approach whereas the explicit appeal attempts to establish harmonious unity between the politician/party and the identity issues and preferences of taste among potential voters (Figure 5.5).[10]

The self-presentation by political parties in the mass media is primarily ori-ented towards immediate pleasing of the senses and emotions of the recipients in order to include them in a monologically defined vision of harmony and mutual affirmation. The appeal may to varying degrees include elements of universally reasoning and subjective experience-reflecting public discourse, but it is first of all propelled by a basic marketing interest and thus by consumerist public

104 Power-Oriented Aesthetic Interventions

Figure 5.5 Twitter Website for Possible Republican Nominee Donald Trump, 5 May 2016.
Source: Shutterstock.

discourse. It is, in other words, not the political judgement of the critical, participating citizen that is being addressed, but rather the disoriented, compensatory need of the private individual to be able to imagine a life situation free of conflict and characterised by stable patterns of identity.

An illustrative example of the tendency towards harmonisation is the development of the terminology of established politics that in terms of creative conflict-denial often reaches the heights of Orwellian newspeak. 'Reform', for instance, is a central concept in democratic politics in general and has traditionally represented a positively defined, progressive improvement of societal conditions. But in later decades the content of the concept has gradually and imperceptibly mutated into being about cutting and reducing established welfare institutions. Comparable to the phenomena *spin* and *framing*, the aim of this predominant political rhetoric is to let the historically founded positive connotations that are associated with the concept of reform harmonise the social conflict material that the programmed reductions imply, and make these appear as indisputably necessary adjustments in the common interest.

Correspondingly, in the prevailing political rhetoric, the positively charged concept 'modernisation' no longer represents visionary political regulation measures but, on the contrary, deregulation and rolling back welfare institutions to the benefit of marketisation of societal relations. Due to this terminological transformation, resistance against this type of policy is not recognised as a

Power-Oriented Aesthetic Interventions 105

relevant political counterpart, but automatically marginalised as anti-modern and old-fashioned – and therefore in advance has a hard time establishing itself as a serious position in political debate. Likewise, the term 'normalisation' has an immediately positive, affirming appeal to common sense, but e.g. in labour market policy, the employer side frequently attempts to monopolise the term, rhetorically rendering the position of the employees 'non-normal', i.e. not pointing to a real conflict of interest, but merely to a delusion that should be abandoned in the interests of everyone.[11]

In other words, harmonising, conflict-denying aestheticisation of political terminology is a crucial power-oriented form of intervention that contributes actively to restricting the developmental possibilities of political judgement of citizens.

The Atmospheric Level

A corresponding dominance of merely agreeable forms of approaches characterises the aesthetic interventions on the 'atmospheric' level.[12] Here, we are dealing with a generalised equipment of the collective space of meaning – and in the present context specifically the space of political practice – with a sensuous and emotional surplus-meaning. At this level, the recipient is not engaging in a projecting dialogue with specific artefacts (e.g. an individual politician) – instead, he/she is exchanging with the whole aesthetic design of the given space of practice in the shape of what we might term an 'atmospheric projection' that modulates the experience of the space and endows it with a specific quality of mood, an atmosphere.

As is the case at the artefact level, the nature of the atmospheric formation of meaning depends on the dialogical meeting between a given subject with specific knowledge resources and experiential qualifications to relate to designed surroundings, and a given object, in this case, a spatial entity with specific physical and aesthetic characteristics: architectural design, materials, light and sound qualities, openness or closedness, interplay of balance and movement, and so forth.

As Reinhard Knodt puts it, individuals with different social and cultural backgrounds will possess different measures of 'atmospheric competence'; and similarly, the other way around, different spatial designs will give the atmospheric projection of meaning qualitatively different types of response. Atmospheric meaning in this sense is neither determined by spatial design nor by arbitrary subjective projections – it takes shape in a complex and conditioned process of exchange between subjective and objective factors.

A predominant way of designing the political space of practice in the public of parliament-oriented mass media appears to be closely related to classic *party space*, as described by Reinhard Knodt.[13] The space of a party holds its meaning in itself. It is basically characterised by its contrast to everyday life's various differentiated and function-specific spaces of practice in which conflicts, ambivalences, and role-defined distance between individuals form the conditions of

106   *Power-Oriented Aesthetic Interventions*

interaction. As opposed to this, party space temporarily suspends these features of interpersonal relationships of everyday life to the benefit of creating a community based on closeness and harmonious unity. By way of a special staging of physical space, the participants' non-everyday dress-code and forms of conduct, and various forms of cultivating and stimulating the senses (subdued light, loud music, refined food, and alcoholic drinks), party space invites a collective atmospheric projection that offers the participants a pleasurable concurrence of emotions.

As a significant dimension of the general tendency towards aestheticisation, the cultural industry – in the mode of consumerist public discourse – attempts to adopt these specific features of party space and expand them to the overall collective space of meaning. In this version, aesthetic intervention amounts to a generalised party-assertion that aims to appeal broadly to immediate, diffuse wishes for non-conflictual intensity and colouring of a monotonous everyday life, but which on the basis of the aesthetics of the agreeable merely affirms standardised patterns of positive, evocative experiences. To a large degree, the invitation to this type of harmonising atmospheric projection forms the aesthetic sounding board of practice in the public of parliament-oriented mass media – as the element in which the general struggle for attention is increasingly taking place. A lucid example of this is the widespread participation by politicians in entertainment programmes on the media. In this type of public space that in terms of genre is devoted to facilitating community, party mood, pure fun, and cosiness, and which therefore is vacuum-cleaned of political conflict material, politicians have the opportunity of marketing themselves as – at the same time – private individuals and public figures of identification at eye level who are able to dance (Figure 5.6), sing, cook, and get a divorce like anyone else. On this account they are expected to gain an apolitical, mood-based sympathy that may be generalisable and thus strengthen their position in mobilising an empathic appeal in political matters as well.

This type of aesthetic intervention fosters consumers rather than citizens. It contributes to depoliticising the political process and weakening the formation of collective political experience, and thereby reduces the capacity of political culture to process differences and handle conflicts dialogically when they occasionally break through the atmospheric harmonisations. In other words, the capability of the political process to establish meaning on its own premises is threatened by this tendency.

The atmospheric level of aesthetic intervention further includes a special phenomenon which we, for lack of a better term, could conceptualise as 'Zeitgeist'.[14] This concept should not be understood as a reminiscence of Hegel's totalising philosophy of history, but as an attempt to conceptually grasp the intangible, yet very real phenomenon that the *access* to public attention is characterised by a marked periodic selectivity whose changing principles seem founded rather on mood-based aesthetic fascination than on arguments and matter-of-fact reasoning.

A pronounced Zeitgeist is not present at all times, and when the phenomenon emerges, it is not necessarily confined to the political field of practice but may

Figure 5.6 Former Labour Shadow Chancellor Ed Balls with Professional Partner in *Strictly Come Dancing*, 2016.

Source: BBC Photo Library.

also be operative in fields like fashion and life-style, ideological and theoretical currents, and orientations in art and general culture. Major changes in the predominant orientation in these discursive fields will always be accompanied by more or less elaborate arguments of reason, but if we want to understand why one type of argument at a certain time holds a high standing while another, factually equally qualified, argument is automatically marginalised and why the positions at another time may be reversed, we need to reflect on the changes' dimension of the Zeitgeist.

The Zeitgeist works in accordance with the principles of atmospheric projection: it endows specific positions in the collective space of meaning with a sensuous-emotional, imaginative surplus value, an intensified quality of mood that indeterminately profiles these positions and associates them with an aura of supremacy that promises a relationship of pleasurable harmony with the world at large. In other words, the Zeitgeist provides the framework for a broadly appealing community of fascination based on the aesthetics of the agreeable or on the delimiting principles of idiosyncratic judgement. The raw material for the formation of the Zeitgeist is delivered by the general tendency towards culturalisation, i.e. the multiplicity of dynamic, initially amorphous identity-seeking processes to which the societal processes of individualisation and modernisation give rise.

As pointed out earlier, identity-seeking processes may in principle draw on cognitive as well as moral and aesthetic discourses; however, a Zeitgeist emerges

108 *Power-Oriented Aesthetic Interventions*

when the aesthetic dimension of these seeking processes forms collective patterns of fascination and orientations of taste that temporarily obtain a hegemonic position in public space. When such integrative, aesthetically profiled channelling of the sensuous-emotional dimension of the identity work of major parts of the population occasionally occurs, it is of crucial importance as to which forms of practice and which formations of meaning enjoy high standing in public space – and which have problems even being taken note of. The Zeitgeist thus represents an aesthetic context factor that conditions individual identity work as well as societal meaning formation in a broad sense.

The Zeitgeist emerges and changes in interplay with the development of general conditions of society. Crucial determinants in the emergence of a Zeitgeist are the areas of society that at the given time are characterised by drive and progress and from which therefore a forceful social dynamic emanates. These progressing areas of society attract great attention in political life, in the media, and in the imagination of the ordinary citizen, where somehow being connected to such dynamic field is associated with positive expectations of the future and social prestige. Therefore, a generalised high status is ascribed to the agents who are placed at the centre of this cultural field of power: they are positioned as society's trendsetters whose self-presentation and preferences of taste count as the 'answer of the time' to the collective issue of orientation. As long as the drive and the success last, a self-reinforcing atmospheric appeal emanates from this constellation that is not substantially defined but exercises attraction and convinces by way of the power of aesthetic fascination.

These dynamic fields of power may arise within different frameworks. Most obviously, in the context of the market where strong economic growth and rising opportunities of employment and consumption frequently endow the branches of growth in question with an imaginative surplus value. An illustrative example is the 'hype' around the IT industry in the late 1990s and the messianic perspectives for the development of culture and society at large that digital gadgets and appliances were charged with, by way of a collective atmospheric projection. Or the real estate bubble of the 2000s where the exponentially rising prices and the unlimited access to cheap loans contributed to the formation of a euphoric consumerist Zeitgeist (among real estate owners) that was intensely applauded by politicians, the financial sector, and the mass media. In the periods in question, the hegemonic, imaginative ascription of a positively charged surplus meaning to the IT industry and the real estate market made it virtually impossible to attract public attention to critical reflection and the consideration of political alternatives. Economists who warned about the danger of a major financial crisis during the real estate euphoria were largely ignored by the broad, heterogeneous coalition of special interests that benefited from the bubble. In other words, the immediate favouring of the short-sighted self-interest of major parts of the population combined with the Zeitgeist-based expectation that matters could only move forward and upward, made predominant public opinion completely immune to matter-of-fact argumentation that today, after the evaporation of euphoria, seems evidently sane.

Also in the context of government, a dynamic power field may occasionally emerge that gives rise to a Zeitgeist. For instance, the comprehensive improvement of the welfare state in a number of Western countries in the 1960s and 1970s and the associated growth in employment and the rise in the general standard of living were accompanied by a collective faith in progress that, in terms of fascination power, was comparable to the mentioned examples from the market context. Further, in the context of government, a Zeitgeist based on the fascination of the exercise of power in itself may occasionally arise. For instance, the determined military response by the Western countries to the challenge from international terrorism in the 2000s invited an atmospheric projection based on aesthetic fascination with the sharply profiled exercise of power and the polarising quality of mood (Good vs. Evil) that it produced in society as a whole. In that type of context, critically nuancing arguments have all the odds against them – not only in terms of parliamentary strength but also in terms of the atmospheric conditions of the Zeitgeist.

Finally, a Zeitgeist may develop in the context of civil society movements as was the case, for example, in the cultural and political uprisings in the late 1960s and early 1970s. Underlying the concrete struggles with authorities and traditional power structures was a sounding-board in the shape of a collective mood that was established by way of an atmospheric projection and propelled by collective identity work. A Zeitgeist based on this mood endowed the anti-authoritarian uprising and the associated visions of alternative life-forms and societal structures with positive fascination and deprived more traditional political and cultural positions of glamour and standing. A similar – but in terms of political orientation completely opposite – process seems to be unfolding in the nationalist populist movements that are presently developing in a number of Western countries.

To be sure, politics is not reducible to atmosphere and a Zeitgeist – it is always in its core about concrete struggles and reflective organisation of power and interests.[15] But when a hegemonic Zeitgeist exists, it nevertheless plays a crucial role as a context factor of the political process in as far as political themes and positions that are favoured by the fascination power of the Zeitgeist have an obvious advantage over others in terms of the ability to attract public attention and place themselves in a position of strength.

However, in itself, the Zeitgeist is not reflective or dialogic in terms of universally reasoning and subjective experience-reflecting public discourse. As is characteristic of the aesthetics of the agreeable and idiosyncratic judgement in general, the atmospheric projection of the Zeitgeist does not interact with political judgement; hence, it does not contribute to the reflective formation of experience and is therefore not constitutive of empowered political communities. Due to its volatility, it rather appears as an inscrutable manager of access to public attention.

When a Zeitgeist has been established, it forms a general condition for the political process, but in a democratic perspective its most pronounced function is the selective mark on the conditions of access to the public of parliament-oriented mass media, since its filter of aesthetic fascination thereby exercises a

110   *Power-Oriented Aesthetic Interventions*

crucial influence on civil society positions' possibilities of gaining attention and success in terms of political contents.

The dynamic of the Zeitgeist further inspires currents in political science and among political commentators and spin-doctors to create a totalising, aestheticised image of the voters as an inscrutable force of nature that is commanded entirely by volatile moods – the movements of which only these especially well-informed experts are able to interpret.[16] The never-ending stream of opinion polls that systematically address individuals as segmented, self-centred consumers and thus neglect their capability of engaging in dialogue and reflecting as citizens, deliver the meagre data on which these experts build their imaginative interpretations and predictions of changes of moods and emotional inclinations in the irrational ocean of voters – to which politicians then attempt to adjust their public proposals. This is a well-established circuit that grants legitimacy to politicians, commentators, and opinion pollsters, but it creates a mystified and reduced image of public opinion formation and therefore does not contribute to the development of political judgement in society.

Aestheticisation and Political Culture

In summary, political positioning and power struggles are increasingly carried out with aesthetic means: the performance of the individual politician, his/her ability to communicate enthusiasm, attract sympathy, demonstrate quick wit, rhetorically make problems disappear, look good on TV, and so on, tend to replace political content in the struggle over political power. These power-oriented types of aesthetic intervention that dominate the staging of politics in the mass media represent a dedifferentiating aestheticisation in the sense that the appeal to senses and emotions is intensified at the expense of the appeal to reason and reflection on political content. Political discourse, the capability of which to deal with reality in a qualified way rests on the integration of matter-of-fact knowledge, universalist ethics, and a generalising reflective processing of senses and emotions, is consequently reduced to the provider of aesthetically pleasing experiences in competition with the offers of the entertainment industry. The capacity of political discourse to create meaning on genuinely political terms, i.e. the reason-based mediation between conflicts of interests and the common good, is thus undermined.

Correspondingly, these types of intervention represent restricted scenarios of politico-cultural experience formation in as far as they address the individual as a self-centred consumer – rather than challenging him/her via the aesthetic judgement of taste or the aesthetics of the sublime into developing political judgement and reflecting on himself/herself as an empowered, participating citizen.

As pointed out earlier, the politico-cultural experience formation of society depends on the interplay and the hegemonic relationship between all four types of publics, and we should therefore not draw generalising conclusions on the basis of this characterisation of prominent tendencies in the public of

Power-Oriented Aesthetic Interventions 111

parliament-oriented mass media. But due to the pivotal status of this public in the parliamentary political process and as the central forum for processing common experiences of society – and thereby its position as the condition of competition for the efforts of civil society publics in order to influence the decision-making process – this tendency towards aestheticising politics can be assumed to have quite comprehensive implications for society's political culture as a whole.

Notes

1 Wolfgang Iser, *Der Akt des Lesens* (München: Wilhelm Fink Verlag, 1976).
2 Wolfgang Ullrich (ed.), *Macht zeigen. Kunst als Herrschaftsstrategie* (Berlin: Deutsches Historisches Museum, 2010).
3 Dieter Prokop, *Der kulturindustrielle Machtkomplex* (Köln: Herbert von Halem Verlag, 2005). In this sense, it is explicitly considered a crucial problem in the public of parliament-oriented mass media, if a politician does not possess an amount of charisma substantial enough to make an impact in the media, thus attracting attention to his/her person and, as a derived effect, to his/her party and its policy. The question of the quality of the content of political ideas and proposals is granted considerably less attention.
4 Dieter Prokop, *Ästhetik der Kulturindustrie*, Kulturanalysen vol. 11 (Marburg: Tectum Verlag, 2009).
5 Joseph N. Cappella and Kathleen Hall Jamieson, *Spiral of Cynicism: The Press and the Public Good* (Oxford: Oxford University Press, 1997); Nick Davies, *Flat Earth News* (London: Random House, 2008).
6 Bernhard Peters, *Der Sinn von Öffentlichkeit* (Frankfurt am Main: Suhrkamp, 2007).
7 Samuel P. Huntington, *The Clash of Civilizations and the Making of World Order* (New York: Simon & Schuster, 1996).
8 Lisa S. Villadsen, 'One Should Not Say Anything with Which One's Enemies Agree: Norms of Rhetorical Citizenship in Danish Foreign Policy Debate', in S.A. Nohrstedt (ed.) *Communicating Risks: Towards the Threat Society?* (Göteborg: NORDICOM, 2010).
9 Fritz Breithaupt, *Kulturen der Empathie* (Frankfurt am Main: Suhrkamp, 2009); Anker Brink Lund, 'Mediedebat som politisk mantra', in Henrik Kaare Nielsen and Finn Horn (eds), *Kritik som deltagelse* (Aarhus: Klim, 2006).
10 George Lakoff, *Don't Think of an Elephant!* (White River Junction, VT: Chelsea Green Publishing, 2004).
11 For instance, this was the position of the Danish public employers in the 2013 conflict with the teachers' union over a new settlement on work hours.
12 For the general debate on atmosphere, see e.g. Gernot Böhme, *Atmosphäre. Essays zur neuen Ästhetik* (Frankfurt am Main: Suhrkamp, 1995) and Reinhard Knodt, *Ästhetische Korrespondenzen* (Stuttgart: Reclam, 1994). For reasons of space, I will not be elaborating on the difference in terms of the ontology of the phenomenon of atmosphere between the positions of Böhme and Knodt. I will primarily draw on the latter and combine this inspiration with the concept of reception aesthetics presented above.
13 Knodt, *Ästhetische Korrespondenzen*, op. cit. p. 65ff.
14 Henrik Kaare Nielsen, *Æstetik, kultur og politik* (Aarhus: Aarhus University Press, 1996), p. 129ff.
15 See also Niels Albertsen, 'Atmosphere: Power, Critique, Politics', in Nicolas Rémy and Nicolas Tixier (eds), *Ambiances, Tomorrow*. Proceedings of 3rd International Congress on Ambiances, September 2016, Volos, Greece, vol. 02, International Ambiances Network and University of Thessaly.
16 Prokop, *Ästhetik der Kulturindustrie*, op. cit., p. 287ff.

112 *Power-Oriented Aesthetic Interventions*

References

Albertsen, Niels (2016) 'Atmosphere: Power, Critique, Politics', in Nicolas Rémy and Nicolas Tixier (eds), *Ambiances, Tomorrow*. Proceedings of 3rd International Congress on Ambiances, September 2016, Volos, Greece Vol. 2, International Ambiances Network and University of Thessaly.

Böhme, Gernot (1995) *Atmosphäre. Essays zur neuen Ästhetik*, Frankfurt am Main: Suhrkamp.

Breithaupt, Fritz (2009) *Kulturen der Empathie*, Frankfurt am Main: Suhrkamp.

Brink Lund, Anker (2006) 'Mediedebat som politisk mantra', in Henrik Kaare Nielsen and Finn Horn (eds), *Kritik som deltagelse*, Aarhus: Klim.

Cappella, Joseph N. and Kathleen Hall Jamieson (1997) *Spiral of Cynicism: The Press and the Public Good*, Oxford: Oxford University Press.

Davies, Nick (2008) *Flat Earth News*, London: Random House.

Huntington, Samuel P. (1996) *The Clash of Civilizations and the Making of World Order*, New York: Simon & Schuster.

Iser, Wolfgang (1976) *Der Akt des Lesens*, München: Wilhelm Fink Verlag.

Knodt, Reinhard (1994) *Ästhetische Korrespondenzen*, Stuttgart: Reclam.

Nielsen, Henrik Kaare (1996) *Æstetik, kultur og politik*, Aarhus: Aarhus University Press.

Peters, Bernhard (2007) *Der Sinn von Öffentlichkeit*, Frankfurt am Main: Suhrkamp.

Prokop, Dieter (2005) *Der kulturindustrielle Machtkomplex*, Köln: Herbert von Halem Verlag.

Prokop, Dieter (2009) *Ästhetik der Kulturindustrie, Kulturanalyse*n vol. 11, Marburg: Tectum Verlag.

Ullrich, Wolfgang (ed.) (2010) *Macht zeigen. Kunst als Herrschaftsstrategie*, Berlin Deutsches Historisches Museum.

Villadsen, Lisa S. (2010) 'One Should Not Say Anything with Which One's Enemies Agree: Norms of Rhetorical Citizenship in Danish Foreign Policy Debate', in S.A. Nohrstedt (ed.), *Communicating Risks: Towards the Threat Society?* Göteborg: NOR-DICOM.

6 Artistic Interventions in the Field of Political Practice

It does not necessarily imply sophisticated, avant-gardist effects from the tradition of high art for an aesthetic approach to challenge and stimulate the recipient's political judgement. The approach can also be conceptualised as an elaboration of the aesthetic forms of popular culture that traditionally have balance, order, and harmony as central motifs.[1] The emotions that are being aroused and that spontaneously seek pleasure in these forms can, on the basis of the aesthetic judgement of taste, be processed towards a qualified sense of reality by way of taking them seriously. This would imply establishing an interplay with the universalising categories of reason, making them reflective, and bringing them into dialogue with the conflicts and ambivalences with which they are intertwined in the concrete life context of the recipient. Alternatively, the emotions can, on the basis of the aesthetics of the sublime, be confronted with sudden, overwhelming ruptures of established expectations of order and meaning and be invited to engage in an open, reason-based seeking process that reflects the conditions of possibility of reshaping order on new premises.

In other words, the challenge for a political communication that aims to strengthen political judgement, and thus a reason-based public discourse, is to design the political approach aesthetically as a multidimensional field of tension which – instead of rendering complex matters unambiguous – makes a plurality of possibilities visible, balances reflectively between them, and thereby opens the horizon of public exchange to nuancing debate and collective learning processes.

The forms of aesthetic intervention that in the following – for lack of a better term[2] – will be called 'artistic' do not all define themselves in relation to the established institution of art and the associated discourses of quality and recognition – nor is this relationship pertinent in the present context. But in their interventions in the political field of practice, they employ forms of expression and reflection that stem from or are inspired by artistic practices.[3] In other words, this type of aesthetic intervention in the political field of practice differs considerably from what we have been dealing with above.

The main difference can be illustrated on the basis of the presented model of the political process in modern democratic society: as outlined above, the polarising and the harmonising form – as the predominant forms of aesthetic

114 *Artistic Interventions in Political Practice*

intervention in the public of parliament-oriented mass media – both intervene on the conflict level of the political process (level A) (see Chapter 2) where they are implemented in order to affect power relations and the formation of compromises; and as an indirect effect, they influence the politico-cultural formation of experience (level B).

In contrast, artistic interventions are ideal-typically characterised by not being oriented towards power politics. When art intervenes in politics, it happens via the discursive field of cultural practice, where art by way of its specific formal and thematic tools creates 'twisted' ways of perceiving and experiencing, leading to 'odd' new insights. On this basis, art offers its own, specific – indeterminate, but nevertheless critical – space of reflection as a mirror to other discursive fields, including the political. In other words, artistic intervention represents a specific mode of processing society's conflict experiences, which, in art's ambiguous way, challenges the established patterns for processing conflicts and the associated politico-cultural horizon of expectation. Interventions typically target practices and formations of meaning in the governmental decision-maker public, in the public of parliament-oriented mass media, or in manifestations of consumerist public discourse in physical, medial or virtual space. As an effect, these formations of meaning are highlighted in an indeterminate fashion and thus put at the disposal of critical public discourse in both the universally reasoning and the subjective experience-reflecting senses.

Phrased differently, power-oriented aesthetic interventions represent an attempt to channel the sensuous and emotional dynamic of identity work that constitutes the raw material of the political, into institutional politics as a resource in power struggles. Artistic interventions, on the contrary, do not relate to institutional politics, but process the political on their own terms and challenge it to self-reflect. Artistic interventions often bring matters to a head in an *aesthetic* sense, and in this way they call for radical problem awareness and for investigating possible alternatives to the status quo. But such interventions leave the determination of the possible *political* consequences of enhanced problem awareness to political discourse and the interplay with political judgement.

Artistic interventions thus address the critically reasoning citizen as a model recipient, attempting to establish an enlightened dialogue on the common concerns of society on aesthetic terms. Their space of action is general public debate in its capacity as mediator between the conflictual and the consensual level of the political process – in other words, in relation to the presented model, art intervenes in the experience-processing interplay between the levels. On the basis of the indeterminately challenging discourse of aesthetic practice, artistic interventions therefore contribute to opening established formations of meaning, to renewed processing of the conflictual experience of society, and to the further development and transformation of political culture – but without relating directly to the struggles of power and distribution of resources on the level of conflict (A).

In the following, a number of significant examples of artistic intervention in the political field of practice will be analysed. The selected examples cover a broad spectrum of interventions in terms of both period and genre, but the

Artistic Interventions in Political Practice 115

selection does not claim to exhaust the field. As mentioned above, a distinction will be made between, on the one hand, an artefact level where specific, well-defined aesthetic practices intervene in the meaning formation of political practice; and, on the other, a generally framing, atmospheric level where public spaces in a broad sense – city spaces, local environments, medial and virtual spaces – are submitted to aesthetic intervention in order to challenge and stimulate them as cultural framing conditions for public interaction and for the emergence of citizen identity. In themselves, these public spaces of course have specific artefactual characteristics, but in this context, focus will be on their potential for catalysing general atmospheric projections.

The Artefact Level

With respect to aesthetic interventions on the artefact level, parts of the research literature operate with a distinction between *provocation* as a term for direct, confronting intervention and *subversion* as a term for a non-confronting intervention that instead undermines established formations of meaning by causing astonishment and reflection.[4] When pointing to a difference in terms of modality, this distinction is useful, but in practice we must understand it as analytical, since artistic intervention, as defined above, may imply elements of both provocation and subversion.

Further, not all concrete aesthetic practices that define themselves as political live up to the ideal principles of artistic intervention as an indeterminately opening challenge to established formations of meaning – just as not all aesthetic practice that actually meets these standards defines itself as political. To exemplify the former, one could mention the multiplicity of political, artistic activities in the 1970s, where the predominant, determining effort to 'take the correct stand in the class struggle' often obstructed any possibility of forming meaning on the basis of opening, non-determining, aesthetic discourse. On the contrary, intervention was *supposed* to be determining and goal-orientated in order to change the balance of power and the distribution of resources on the level of conflict (A). In reality, this type of intervention was thereby defining itself out of the field of aesthetic discourse and into the field of political discourse – where it usually was not able to contribute anything of interest, either; that is to say, the message could be adequately expressed within political discourse.

A more sophisticated version of this type of aesthetic intervention is the tradition of political satire that includes, e.g. the photo montages by John Heartfield from the 1930s (Figure 6.1) and the 'culture jammings' by Adbusters and German artist Klaus Staeck in the present.

The simple but effective aesthetic technique at work here consists in challenging political or commercial power by reproducing its aesthetic self-presentation, while simultaneously integrating textual or figurative elements of meaning that undermine this self-presentation and expose it as contradictory or even mendacious. In decoding this ambiguity of the expression, the recipient is granted a certain space to seek reflective judgement, but the space is relatively

Figure 6.1 John Heartfield, *Der Sinn des Hitlergrusses* (1932).
Source: Scala Picture Library/VISDA.dk.

narrow, and the montages first of all address the already agreeing sympathiser as model recipient, thus in reality offering a pleasurable affirmation on the basis of private judgement. In other words, in this tradition of aesthetic intervention, a given, unequivocal political message is equipped with a sensuously and emotionally appealing surplus meaning, but the potential of aesthetic experience seems to be limited.

The American activist duo *The Yes Men* have taken this tradition further. The main principle of their actions is to create uncertainty regarding the identities of social agents. For instance, they appear at international conferences and in the mass media claiming to represent the WTO and argue seemingly seriously that the WTO now recommends a new and highly improved form of slavery as a counterweight to the devastating consequences that free trade policy has imposed on the African countries. Similarly, they accepted full responsibility for the poison disaster in Bhopal in 1984 in the name of Dow Chemicals. These interventions draw their appeal from the real schisms to which they point, e.g. between the general politico-cultural consensus that polluting companies should take responsibility for the consequences of their activities and the widespread knowledge of companies in reality trying to escape this liability. In the light of this schism, it would in principle be imaginable that Dow Chemicals had finally decided to accept its responsibilities – but can this really be true? Evidently, the company subsequently had a hard time denying the story and making its maintained position appear legitimate to the public.

The uncertainty and bewilderment that this type of intervention creates among the political public stimulate the seeking movement of reflective judgement, but at the same time it channels it into given lines of thinking: The Yes Men do more than destabilise established identities and prompt critical reflection – they also prescribe specific alternatives. 'Identity correction' is the declared purpose of their interventions in organisational identities that they regard as associated with immoral or mendacious practice. Similar to the satirical tradition mentioned above, their aesthetic discourse serves a given position in a predefined political scenario by attracting attention to it. Here, however, the implicit model recipient is not a sympathiser practising private judgement, but a citizen committed to the values of a common political culture, to a political *sensus communis* as suggested by The Yes Men. In this way, the aesthetic intervention dynamises political discourse and highlights its dimension of consensual ethics.

Electoral Guerilla Theatre is a colourful tradition that dates back to the 1960s (represented, among others, by the Dutch Provo movement).[5] The aesthetic intervention consists in officially running for parliament, including conducting an election campaign – not with the purpose of getting elected, but in order to throw a critical light on established politics and its candidates by way of satire and irony and thereby initiate reflection concerning the ethics and the functioning of the political system.

An intervention in this tradition was designed by Michael Moore in 2009, when he campaigned to nominate the house plant *Ficus* for the primaries in New Jersey. He argued that the candidates of the established parties are being re-elected again and again without contest, even although they are full of hot air, go back on their election promises, are in the pocket of rich lobbyists, and give priority to senseless rises in the military budget at the expense of health and education. Consequently, he claimed that 'the American people deserve better' and that Ficus would represent a positive alternative. Here, the artistic intervention serves to create a public platform for a critique of the established political system that pinpoints discrepancies between the ideals of democracy and the actual practices of the elected. The implicit addressee is the critically reflective citizen who – on the basis of the assumption of a political *sensus communis* – is invited to practise political judgement and engage in strengthening the position of consensual democratic values in the political process.

Another example in this tradition is the election campaigns that the Danish comedian Jacob Haugaard ran in the 1980s and 1990s as a candidate for the anarchistic *Union of Consciously Work-Shy Elements.* In contrast to Michael Moore's intervention whose satire was based on a devotion to genuine democratic ideals and explicitly aimed to restore them to favour, Haugaard's intervention as a point of departure denied institutional politics any sense and legitimacy.

118 *Artistic Interventions in Political Practice*

With mottos like, 'If work is supposed to be healthy, then give it to the sick' and election promises like 'Tail wind on bike paths' and 'Nutella in the field rations', the campaigns presented a nihilistic humour that undoubtedly possessed a high value of entertainment, but they first of all addressed the already agreeing sympathiser as implicit recipient and they can hardly be assumed to have contributed to developing political judgement in general.

However, amusement came to an abrupt end, when Haugaard, in spite of all the odds, got so many votes in the elections for the national parliament in 1994 that he won a seat as an independent MP. In the TV coverage on election night, a perplexed Haugaard, on the verge of tears, reproachfully addressed his voters with the words 'It was supposed to be a joke!'[6] But the trap had snapped shut, and the newly hatched MP had to find his feet in parliament where the demand for anti-political satire was limited. To the astonishment of his anarchistic base of support, Haugaard subsequently developed a strong sympathy for a small, traditional, middle-class party. This example illustratively confirms a basic dogma in the concept of Electoral Guerilla Theatre: intervention is about the campaigning, *not* about getting elected.

The action in New York in September 2011 that initiated the *Occupy Wall Street* movement was announced on a poster created by *Adbusters* (Figure 6.2).[7] This photo montage combines various symbolic elements: the aesthetic symbol of Wall Street, the statue of the stampeding bull, moving aggressively and recklessly forward, lucidly representing financial capital as a societal agent; balancing on top of the bull's head, a graceful female ballet dancer, whose delicate body and sophisticated posture mark a clear-cut contrast with the bull's expression of pure brutal force, but at the same time she demonstrates superiority by way of her controlled, balanced expression and perhaps even indicates the possibility of a civilising subjugation of the beast; and, finally, the blurry civil war scenario in the background where unidentifiable figures with gas masks and sticks move forward through clouds of teargas, appearing to push the composite sculpture of bull and ballet dancer ahead in front of them. The montage is ambiguous in its appeal: does it invite to a democratic, civilised action that by means of imagination and disciplined artistic finesse takes the bull by its horns and attempts to lead it in a more constructive direction? Or does it propose a violent confrontation with finance capital and state power? The verbal motto of the montage, 'What is our one demand?', is correspondingly completely open to any ascription of meaning.

In combination with the contemporary frustration among citizens regarding the financial sector and its active role in causing the financial crisis, this open, aesthetically profiled approach is liable to have had a major impact on the movement's public resonance and its appeal to a multiplicity of activists with quite different motives and backgrounds.[8] However, as the movement made experiences with the authorities and not least the police, the imaginative ambiguity of its appeal tended to yield in favour of a more unambiguous identity of resistance whose primary content was the perpetuation of the occupation.[9]

In this process, the dichotomous thinking that is one element among other in Figure 6.2, became more predominant in the worldview of the movement.

Figure 6.2 Adbusters, 'What Is Our One Demand?' (2011).
Source: Adbusters Media Foundation.

120 *Artistic Interventions in Political Practice*

The dichotomy is also expressed in the central slogan, 'We are the 99%', that alludes to the obvious, monumental inequality in terms of income and property between the richest 1 per cent of citizens and the remaining 99 per cent of the American population. The slogan appeals broadly and openly to (almost) all citizens and suggests that they form a homogeneous entity with common interests confronting a tiny minority that has illegitimately taken control of society's common goods. However, the fact that the attempts of the broad middle class to secure for themselves the maximum return of investments and pension savings was an important factor in bringing about the financial crisis remains in the dark in this diagnosis.[10] In other words, 'the 99%' is a harmonising aesthetic construction that undoubtedly holds an immediate potential for mobilisation, but does not contribute to qualifying political judgement.

The dichotomous tendency is also symptomatically expressed in Corey Ogilvie's video work 'I am not moving',[11] that has achieved great attention and recognition as a documentation of crucial, identity-forming experiences in the Occupy movement. Using the same aesthetic technique as the tradition of John Heartfield *et al.*, the video presents a montage in which, on the one hand, President Barack Obama and Secretary of State Hillary Clinton pompously and emphatically praise the Arab Spring and all humans' inalienable rights to raise their demands in public; and in which, on the other hand, Occupy activists are brutally beaten and have their basic human rights violated by the police in the streets of New York at an action on 24 September 2011. By way of this confrontation, the work lucidly throws the hypocrisy of official US policy in relief, but the overall meaning formation that constitutes its offer of dialogue to the recipient, is firmly framed by political intentionality and thus lacks scope for the unfolding of the nuancing potential of aesthetic experience. The work primarily addresses the already agreeing sympathiser.

In connection with the American presidential elections in 2000 and 2004, the Austrian artist group *Ubermorgen* conducted the actions *Vote-Auction* and *Sell-TheVote*.[12] An Internet campaign launched as an auction offered to sell American constituents' votes for the presidential elections to the highest bidder. The stated purpose was to give *the consumer*, i.e. the vote-buyer, a more active and effective role in the bureaucratic election system of the USA. In other words, the actions intervened in the relationship between democracy and capitalism which in the hegemonic neoliberal ideology is routinely presented as unproblematic or even as one and the same thing: 'the democratic market economy'.

Under the motto 'Bringing democracy and capitalism closer together', these actions took this explicit self-conception of established power literally and radicalised it by means of irony, with the result that its real consequences appeared in their obvious absurdity: the reduction of democracy to commercial transactions and the transformation of the citizen into a self-centred consumer. As might be expected, this caused some furore: in a number of federal states the authorities initiated legal measures in order to prevent a possible undermining of the legitimacy of the election system, and several American media organisations, including CNN, bewildered and slightly alarmed, devoted their attention to this

Artistic Interventions in Political Practice 121

foreign intervention in the American election system in the name of the free market.

The experimental, indeterminately open nature of the intervention does not point out authoritative alternatives to the status quo, but merely lets the formations of meaning of power reveal their inner contradictions, thereby prompting critical reflection and a search in regard to possible alternative designs for political democracy, making this intervention an example of a mutually beneficial interplay between aesthetic and political discourse.

Another example of a successful artistic intervention in political meaning formation is Jimi Hendrix's instrumental interpretation of 'Star-Spangled Banner' at the Woodstock Festival in 1969. The institutionalised aesthetic patterns of expectation related to national anthems are centred around politico-cultural harmony, community, and concordance. But against the backdrop of the Vietnam War, Hendrix undermined the national anthem's assertion of harmony by including long, disharmonious improvised passages with highly distorted guitar imitations of bombers, detonating grenades, and cries of pain in his musical expression. In this interpretation, the official aesthetic self-presentation of the United States bears testimony to anything but the proclaimed political mission for peace and democracy, and the martial aggressiveness with which the expression of the national anthem is charged thus also points inward into American society, to a national community dangerously divided against itself. Correspondingly, oppositely charged sensuously and emotionally rooted formations of meaning are played off against each other (longing for harmonious community vs. fear of aggression, violence and social disintegration), thus inviting the recipient to an ambivalent seeking movement concerning the nature of societal relations. Apart from delivering a hitherto unsurpassed piece of basic research into the expressive potential of the electric guitar, Hendrix takes a politico-culturally well-defined genre as his starting point and by way of aesthetic means dissolves it from within, thereby opening new possibilities of meaning.

A special type of artistic intervention in politics, which similarly holds an element of the aesthetics of the sublime in its approach, initiates events that include the recipients in actions and lead to common processes of experience. As an example, we could mention the Danish political theatre group *Solvognen* and their 'Army of Santa Clauses', which in December 1974 performed happenings in Copenhagen. The most spectacular event took place in the Magasin du Nord department store, where the Santas took commodities from the shelves and freely gave them away to by-standing children and adults, with the merry Christmas message of warm-heartedness and generosity as their motto. Subsequently, the public experienced the realities of capitalism, as security guards and shop assistants tore the presents out of people's hands in the name of private property, and as Santa Claus – the children's friend and the incarnation of jollity, harmonious fellow-feeling, and Christmas cosiness – was brutally hand-cuffed and taken away by the police under charges of disturbing the peace and violating private property.

This scenery effectively played several established, emotionally anchored formations of meaning off against each other, but without closing this freshly

122 *Artistic Interventions in Political Practice*

opened space of reflection by way of a determining moral. Here, the public was invited to engage in a genuine process of aesthetic experience in a conflictual interplay between aesthetic and political discourse in which their respective autonomies were maintained, and at the same time, basic, potentially violent social power relations were exposed under the Christmas decorations.

Solvognen used the same aesthetic strategy at their action in Rebild on 4 July 1976. The annual celebration of Danish-American friendship was especially solemn that year due to the 200-year anniversary of American independence. The scene of the celebration was, as always, the beautiful hills of Rebild that form a natural amphitheatre; speakers, musicians, and notables perform on a podium at the base and the audience are seated on the slopes.

In the middle of the celebration, 40 American Indians on horseback suddenly appeared on the top of the slopes. This intervention manifested in a sensuously concrete way the fact that one part of society and national history, the indigenous American people, was not invited to the party. The action, in other words, aimed at initiating an aesthetic process of experience that made the image of the USA ambiguous. To the official glossy image of the successful and powerful object of celebration was added a repressed historical dimension of chauvinism and discrimination of minorities – here, with concrete reference to the violent marginalisation and decimation of the native population. When the police, assisted by upset civilians, physically attacked the uninvited guests, tore the actors off their horses, beat them, and subsequently sent them to jail, they were in reality re-enacting and reviving, in a sensuously and emotionally aggressive way, the historical fate of the Native Americans, and thus contributing to further radicalise the potential of aesthetic experience of the action.

The aesthetic interventions by *Solvognen* obviously have a political bias, but what distinguishes this type of action from some of the interventions mentioned above is that its approach is not merely communicative, but stages an aesthetic process of experience in which the audience becomes a participant and is placed with body and mind in the middle of conflicts and ambivalences that both culturally and politically permeate present society. The intervention makes these conflicts and ambivalences inescapable and prompts the audience to relate to them with senses, emotions, and intellect.

The intervention by *The Yes Men* at Roskilde Festival 2016 had similar qualities. In secret collaboration with the festival management and the whistle-blower Edward Snowden, the activists addressed the issue of surveillance by putting up signs in the festival area stating what was presented as the official data policy of the festival: all Internet activity at the festival would be monitored, and all digital data, including text messages and phone conversations, would be collected, stored, and passed on to external partners. Further, video cameras and drones would collect data on activity in physical space.

The intervention resulted in comprehensive protests from festival-goers and caused a shitstorm on social media – as intended by The Yes Men. They conceptualised their strategy as 'anger marketing', i.e. motivating people to reflect deeper on a matter by pissing them off. In this case, the massive, incalculable surveillance by authorities and private companies that we are all submitted to in all parts of daily life and that most of us hardly think about, was highlighted by way of an aesthetic reduction of complexity that made it tangible and thereby possible to process reflectively and to address politically. As a first step, the local public space of the festival was charged with the participants' energy of indignation directed towards the fictional data policy of the festival. As a second step, this energy was channelled into generalising, reflective patterns, not least by way of a satellite-transmitted dialogue with Edward Snowden. In this process, genuine public engagement and a common, critical awareness of the reality, the scope, and the implications of ongoing surveillance activity in society at large were created, thus integrating subjective experience-reflecting and universally reasoning public discourse.

A corresponding intervention – limited, however, to the self-conception and practices of the established art institution – was conducted by Santiago Sierra when in 2003 he was entrusted with representing Spain at the Venice Biennial. Sierra staged the Spanish pavilion as completely closed to the outside world by covering the 'España' sign on the façade and bricking up the main entrance. If the public found their way to the back door, they were confronted by guards in uniform who only let people with Spanish passports inside – everybody else was rejected. Here, the privileged, cosmopolitan art public with their own bodies and minds experienced the discrimination and bureaucratic marginalisation that represent the daily state of affairs for less privileged people across the world. Correspondingly, the Spanish public was placed in the experiential ambivalence of, on the one hand, enjoying the privilege of access, and, on the other, overtly participating in a discriminatory practice.

With differences in terms of quality and scope, these examples all challenge formations of meaning in the political field of practice by way of elements of the aesthetics of the beautiful or the aesthetics of the sublime, thus instigating reflective exchange across discursive borders while maintaining the autonomy of discourses. Further, their critical approach is not abstract utopian, but immanent: their indeterminate challenging and opening of political formations of meaning refer to normative potentials which have already been developed and anchored in the politico-cultural formation of experience on the level of consensus (B) (see Chapter 2), and to which politics therefore in principle should be committed. The inconsistencies demonstrated by these aesthetic interventions thus represent real dilemmas for political practice, and in a non-specific way they therefore challenge political life to reflect on possible alternative forms of practice.

However, artistic interventions at the artefact level are continuously being countered and contained by systemic counter-strategies, e.g. in the sense that authorities are always involved in a process of adjusting their preparedness and measures to the challenges that interventions are posing. Further, the aesthetic tools of interventions are instantly absorbed by the described general struggle over attention in public space. Provocative and subversive expressions are on a regular basis being appropriated by market agents who weed out their

124 *Artistic Interventions in Political Practice*

critically intervening dimension and deploy the 'cleansed', spectacular form as an attention-creating factor in any commercial context. In other words, the development in public space is in this sense characterised by an unceasing, effect-straining spiral movement in which aesthetically intervening civil society-oriented counter-discourses have to permanently innovate and reinvent their dialogue-oriented tools, if they want to stay ahead of the colonising movement that at all times emanates from the market's monologic process of meaning formation.

The Atmospheric Level

As is the case on the artefact level, the aesthetics of the agreeable, appealing to immediate pleasure of the senses and longing for harmonious merging with the world, is not necessarily the exclusive principle of meaning formation on the atmospheric level. Similar to the artefact level, the possibility exists of processing the emotions that are aroused and channelled by generalised patterns of moods in a more qualified direction.[13] For instance, the invitation to atmospheric dialogue can be designed ambiguously, thus appealing to reflective judgement with a reference to the aesthetics of the beautiful or the aesthetics of the sublime. The potential of aesthetic discourse in terms of critical reflection and challenging established formations of meaning can in this way be realised in transcending standardised patterns of moods, in that the aroused emotions are brought into interplay with understanding and potentially with political judgement. Hereby, the possibility of processing the individual's own specific experiences is opened and thereby the possibility of gaining a more nuanced and reflective insight into the real opportunities and limitations with regard to the community of experience and interests that characterise the collective space of meaning and the given socio-political constellation. Examples of this are artistic interventions in urban space that challenge the hegemony of consumerist public discourse and attempt to open the space to diversity and dialogic public discourse.[14]

Reinhard Knodt's account of the phenomenon of the belly dance is inspirational for determining the *cultural* potential of an atmospheric projection:

> The point of belly dance, in a certain sense its metaphysical level, is a dynamising process between the dancer and the spectators, the body and the gazes; the crucial question is whether the body is able to stand its ground against the gazes that rest upon it or whether it dissolves into flesh. It is a dramatic process based on movement, eroticism, music, playful eye casts, provocation, withdrawal, aggressiveness, and sublimation – a process that leads to the point where the desire with which the gazes have rested upon the woman has dissolved. Belly dance – any oriental will tell us – is supposed to transform desire into a state of common joy, of festivity, and unites the participants of the process as is the case with any other means of intoxication and stimulation that are used for party purposes.[15]

Of interest in the present context is not the dance as artefact, but its capacity as intervention in a social space and its catalysing effect on interaction in this space. What Knodt describes is a social process in which cultural orientation – in dialogue with the artistic intervention, the aesthetic characteristics of the room, and the accompanying development of a common quality of mood – is transformed from the aesthetics of the agreeable (based on each spectator's immediate sensuous desire for the inciting, scantily dressed dancer) to the aesthetics of the beautiful, thus elevating the experience from the horizon of individual desire and making it a general community-constituting factor. In other words, the process invites an atmospheric projection based on an intuitive experience of a *sensus communis*.

With regard to the atmospheric significance of the aesthetic characteristics of the space of practice (architectonic design, use of materials, conditions of light and sound, openness vs. closure, balance vs. movement, etc.), we can further find inspiration in Knodt's argument concerning our relationship to articles for everyday use: he points out that an involved, meaning-creating exchange with articles for everyday use largely depends on whether the things bear witness to their history, to their process of manufacture, and to the use that was made of them. In other terms, an article of everyday use on which human practice has left its traces in the shape of a patina paves the way for an atmospheric projection of historical connectedness between the producer, prior users, and us as current users. However, this kind of linking and involved experience cannot be catalysed by materials on which human situations of use do not leave their traces, but which instead merely get old and worn out (e.g. veneer or laminated articles and articles made out of plastic or chipboard). The atmospheric projection of meaning has nothing to take hold of and elaborate on in items like this, and our relationship with these things is therefore purely instrumental and devoid of perspectives with regard to our historical and socio-cultural connectedness with other people.

If we transfer this reasoning to contemporary urban space, the main tendency is that the aesthetics of plastic and chipboard predominates. The above-mentioned functional reduction of urban spaces to consumer zones manifests itself in their aesthetic as a lack of history: this aesthetic makes a virtue out of representing an intensified otherness in respect to everyday forms and meanings, but it merely amounts to a levelled, coquettish otherness that does not invite a dialogic experiential exchange, and its fascination is only meant to last until the proposed commercial transaction has been carried out. The glossy, permanently renewed façades are devoid of all traces of connecting and obligating historical contexts of practice. This also applies to the typical reconstructed urban space, where the old houses are shined up so that all evidence that people have used them is wiped out, and they are left as de-historicised references to themselves. This aesthetic and the kind of atmospheric projection to which it appeals do not call for citizens' involvement in our common history and for participation in public affairs, but merely for the fleeting desire of isolated consumers to mirror themselves in the well-designed sets and their persisting promises of sheer happiness and harmony.

126   *Artistic Interventions in Political Practice*

In contrast, a designed approach that by way of the aesthetics of the beautiful provides the atmospheric projection with traces of historical and cultural connectedness, might facilitate an experience of cultural community that, like the belly dance example, refers to an intuitive notion of a *sensus communis* and thus holds the potential for the dialogic orientation that characterises subjective experience-reflecting and universally reasoning public discourse. In this context, we could speak of an invitation to the creation of an identity of *cultural citizenship* among the involved.

To be sure, there is no guarantee that such community-constituting atmospheric transformation will emerge in physico-spatial interaction, but in principle it is a possibility, and when transformation does take place, it forms a valuable background resource for the possible development of democratic public discourse. Likewise, there is no guarantee that a successful experience of cultural community also will lead to political dialogue in the space of practice in question.[16] This would require the emergence of an atmospheric projection that not only refers to the notion of an aesthetic *sensus communis*, but also brings this into interaction with political judgement and the associated reflection of the concurrency of conflict and politico-cultural community. Here, we could speak of an invitation for the formation of an identity as *political citizen.*

As outlined above, public space is permeated by hegemonic conflicts between modernity's overall institutionalisations of social practice. It is, in other words, crucial for the perspectives of atmospheric projections in terms of democratic public discourse, whether they relate to the formal, expansive principles of market and state or the communicative principles of civil society as horizon of meaning formation. In practice, we will often be dealing with mixed forms, but in that case the question of dominance between the involved horizons of meaning will determine the type of atmospheric projection and thereby the perspectives concerning the development towards political judgement and democratic public discourse.

This problem awareness currently appears to be absent in many popular theoretical and political discourses on 'creativity of everyday life', 'the user/consumer as co-creator/produser/prosumer', 'DIY', 'participatory culture', etc. With its point of departure in the reflective, active choice of consumption and life-style, in the possibilities of Web 2.0 and the social media, and in local interventionist projects in urban space, these discourses project an unequivocally positive democratic development.[17] However, as argued above in the context of the Internet and the social media, this means jumping to conclusions. Participation, including discursively highly valued 'interactivity', can unfold on quite different terms and within a variety of horizons of meaning (market, state, civil society) – comprising premises that the participants are not always able to estimate.[18]

In other words, it cannot be settled in abstract terms whether participation strengthens democratic public discourse – a concrete analysis of the context of the process of participation in question is needed. Such a context analysis includes the question whether the framing of participation is closed (with a solid

Artistic Interventions in Political Practice 127

structure and agenda) or open (with the possibility of new developments, learning processes, and the agents influencing the process).

That participation in public space basically implies engaging in a relationship of struggle with regard to hegemonic meaning formation, is lucidly illustrated by the heterogeneous tradition of *Street Art*[19] and likewise by the international experiences with conflicts of interests concerning the implementation of digital screens in urban space: are the screens supposed to facilitate private advertising purposes, commercial entertainment, official authority communication, surveillance, or civil society and artistic participation?[20]

A contemporary form of artistic intervention that engages in this issue is *relational aesthetics.*[21] This practice positions itself critically towards the instrumentalising shaping of societal relations by the market and the state and defines itself in the tradition of artistic avant-garde movements, including their visions of emancipation as a unification of art and life. However, in contrast to its historical predecessors, relational aesthetics is not a proponent of a totalising revolutionary perspective that aims to dissolve all discursive differentiations. Instead, it seems fair to speak of a pragmatic self-conception that takes its point of departure in the creation of concrete, local mini-publics as the objective of interventions.

Relational artistic practice does not create works in the sense of traditional artefacts, but initiates and facilitates a 'production of social relations' in a concrete public space where the audience of art in an interactive process is transformed from spectators to participants. The intervention's reflective establishment of new relations and meetings between people indeterminately challenges the everyday routine of specific ways of perceiving and practising social relations and thus opens the possibility of processes of empowerment and reflection of alternatives to the social relations of normality. The original perspective in relational aesthetics, in other words, is the creation of an awareness among the participants of *the relational potential* in public space.[22]

When interventions by relational aesthetics are successful, they are able to catalyse a collective atmospheric projection among the participants that is reflective by nature and draws on the aesthetics of the beautiful. Its frame of reference is the notion of a *sensus communis* but on displaced and questioned premises, and it operates in the open seeking movement of reflective judgement with regard to alternative principles of sociality. However, it appears to be disputable whether all aesthetic interventions that define themselves as relational, actually meet these criteria. For instance, the atmospheric quality of invitations like Rikrit Tiravanija's serving of Thai food to the audience rather seems to appeal to the aesthetics of the agreeable.[23]

Correspondingly, in the light of the argument above, one must question relational aesthetics' general understanding of sociality-creating interventions as political per se, and of dialogic relations as by definition synonymous with both harmonious community and democratic public discourse. As outlined above, this type of collective atmospheric projection forms a potentially productive sounding board for the development of democratic public discourse, but such development also requires an interplay with political judgement's conflict-reflecting way

128 *Artistic Interventions in Political Practice*

of operating. This perspective is not incompatible with relational interventions, but, on the other hand, it does not appear to play any explicit role in the concept. Two related examples that actually reflect this perspective may illustrate the potential of this type of intervention:

The Danish artist Kerstin Bergendal creates site-specific interventions with the purpose of establishing *commons*, i.e. spaces for public participation and community. She aims to facilitate a civil society-oriented use of public space as opposed to the design of public space and interaction represented by the market or state bureaucracy.

In an elaborate process of research that comprises extensive dialogue with the citizens who are affected by and have interests in a given local development project, Bergendal works out a utopian but still feasible counter-concept to established city planning's bureaucratically and commercially inclined plans for the area. She bases her counter-concept on her experiences from the research process regarding interests, needs, conflicts, resistance, and counter-visions related to the locality and its development. The primary focus of the counter-concept is to ensure the conditions of possibility for a continuing public exchange among the citizens in the area. The process further integrates dialogue between citizens, experts, and representatives of the authorities, contributing to mutual enlightenment and understanding and strengthening the position of the counter-concept in the political decision-making process.

Bergendal's practice shares many features with the political tradition of deliberative democracy in regard to the needs of civil society and the establishment of a constructive public dialogue between citizens, experts, and decision-makers. But whereas the concept of deliberative democracy has its focus on conducting a dialogue according to universally reasoning public discourse, Bergendal's interventions are aesthetically shaping measures that change the sensory appearance of the locality, its framing, infrastructure, and spatial design, and thereby enhance its attractiveness, accessibility, and utility in terms of participation and public dialogue. Bergendal's interventions are based on the assumption of a *sensus communis*: they invite the recipient to engage in public interaction as a citizen in an arena that is designed for the purpose, but they make no claims to determine the contents of the interaction. This perspective remains open as a challenge to the concrete dialogues of the agents and their process of experience formation.

Superkilen is a recently designed urban space in Copenhagen, created by the artist group Superflex and the architectural firm Bjarke Ingels Group (BIG). Relational aesthetics' understanding of the creation of social relations was reflected in the concept from the start, and the socially vulnerable and ethnically diverse nature of the surrounding neighbourhood has played a central role throughout the developmental process. Superkilen comprises three connected spaces, each with its own colour tone and surface: a square for sports and cultural activities, a market place, and a park area. The inhabitants of the neighbourhood have been involved in the creation of the new urban space; for instance, in collaboration with the artists and architects, inhabitants have been

Artistic Interventions in Political Practice   129

active in selecting objects like benches, street lamps, dustbins, and plants modelled in concordance with the corresponding objects in the more than 50 countries that the inhabitants of the neighbourhood come from. In some cases, objects were even brought to Copenhagen from the home country.

Superkilen has become internationally renowned and won awards as an outstanding design of an urban space in a globalised, multi-cultural city. A space that simultaneously invites the creation of a universal cultural community and lets diversity express itself. The implicit recipient addressed by Superkilen is the open-minded, cosmopolitan citizen who is invited to participate in a collective atmospheric projection that creates a specific quality of mood by integrating the notion of a *sensus communis* with a positive valorisation of diversity.

As pointed out earlier, artistic interventions in the political field of practice are characterised by not being oriented towards power politics. They are not associated with any project of order, but challenge established orders and formations of meaning indeterminately, make a multiplicity of possibilities visible, and – with the critically reflective citizen as model recipient – invite public debate and common learning processes. This type of artistic intervention, in other words, holds positive potential with regard to integrating universally reasoning and subjective experience-reflecting public discourse – and thus to contributing to the development of deliberative democracy.

Whether empirical recipients accept the invitation is another question that cannot be answered while generalising on the basis of the implicit model recipient of the aesthetic approach. As mentioned earlier, the empirical process of reception encompasses considerable scope for individual idiosyncrasies, sociocultural differences in respect to knowledge and experience-based dispositions for reception, situation-specific distractions, and so on. But the artefact's or the space's invitation to dialogue nevertheless constitutes an important conditioning frame for empirical reception processes, and from this perspective the aforementioned artistic interventions seem to represent constructive invitations to engage in the common concerns of society.

In different ways, the examples prompt an indeterminate reflective exchange between aesthetic and political discourse, while at the same time allowing them to maintain their autonomy. Furthermore, their critical approach is not abstract-utopian, but immanent: their indeterminate challenging and opening of established political meaning formations offers the recipient an aesthetic experience based on reflective judgement and the assumption of a *sensus communis*, thus creating a dialogue with normative potentials that are rooted in the politico-cultural experience formation of democratic societies, and which politics is therefore in principle obliged to honour. Aesthetically pinpointed inconsistencies represent real dilemmas for political practice, and they therefore challenge it indeterminately to reflect on possible alternative forms of practice.

Evidently, however, much depends on the political practices that in reality develop in the wake of artistic interventions. If constructive, dialogic forms of practice emerge, they can contribute to developing a cultural community, but as mentioned above, this does not automatically imply the rise of a politically

130 *Artistic Interventions in Political Practice*

reflecting community. The establishment of a successful democratic public discourse requires not only constructive, dialogical forms of practice and appreciation of diversity but also a universalist political culture and an associated reason-based political judgement that is capable of reflecting on conflicts and processing them in the view of the common good. Artistic interventions, in other words, cannot replace more classic forms of political practice and experience, but they may open their established formations of meaning and prompt them to rethink practices and create new experiences.

Notes

1 Dieter Prokop, *Ästhetik der Kulturindustrie*, Kulturanalysen vol. 11 (Marburg: Tectum Verlag, 2009).
2 The term 'creative' which is used by some scholars in the field, appears to be both vaguely defined and to a large extent occupied by management newspeak, therefore, it is not regarded as adequate in the present context.
3 Sources of inspiration can, for example, be artistic avant-garde movements or the types of discretely subversive aesthetic expression that have been developed by critical artists working under totalitarian regimes.
4 For example, Thomas Ernst *et al.*, *SUBversionen. Zum Verhältnis von Politik und Ästhetik in der Gegenwart* (Bielefeld: transcript Verlag, 2008); Nina Bandi *et al.*, *Kunst, Subversion, Krise. Zur Politik der Ästhetik* (Bielefeld: transcript Verlag, 2012). See also Stephen Duncombe, *Dream* (New York: The New Press, 2007); Silas Harrebye, *Social Change and Creative Activism in the 21st Century* (Basingstoke: Palgrave Macmillan, 2016); and Andrew Boyd (ed.), *Beautiful Trouble: A Toolbox for Revolution* (New York: OR Books, 2012).
5 L.M. Bogad, *Electoral Guerilla Theatre* (London: Routledge, 2005).
6 Quote based on my recollection and in my translation.
7 The action was inspired by the Arab Spring of the winter 2010–2011, where the physical occupation of city space had played a crucial role in the success of the popular movements. In accordance with this model, the activists occupied Zuccotti Park in the financial district of New York on 17 September 2011 and held the occupation until 15 November 2011 where it was dissolved by force. During the occupation, an anarchistic movement developed under the name 'Occupy Wall Street'. It attracted major public attention and spread to a large number of other countries and cities throughout the world.
8 See Stephen Duncombe, 'Affect and Effect: Artful Protest and Political Impact', in Henrik Kaare Nielsen, Christina Fiig, Jorn Loftager, Thomas Olesen, Jan Lohmann Stephensen, and Mads P. Sorensen (eds), *The Democratic Public Sphere. Current Challenges and Prospects* (Aarhus: Aarhus University Press, 2016).
9 This developmental pattern is well known from many other social movements. Cf. Henrik Kaare Nielsen, *Demokrati i bevægelse* (Aarhus: Aarhus University Press, 1991).
10 Christoph Deutschmann, 'Die Finanzmärkte und die Mittelschichten: Der kollektive Buddenbrooks-Effekt', *Leviathan* 36 (2008).
11 To be found on www.vimeo.com (accessed 1 October 2017).
12 See www.vote-auction.net (accessed 1 October 2017).
13 Ilka Becker, 'Einblendung', in Tom Holert (ed.), *Imagineering* (Köln: Oktagon Verlag, 2000).
14 Nikolaus Hirsch and Markus Miessen (eds), *What Is Critical Spatial Practice?* (Berlin: Sternberg Press, 2012).

Artistic Interventions in Political Practice 131

15 Reinhard Knodt, *Ästhetische Korrespondenzen* (Stuttgart: Reclam, 1994), p. 156 (my translation).
16 Tom Nielsen, 'Democratic Urban Spaces in the Nordic Countries?' *Arbejdspapir nr. 4 fra AU IDEAS Pilotcenter: Den demokratiske offentlighed*, Aarhus Universitet, 2013. Available at: www.offentlighed.au.dk; Michael Schudson, 'Why Conversation Is Not the Soul of Democracy' *Critical Studies in Mass Communication*, 14(4) (1997).
17 For example, Birgit Richard and Alexander Ruhl (eds), *Konsumguerilla* (Frankfurt am Main: Campus, 2008); Hanno Rauterberg, *Wir sind die Stadt! Urbanes Leben in der Digitalmoderne* (Frankfurt am Main: Suhrkamp, 2013); Henry Jenkins, Mizuko Ito, and danah boyd, *Participatory Culture in a Networked Era* (Cambridge: Polity Press, 2016).
18 Christian Fuchs, *Social Media* (London: Sage, 2014); Nico Carpentier, *Media and Participation: A Site of Ideological-Democratic Struggle* (Bristol: Intellect, 2011); Steven Griggs, A. Norval, and H. Wagenaar (eds), *Practices of Freedom: Decentred Governance, Conflict and Democratic Participation* (Cambridge: Cambridge University Press, 2014); Patrizia Nanz and Claus Leggewie, *Die Konsultative. Mehr Demokratie durch Bürgerbeteiligung* (Berlin: Wagenbach, 2016); Alex Demirovic (ed.), *Transformation der Demokratie – demokratische Transformation* (Münster: Westfälisches Dampfboot, 2016).
19 Kristoffer Horn, 'Street art – civil ulydighed, kunst og kreative interventioner i byens rum', in Cecilie Eriksen (ed.), *Ulydighed og etisk dynamik* (Aarhus: Klim, 2013).
20 Scott McQuire, Meredith Martin, and Sabine Niederer, *Urban Screens Reader* (Amsterdam: Institute of Network Cultures, 2009).
21 Nicolas Bourriaud, *Relational Aesthetics* (Dijon: Les Presses du Réel, 2002).
22 Solveig Gade, 'Rammen om værket i verden', PhD dissertation, Department of Art and Cultural Studies, University of Copenhagen, 2008.
23 Peter Brix Søndergaard, 'Relationel æstetik: Connecting People?', in Henrik Kaare Nielsen and Finn Horn (eds), *Kritik som deltagelse* (Aarhus: Klim, 2006).

References

Bandi, Nina, Michael Kraft, and Sebastian Lasinger (2012) *Kunst, Subversion, Krise. Zur Politik der Ästhetik*, Bielefeld: transcript Verlag.
Becker, Ilka (2000) 'Einblendung', in Tom Holert (ed.), *Imagineering*, Köln: Oktagon Verlag.
Bogad, L.M. (2005) *Electoral Guerilla Theatre*, London: Routledge.
Bourriaud, Nicolas (2002) *Relational Aesthetics*, Dijon: Les Presses du Réel.
Boyd, Andrew (ed.) (2012) *Beautiful Trouble: A Toolbox for Revolution*, New York: OR Books.
Carpentier, Nico (2011) *Media and Participation: A Site of Ideological-Democratic Struggle*, Bristol: Intellect.
Demirovic, Alex (ed.) (2016) *Transformation der Demokratie – demokratische Transformation*, Münster: Westfälisches Dampfboot.
Deutschmann, Christoph (2008) 'Die Finanzmärkte und die Mittelschichten: Der kollektive Buddenbrooks-Effekt', *Leviathan* 36.
Duncombe, Stephen (2007) *Dream*, New York: The New Press.
Duncombe, Stephen (2016) 'Affect and Effect: Artful Protest and Political Impact', in Henrik Kaare Nielsen, Christina Fiig, Jorn Loftager, Thomas Olesen, Jan Lohmann Stephensen, and Mads P. Sorensen (eds), *The Democratic Public Sphere: Current Challenges and Prospects*, Aarhus: Aarhus University Press.

132 *Artistic Interventions in Political Practice*

Ernst, Thomas, Patricia Gozalbez Cantó, Sebastian Richter, Nadja Sennenwald and Julia Tieke (2008) *SUBversionen. Zum Verhältnis von Politik und Ästhetik in der Gegenwart*, Bielefeld: transcript Verlag.

Fuchs, Christian (2014) *Social Media*, London: Sage.

Gade, Solveig (2008) 'Rammen om værket i verden', PhD dissertation, Department of Art and Cultural Studies, University of Copenhagen.

Griggs, Steven, A. Norval, and H. Wagenaar (eds) (2014) *Practices of Freedom: Decentred Governance, Conflict and Democratic Participation*, Cambridge: Cambridge University Press.

Harrebye, Silas (2016) *Social Change and Creative Activism in the 21st Century*, Basingstoke: Palgrave Macmillan.

Hirsch, Nikolaus and Markus Miessen (eds) (2012) *What Is Critical Spatial Practice?* Berlin: Sternberg Press.

Horn, Kristoffer (2013) 'Street art – civil ulydighed, kunst og kreative interventioner i byens rum', in Cecilie Eriksen (ed.), *Ulydighed og etisk dynamik*, Aarhus: Klim.

Jenkins, Henry, Mizuko Ito, and danah boyd (2016) *Participatory Culture in a Networked Era*, Cambridge: Polity Press.

Knodt, Reinhard (1994) *Ästhetische Korrespondenzen*, Stuttgart: Reclam.

McQuire, Scott, Meredith Martin, and Sabine Niederer (2009) *Urban Screens Reader*, Amsterdam: Institute of Network Cultures.

Nanz, Patrizia and Claus Leggewie (2016) *Die Konsultative. Mehr Demokratie durch Bürgerbeteiligung*, Berlin: Wagenbach.

Nielsen, Henrik Kaare (1991) *Demokrati i bevægelse*, Aarhus: Aarhus University Press.

Nielsen, Tom (2013) 'Democratic Urban Spaces in the Nordic Countries?', *Arbejdspapir nr. 4 fra AU IDEAS Pilotcenter: Den demokratiske offentlighed*, Aarhus Universitet. Available at: www.offentlighed.au.dk.

Prokop, Dieter (2009) *Ästhetik der Kulturindustrie*, Kulturanalysen vol. 11, Marburg: Tectum Verlag.

Rauterberg, Hanno (2013) *Wir sind die Stadt! Urbanes Leben in der Digitalmoderne*, Frankfurt am Main: Suhrkamp.

Richard, Birgit and Alexander Ruhl (eds) (2008) *Konsumguerilla*, Frankfurt am Main: Campus.

Schudson, Michael (1997) 'Why Conversation Is Not the Soul of Democracy', *Critical Studies in Mass Communication*, 14(4).

Søndergaard, Peter Brix (2006) 'Relationel æstetik: Connecting People?' in Henrik Kaare Nielsen and Finn Horn (eds), *Kritik som deltagelse*, Aarhus: Klim.

7 Current Developmental Perspectives of Public Discourse

As has been argued in the theoretical and analytical investigations above, the interrelationship between aesthetic and political discourse may assume a variety of forms. It further depends entirely on the nature of the aesthetic intervention in question whether the interplay provides political discourse with new, positive possibilities of creating critical reflection, socio-political engagement, and a common capacity to imagine politically qualified alternatives to the status quo, or whether it, on the contrary, deprives political discourse of its dimension of matter-of-fact orientation, conflict-processing, and reference to reason, thus replacing it with merely pleasing appeals to senses and emotions.

On the basis of a variety of significant examples, the argument was made that the predominant public of parliament-oriented mass media – in the intersection between intensified media competition and power and prestige struggles among professional political agents – to a large degree functions as a vehicle for aestheticising political practice in the sense that political content in the approach to voters tends to fade away behind spin, effect-straining staging, depoliticising harmonisation, spectacular polarisation, etc. In this perspective, it was argued, public interaction is at risk of being reduced to a branch of the entertainment industry and the citizen transformed into a consumer, shopping for private pleasure and for affirmation of prejudices.

In other words, to the extent that this type of approach is colonising public space, collective processing of experience on the terms of political discourse will have a hard time developing, and democratic political culture will be in danger of eroding. Furthermore, the governmental decision-maker public remains monologically committed to the strategic interests of the state and is therefore not substantially open to engage in the deliberation of arguments. Consequently, neither the parliament-oriented mass media public nor the governmental decision-maker public have strong incentives to change the current constellation.

If this diagnosis appears plausible, the question arises as to which options this situation entails, with respect to the further development of public discourse and democratic political culture. Such a development would have to be established by way of civil society publics putting pressure on the parliament-oriented mass media public and the governmental decision-maker public. A strengthening of public opinion formation from below, integrating both the universally reasoning

134   *Current Developmental Perspectives*

and the subjective experience-reflecting public discourse would be able to challenge the politicians' and the media's reduction of political debate to a barren power struggle, thus shifting the balance of debates in the parliament-oriented mass media towards searching for good solutions to common problems. An important step would be to establish civil society pressure on the public service media and the publicistic media in order to make them reflect on their *raison d'être* and make them move away from market calculation as main editorial principle. Apart from civil society pressure, such strengthening of the media's obligation to facilitate high quality public debate would require increased direct or indirect state subsidies for media that are willing to take on this responsibility for the general public.

A crucial precondition for establishing this type of civil society pressure would be to create forums at the grassroots level in which a strengthened public opinion formation can develop and express itself. Social movements and civil society grassroots initiatives that continuously emerge, develop, transform, and fade away in the course of concrete social and cultural struggles, are obviously important agents in this game, but they emerge and develop following their own context-specific premises and cannot meaningfully be endowed with any given role in a general strategic perspective to strengthen democratic public discourse. The same applies to artistic interventions, which, as has been shown, in principle have the potential to challenge established formations of meaning and to catalyse reflection on alternatives to the status quo, but the realisation of this potential cannot meaningfully be anticipated strategically, either.

To some extent, however, this option is present with regard to the type of citizens forums, on the basis of which the tradition of deliberative democracy operates.[1] In contrast to the static registration of isolated individuals' immediate, monological expression of opinions by the opinion polls, deliberative democracy creates a dialogical context in which participants experience that their position actually matters to a debating community, in which a joint reflection on different positions takes place, and in which an informed opinion formation is therefore able to develop. The basic model is that a representatively selected group of citizens gather in a physical location over several days in order to discuss a concrete political issue. They are supplied with all the relevant information material, take part in group discussions, and are involved in face-to-face dialogue with experts and politicians who are working on the political issue in question. The participating citizens' diverse backgrounds and different perspectives on the subject matter contribute to qualifying experts' and politicians' overall models of problem solution – and vice versa. The general experience is that ordinary citizens in such mini-publics are capable of debating complex issues soberly and competently, listen to arguments, nuance their own arguments – and occasionally are convinced by a better argument. In other words, participating citizens are enabled to actively form a qualified opinion, weigh a multiplicity of possible alternatives, and identify with the responsibilities of the role as citizen.

As is the case with regard to public space in general, such mini-publics do not offer any guarantee that participation will take place on the self-defined terms of

Current Developmental Perspectives   135

the involved citizens. As outlined above, social practice in general is always characterised by a conflictual interplay between interests and considerations stemming from the market, the state, and civil society, and in the work of each concrete citizens forum the hegemonic interrelationship between these factors will be important to the developmental possibilities and democratic perspectives of the deliberative process. If participation is framed top-down on the basis of the agendas of politicians, administrators, and experts, citizens forums will be reduced to just another type of monological governance, in which special interests are bargaining or in which participating citizens are taken hostage by already fixed technocratic policies.[2] If, conversely, the relationship of power in terms of framing participation is in favour of civil society and the involved citizens, the agenda can be defined bottom-up, and a genuine deliberative dialogue will be able to unfold. The present argument regards this latter scenario as a crucial condition of the possibility of developing political judgement on a broad basis in society.

Evidently, it is initially only the participants in concrete citizens forums who will obtain this qualification of their political judgement. But with the right processing and dissemination by the media, the opinion formation that takes place in these citizens forums is liable to have qualifying effects on the opinion formation of the population at large. Furthermore, the conceptualisation of deliberative processes needs adjustment in terms of granting the participating citizens a more extended influence on the framing of content, the choice of experts, etc., but all in all, according to present experience, much can be said for institutionalising deliberative citizens forums as exemplary laboratories to develop democratic virtues, political judgement – and more qualified political decisions. To the extent that such development gains ground, it will pose a strong, matter-of-fact-oriented pressure on politicians and journalists/editors in the parliament-oriented mass media public and on the governmental decision-maker public.

However, this developmental perspective presently appears to be challenged by political currents that might pull society in entirely different directions. The democratic model of Western societies has for some time been facing a severe crisis.[3] Due to their self-disempowering submission to the demands of market agents, representative institutions and associated expert systems are losing credibility and legitimacy in the eyes of many citizens, civic engagement in the institutional democratic process is dropping, and significant counter-tendencies in civil society tend to orientate themselves towards more or less authoritarian or nationalistic populist positions rather than towards open deliberation, public discourse, and qualified political judgement. Further, a diversity of political grassroots activism based on fundamental distrust of the established political system is spreading.

Technocratic neoliberalism that has been hegemonic in defining the terms and interpreting the perspectives of capitalist globalisation since the 1980s seems to be imploding on its own inner contradictions. It is not successful in meeting its own claims of providing economic growth and raising the general standard of living, and counter-productive effects that have accompanied this politico-economic model all along are becoming increasingly manifest: massive

136   *Current Developmental Perspectives*

inequality in the distribution of resources and life opportunities both on a global scale and internally in Western societies; concentration of huge wealth in the hands of the few; precarisation of the life conditions of large parts of the middle and working classes and outright marginalisation of people who are not 'useful' in market terms; exposing society as a whole to the incalculabilities of a globalised finance market beyond any political control; and continuing destruction of the environment and the climate of the planet.

The alleged 'necessities' of neoliberal economy as interpreted by political elites and associated expert systems no longer appear convincing to those parts of the population who are increasingly finding themselves the losers of this type of globalisation. Interconnected with this development, new societal conditions of creating and authorising knowledge have emerged that are contributing to weakening the hegemonic position of established institutions. Attempts to develop new forms of participation and governance that bring democracy up to date are bound to reflect this interconnectedness of institutional crisis and changing conditions of knowledge.

The Internet and the social media have been instrumental in bringing about these new conditions of knowledge. They have created an infrastructure that allows all citizens of democratic countries to freely access, compose, and disseminate any kind of information on their own conditions and thus to become co-creators of knowledge. In the so-called 'post-factual society',[4] the barrier between the layman and the expert tends to dissolve. Laypersons increasingly refuse to recognise official authorities of knowledge and instead refer to their own self-generated knowledge (e.g. on vaccination or climate change) and to closed circuits of opinions in Internet echo chambers. In principle, the floodgates are open to anyone authorising their own private opinion as facts – including political or commercial agents strategically spreading lies in order to strengthen their position in the struggle over attention, resources, and power.

From a democratic perspective, this is a highly ambivalent process: on the negative side, dialogical public discourse as such is under pressure and risks being replaced by monological special interests struggling solely for their own individual causes. As a consequence, it is becoming increasingly difficult to establish universally recognised societal standards and priorities. The discursive frame of the common good, the notion of the better argument, and the idea of political debate as both a struggle and a search for adequate common solutions tend to be marginalised by overt power politics. The social media are ideal platforms for this type of political practice: monological self-presentation as a political power player can take place undisturbed by dialogical challenges from opponents and journalists, and the editorial process imposing assessments of quality and relevance. The traditional authority of the mass media is being severely challenged by this development and, as pointed out above, such a challenge in many respects seems to be well deserved. In this context, however, it happens at the cost of the obligation to common standards of debate.

This state of affairs has paved the way for populist appeals in the political field of practice. In accordance with the analysis by Jan-Werner Müller,[5] I use

Current Developmental Perspectives   137

the term 'populism' in the specific sense of a politico-ideological power discourse that reduces societal complexity to a dichotomy between an illegitimate 'elite' and a true, homogeneous 'people'. By taking out a patent on interpreting and representing the people, populist discourse grants itself a monopoly on the moral right to power, thus denying all other political positions democratic legitimacy.

In a number of Western democracies, populism is presently manifesting itself as a highly effective discourse for framing political debate, thus forcing the rest of the political spectrum to relate to – and thereby involuntarily intensify – the populist agenda. This constellation is fuelled by the fact that the dichotomising discourse addresses real experiences in major parts of the population with life-world interests being marginalised in favour of systemic 'necessities' (liberalisation of the labour market with loss of job security and a race towards the bottom as a consequence; decreasing public welfare; technocratic planning measures destroying traditional life contexts; submission of ordinary citizens' basic conditions of housing and pensions savings to volatile, incalculable financial markets; increasing environmental and climate problems due to unleashed capitalist expansion, etc.).

These real experiences of colonisation have been neglected and repressed by the broad neoliberalist consensus in established political life that insists on there being 'no alternative' to technocratic, market-conforming policy. Various social movements (the World Social Forum, ATTAC, Occupy Wall Street, etc.) have occasionally given voice to these life-world experiences and demanded changes in policy, and like any other representations of alternative societal rationalities, they have been marginalised as irrational and irresponsible by the political establishment. As an effect of this monologic exclusion of attempts to promote a critical, reason-based debate on possible alternatives to technocratic neoliberalism, the general, repressed life-world dynamics have been seeking other channels and are now – as a mere reflex of marginalisation – to some extent surfacing in forms that display non-reflective, immediate emotions and inclinations (post-fact argumentation, nationalism, xenophobia, sexism, etc.). In other words, in current public debate, reason tends to be reduced to technocracy, and civic engagement to emotions and aesthetic fascinations. Thus, the perspective of integrating reason and emotion in developing political judgement is undermined.

The achievement of the present populist currents is that they have been able to give voice to this diverse pool of life-world frustrations and to channel related identity work and subjective impulses of resistance into clear emotion-based patterns that obviously convince and engage large sections of the population. The populists address questions of political content (inequality, injustice, corruption, elitism, immigration, national tradition and values, etc.), but by way of their monologic, polarising emotional appeal, they submit these contents to aestheticised forms that channel identity dynamic and subjective experiences into a dichotomous worldview incapable of reflecting the complex challenges of contemporary society in a nuanced, dialogical manner. In other words, populism represents a version of the political in which the common good is conceptualised

138   *Current Developmental Perspectives*

as an indisputable, predefined entity that populist discourse holds a monopoly on interpreting, and that forms the basis of monologic discursive demarcations against the alleged enemies of 'the people': 'the media', 'the elite', and 'immigrants'. Populist discourse draws on the same dynamics and experiences as subjective experience-reflecting public discourse would do, but due to its constitutive restriction to non-reflective, emotion-based dichotomies, populist discourse remains a particularistic, potentially totalitarian claim to power.

In other words, in contemporary Western populism, the general subjective impulses of resistance generated in late modern everyday life and the life-world experiences of precariousness and marginalisation caused by technocratic neo-liberalism are being addressed and offered a clear pattern of orientation. In recent years, this type of channelling of experiences of frustration and disempowerment has gained a self-reinforcing momentum that is constituting a negatively defined Zeitgeist: an anti-establishment Zeitgeist. This development is fuelled by general, basic conflicts and actual experiences in contemporary society, but populist discourse specifically politicises these matters by way of a collective atmospheric projection that – on the basis of sensuous and emotional appeals that mobilise private judgement – reduces society to a dichotomous entity and suggests correspondingly simple solutions to complex problems.

Evidently, this line of development represents a threatening decay of public discourse and political judgement in society. However, the perspectives of the present crisis of established political institutions and expert systems should not be reduced to post-factual arbitrariness and populist excesses. On the positive side, the crisis at the same time entails a perspective of emancipation from traditional authorities of knowledge and empowerment of citizens to make their own assessments and choices: the weakening of traditional hierarchies and monopolies of knowledge also holds the potential for innovation of democracy, based on decentralised participation and citizen-generated knowledge. This perspective is not just theoretical by nature: parallel to the crisis of established institutions, a multiplicity of grassroots initiatives are developing that can be analysed as drafts for future democratic practices.[6] These tendencies include everyday-oriented participatory cultures, horizontally organised activism on a variety of political subjects on different levels of society unfolding in both physical, medial, and virtual space, decentralised communities of practice working on environmental issues, sharing economy, gender issues, ethnicity issues, DIY communities, etc.[7]

In other words, in contemporary Western democracies, the political not only assumes the shape of authoritarian populism, but also it manifests itself as a rich variety of civil society initiatives from below that are struggling for alternatives to the status quo, based on an inclusive notion of the common good. A further development and realisation of this democratic potential would require that these diverse, partial civil society publics enter a process of exchange, collaboration, and constitution of a common public, both inwardly and outwardly. Initially, the main challenge would be to learn to handle the conflicts that will necessarily arise in this process – without losing sight of either the individual issues or the common perspective. Democratic public discourse does not work without the

Current Developmental Perspectives 139

agents' ability and willingness to practise self-transcending reflection on common concerns (*Bildung*) and exercise political judgement.

As proposed earlier, democratic public discourse relies on a productive interplay between subjective experience-reflecting and universally reasoning public discourse. In the concrete processes of politicisation, subjective experience-reflecting public discourse is mostly at the forefront, processing sensuous and emotional qualities of individual identity work towards a dialogic exchange with arguments of reason and a reflection of the common good – thus gradually building bridges to the universally reasoning public discourse. If successfully integrated into this type of reflective process, sensuous and emotional engagement is the foundation of the political in a genuinely democratic sense of the term – and in no way reducible to populism.

The concept of deliberative democracy and the practice of deliberative mini-publics, however, seem to be in need of adjustment on this point. It primarily works on the basis of the universally reasoning public discourse and issues that have already been put on the agenda by established politics.[8] A productive perspective for further developing deliberative practice would be, to a higher degree, letting deliberative mini-publics work departing from the subjective issues and reflective potentials of the participants – and develop the qualifying universal perspectives in interaction with this point of departure.

As has been argued above, artistic interventions may play a productive role in such processes if they engage in a dialogic exchange with political discourse that opens new perspectives and ways of reflecting on political matters. But aesthetic discourse in itself cannot replace political discourse's complex mediation between a multiplicity of conflicts and the reflection of the common good of society. This crucial operation calls for political judgement, not aesthetic judgement.

Notes

1 See the descriptions in John Dryzek, *Foundations and Frontiers of Deliberative Governance* (Oxford: Oxford University Press, 2010); James Fishkin, *The Voice of the People* (New Haven, CT: Yale University Press, 1995); Hélène Landemore, *Democratic Reason* (Princeton, NJ: Princeton University Press, 2013); Jane Mansbridge and John Parkinson (eds), *Deliberative Systems: Deliberative Democracy at the Large Scale* (Cambridge: Cambridge University Press, 2012); Mark E. Warren, 'Can We Make Public Spheres More Democratic through Institutional Innovation?' in Henrik Kaare Nielsen, Christina Fiig, Jorn Loftager, Thomas Olesen, Jan Lohmann Stephensen, and Mads P. Sorensen (eds), *The Democratic Public Sphere: Current Challenges and Prospects*, Aarhus: Aarhus University Press, 2016). The same potential applies to the specific type of artistic interventions that Kerstin Bergendal represented in Chapter 6.
2 Louise Phillips, Anabela Carvalho, and Julie Doyle (eds), *Citizen Voices: Performing Public Participation in Science and Environment Communication* (Bristol: Intellect, 2012).
3 John Keane, 'Monitory Democracy?' in Sonia Alonso, John Keane, and Wolfgang Merkel (eds), *The Future of Representative Democracy* (Cambridge: Cambridge University Press, 2011); Simon Tormey, *The End of Representative Politics* (Malden, MA: Polity Press, 2015).

140   *Current Developmental Perspectives*

4 Farhad Manjoo, *True Enough: Learning to Live in a Post-Fact Society* (Hoboken, NJ: John Wiley and Sons, Inc., 2008); Ari Rabin-Havt, *Media Matters, Lies, Incorporated. The World of Post-Truth Politics* (New York: Anchor Books, 2016).
5 Jan-Werner Müller, *What Is Populism?* (Philadelphia, PA: University of Pennsylvania Press, 2016).
6 Steven Griggs, A. Norval, and H. Wagenaar (eds), *Practices of Freedom: Decentred Governance, Conflict and Democratic Participation* (Cambridge: Cambridge University Press, 2014).
7 Patrizia Nanz and Claus Leggewie, *Die Konsultative. Mehr Demokratie durch Bürgerbeteiligung* (Berlin: Wagenbach, 2016).
8 Thomas Wagner, 'Der Mitmachfalle den Kampf ansagen', in Alex Demirovic (ed.), *Transformation der Demokratie – demokratische Transformation* (Münster: Westfälisches Dampfboot, 2016).

References

Dryzek, John S. (2010) *Foundations and Frontiers of Deliberative Governance*, Oxford: Oxford University Press.

Fishkin, James (1995) *The Voice of the People*, New Haven, CT: Yale University Press.

Griggs, Steven, A. Norval, and H. Wagenaar (eds) (2014) *Practices of Freedom: Decentred Governance, Conflict and Democratic Participation*, Cambridge: Cambridge University Press.

Keane, John (2011) 'Monitory Democracy?' in Sonia Alonso, John Keane, and Wolfgang Merkel (eds), *The Future of Representative Democracy*, Cambridge: Cambridge University Press.

Landemore, Hélène (2013) *Democratic Reason*, Princeton, NJ: Princeton University Press.

Manjoo, Farhad (2008) *True Enough. Learning to Live in a Post-Fact Society*, Hoboken, NJ: John Wiley and Sons, Inc.

Mansbridge, Jane and John Parkinson (eds) (2012) *Deliberative Systems: Deliberative Democracy at the Large Scale*, Cambridge: Cambridge University Press.

Müller, Jan-Werner (2016) *What Is Populism?* Philadelphia, PA: University of Pennsylvania Press.

Nanz, Patrizia and Claus Leggewie (2016) *Die Konsultative. Mehr Demokratie durch Bürgerbeteiligung*, Berlin: Wagenbach.

Phillips, Louise, Anabela Carvalho, and Julie Doyle (eds) (2012) *Citizen Voices: Performing Public Participation in Science and Environment Communication*, Bristol: Intellect.

Rabin-Havt, Ari (2016) *Media Matters, Lies, Incorporated. The World of Post-Truth Politics*, New York: Anchor Books.

Tormey, Simon (2015) *The End of Representative Politics*, Malden, MA: Polity Press.

Wagner, Thomas (2016) 'Der Mitmachfalle den Kampf ansagen', in Alex Demirovic (ed.), *Transformation der Demokratie – demokratische Transformation*, Münster: Westfälisches Dampfboot.

Warren, Mark E. (2016) 'Can We Make Public Spheres More Democratic through Institutional Innovation?' in Henrik Kaare Nielsen, Christina Fiig, Jorn Loftager, Thomas Olesen, Jan Lohmann Stephensen, and Mads P. Sorensen (eds) *The Democratic Public Sphere: Current Challenges and Prospects*, Aarhus: Aarhus University Press.

Index

Page numbers in **bold** denote figures.

9/11 terrorist attacks 84, 101, 102

absolutism 5, 8, 9–10
activism 24, 135, 138
Adbusters 115; Occupy Wall Street poster
118, **119**
Adorno, Theodor W. 2
aesthetic discourse 4, 16, 53, 63, 74–6, 77,
79, 88, 139; intervention of *see* artistic
intervention; public of parliament-
oriented mass media, aesthetic
intervention in; marginalising of the
political 92, 93; and political community
80–5
aesthetic experience 4, 76–8; potentials
and limitations of 88–9
aesthetic fascinations 52, 58, 75, 81, 106,
107, 108, 109–10, 137
aesthetic intervention *see* artistic
intervention; public of parliament-oriented
mass media, aesthetic intervention in
aesthetic judgement of taste 81–4, 86, 87,
88, 110, 113
aesthetic practice 2, 76, 77
aesthetic *sensus communis* 82, 86, 126
aesthetic theory 15
aestheticisation 2, 53–4, 76, 78, 93, 97,
110–11; mass media 58–9
agora 54
agreeable, the 80–1, 83–4, 88, 99, 106,
107, 109, 124, 127
Al-Qaeda 102
'anger marketing' 122
anti-globalization 37
Arab Spring 61, 120, 130n7
architecture, as aesthetic demonstration of
power 10

Arendt, Hannah 20, 45, 85
arguing principle 24, 26, 46, 48, 49
aristocracy 7, 8
Aristotle 85
art, expert culture of 76
art scene 76
artefact level of aesthetic/artistic
intervention 98–105, 115–24
artefacts, aesthetic 77–8
articles of everyday use 125
artistic intervention 113–32, 134, 139; at
artefact level 115–24; at atmospheric
level 124–30; in urban space 124
artworks: politicians' choice of 94;
representation of political power in 3,
4–8
atmosphere 111n12
atmospheric competence 105
atmospheric level of aesthetic/artistic
intervention 4, 98, 105–10, 124–30
ATTAC 137

Barber, Benjamin 2
bargaining 23, 48, 101, 135
Baudrillard, Jean 2
Bauman, Zygmunt 2
beauty/the beautiful 81–2, 123, 124, 125,
126, 127
belly dance 124–5, 126
Benjamin, Walter 2
Bergendal, Kerstin 128
Bhopal disaster (1984) 116
Bildung 7, 76–7, 81, 83, 84, 139
bio-power 16
Bjarke Ingels Group (BIG) 128
blogging 63
blogosphere 63, 96

142   *Index*

Bourdieu, Pierre 16, 29, 33, 74, 75, 82–3
bourgeois public sphere 25, 26–7, 28
Breithaupt, Fritz 34
Brexit campaign (2016) 59
Bubner, Rüdiger 88
bureaucracy 25

capitalism 25, 37
citizens forums *see* mini-publics
citizenship 88, 89; active 24; cultural 126
civic engagement 2, 25–38
civil rights 102
civil society 43, 46, 66–7n1, 126, 128,
   135, 138; as communicative principle of
   societalisation 43–5, 46, 126; conflicts
   and power struggles in 67n11; global
   62; and Internet 60, 61–3, 65–6;
   politicians as agents of 48; and the
   Zeitgeist 109, 110
civil society publics 47, 75, 93, 97, 111,
   133–4; *see also* overall civil society
   publics; partial civil society publics
Clash of Civilisations thesis 101
class 47, 83
class relations 29
class struggle 22, 32, 33
Clinton, Hillary 120
closed aesthetic approach 98
collective bargaining 36
collective discourses 30
collective experience 97
collective identity 29, 30, 32, 35, 109
colonisation of life-world 44
commercialisation, of the Internet 60
commodification: of knowledge 52; of
   politics 56–7
common good 20, 24, 25, 44, 65, 80, 87,
   110, 136; as discursive framework for
   practice 21, 38, 46, 81, 83, 90n16;
   populist interpretation of 137–8; versus
   special interests 65, 86, 89, 136
commons 128; enclosure of 52
communicative action 26, 44
competition: mass media 50, 56, 58, 97; in
   public space 53–4
complexity, reduction of 55–6, 103
compromises 22, 23, 24, 93, 94, 114
conflict 19, 20, 21, 22, 23, 24, 25–6, 37,
   46, 47, 48, 114; in civil society forums
   67n11; ethnic 29
conflict regulation, institutionalisation of
   36
consciousness: industries of 28; political
   28

consensus 19, 20, 21, 24, 25, 48, 114, 123;
   ethical 22–3, 46; metaconsensus 26;
   procedural 26
consumer culture 78
consumerist public discourse 28, 29, 44,
   49, 54, 55, 57, 59, 61, 66, 78, 80, 103–4,
   106, 114
consumption 53–4, 108, 126
counter-publics 65
critical theory 75
cultural citizenship 126
cultural community 126
cultural industry 106
cultural movements 36, 53, 109
Cultural Studies 29
cultural theory 15
cultural/political uprisings (1960s/70s) 109
culturalisation 33–5, 54, 107
culturalist essentialism 35
culture jammings 115

Dean, Jodi 60
decision-making process, formal
   institutional 48
Delacroix, Eugène: *La Liberté guidant le
   peuple* **5**, 5, 7
deliberative democracy 3, 23–4, 46, 48,
   49, 128, 129, 134, 139; and public
   sphere 25–6
democracy: liberal concept of 23;
   parliamentary 24, 27; republican
   concept of 23; *see also* deliberative
   democracy
democratic political process 19–24
democratic public discourse 44, 46, 47,
   126, 127, 130, 134, 138–9; and medial
   spaces of practice 57; and physical
   spaces of practice 54, 55; and virtual
   spaces of practice 60–6
democratic struggle, artistic interpretations
   of 5–8
Denmark 8
determinative judgement 86
digital screens in urban space 127
dis-/misinformation 60, 61
discourse(s) 17; collective 30;
   differentiation and conflictual interplay
   of 78–80; *see also* aesthetic discourse;
   political discourse; public discourse
discriminatory practices 27, 123
discursive practice, identity as 31, 32,
   35–6
diversity, recognition of 20, 21
Dow Chemicals 116–17

Index   143

drone attacks 102
Dryzek, John 26

economic field of practice 79
economic power relations 35
election campaigns 12, 34, 117–18
Electoral Guerrilla Theatre 117, 118
emancipation 17, 25, 26, 88, 127, 138
emotion(s) 2, 15, 77, 124, 137; appeal to
14, 53, 76, 78, 88, 92–3, 97, 99, 110;
and populist discourse 137–8
empathy 34, 53
employment growth 108, 109
empowerment 17, 57, 76, 78, 127, 138
enclosure of commons 52
equality 29, 30; *see also* inequality
ethical consensus 22–3, 46
ethical judgement 82
ethical *sensus communis* 82, 86, 87
ethnic conflict 29
ethnic minorities 27
ethnocentrism 89
ethos 87
everyday life 27
experience 30, 32, 33, 35, 37, 77; aesthetic
see aesthetic experience; collective 97;
immediate 57, 59, 64; mediated 57, 59,
64; sensory-based 57
experience society 74
expert publics 50
expert systems 135, 136, 138
extreme groups 95–6

face-to-face interaction 64–5
Facebook 63
family, socialisation process in 27
fascinations, aesthetic 52, 58, 75, 81, 106,
107, 108, 109–10, 137
Fishkin, James 26
foreign policy 101
Foucault, Michel 29
framing 49–50, 103, 104
France, revolutionary 5, 7
Fraser, Nancy 47, 83

gender 27, 29, 47
Germany 7–8
Giddens, Anthony 17
global civil society 62
globalisation 1, 32, 35, 36, 57–8, 135, 136
good society 25
governmental decision-maker public 48,
50, 75, 93, 114, 233; aesthetic
characteristics of 94

grassroots movements 55; *see also* partial
civil society publics
Guantanamo camp 102

Habermas, Jürgen 2, 15, 16, 25–6, 27, 44,
47, 75
habitus 29, 33, 83
Hansen, Constantin: *Den grundlovsgivende
Rigsforsamling* **6**, 8
happiness 7
Hardt, Michael 16
harmonising aesthetic intervention 99,
103–5, 113–14, 133
Haugaard, Jacob 117–18
Heartfield, John 115; *Der Sinn des
Hitlergrusses* **116**
hegemonic relations 23, 24, 25, 29, 44, 45,
46, 79, 135
Hendrix, Jimi: 'Star-Spangled Banner'
(Woodstock, 1969) 121
Henneberg, Rudolf: *Die Jagd nach dem
Glück* **6**, 7–8
heteronomy 27
Hitler, Adolf 10, **11**
Hoffmann-Axthelm, Dieter 57
Horkheimer, Max 2
human rights 23
Huntington, Samuel P. 35, 101

identity 45; collective 29, 30, 32, 35, 109;
as discursive practice 31, 32, 35–6; as
dynamic 31; individual 29–30, 31–2, 35;
negotiation of 30–1; political 34;
political citizen 126; and politicisation
30, 32–6, 37–8; and power 29
identity correction 117
Identity Politics 29
identity work 53, 83, 84; and aesthetic
experience 88, 89; balance-seeking 31,
35; culturalised 33–5, 54; individualised
32–4, 35; late modern 29–38; and social
media 63–4; and the Zeitgeist 107–8
idiosyncratic judgement 95, 103, 107, 109
imagination 54, 86, 87, 118
immediate experience 57, 59, 64
immigrants 138; marginalisation of 36
immigration policy 101
individualisation 32–4, 35, 107
individualism 35
inequality 2, 85, 120, 136, 137
infotainment 59
Instagram 63
institutions: establishment of 20; trust in
55, 56

144 *Index*

intellect 56, 76, 77, 78, 88, 122
intellectual property 52
interactivity 126; face-to-face 64–5; in virtual space 59, 64
interest groups 22
interests: articulation of 79; struggles/conflicts of 22, 83, 87, 89, 93, 110; *see also* special interests
Internet 58, 59–66, 126, 136; and civil society 60, 61–3, 65–6; commercialisation of 60; and consumerist public discourse 61, 66; and democratic public discourse 60–6; and immediate experience 59; interactive potential of 59, 64; as market agent 59, 60; and mediated experience 59; as object of surveillance 59; as ordinary mass media 60–1; private communication on 61; and subjective experience-reflecting public discourse 59, 61, 65; surveillance activity on 59, 66; and universally reasoning public discourse 59, 61, 65
ISIS 102
Islamic terrorism 102
IT industry hype of late 1990s 108

judgement: determinative 86; ethical 82, 83; idiosyncratic 95, 103, 107, 109; political 4, 85–8, 99, 110, 114, 124, 126, 127–8, 139; private 81, 83–4, 99, 100; reflective 84, 86, 87, 115, 117, 124, 127, 129; of taste *see* aesthetic judgement of taste; teleological 87

Kant, Immanuel 4, 75, 80–2, 83, 85, 87
Kluge, Alexander 15, 20, 26, 27–8, 47, 57, 83
Knodt, Reinhard 105, 124–5
knowledge: changing conditions of 136; commodification of 52; mediation of 57; privatisation of 52; second hand 57; sensory-based 57
knowledge society 52

labour movements 32
Laclau, Ernesto 75
Lakoff, George 49, 103
late modern identity work 29–38
legislation 24, 44
legitimacy, political/institutional 1, 20, 48, 94, 137
liberal concept of democracy 23
liberty 5, 7, 8

lies 60, 61
life-style 33, 55, 74, 126
life-world 27, 31, 47, 55, 76, 77, 98, 137, 138; colonisation of 44
logos 87
Louis XIV of France (Sun King) 9, 10
Luhmann, Niklas 75

Maffesoli, Michel 16, 74
Mann, Thomas 7
Marcuse, Herbert 16
Marianne 5, 7
market, the 27, 35, 43, 44, 45, 46, 108, 126, 127, 135; Internet and 59, 60; money-mediated societalisation of 44, 46
mass media 53, 55–9; aestheticising measures, intensification of 58–9; competition in field of 50, 56, 58, 97; complexity reduction 55–6; and personalised representations of politicians 13–14, 56, 97, 98; sensationalism 58; *see also* public of parliament-oriented mass media
meaning formation 16, 59, 74, 77, 79, 98; at artefact level 98, 115; at atmospheric level 105, 115, 124, 126; and *Bildung* processes 76; and the Zeitgeist 108
medial spaces of practice 55–9
mediated experience 57, 59, 64
Menke, Christoph 85
metaconsensus 26
Middle East politics 101, 102
mini-publics 127, 134–5, 139
mis-/disinformation 60, 61
modernisation 32, 75, 107
modernisation rhetoric 104–5
modernity: as discursively differentiated entity 75; Habermas' theory of 75
monologic approach 9, 10, 29–30, 44, 48, 49, 54, 63, 64, 94
monumentalising of power figures 10, 12, 94
mood(s) 4, 78, 106, 124, 125; *see also* Zeitgeist
Moore, Michael 117
Mouffe, Chantal 45, 75
Müller, Jan-Werner 136
multitude 16

nation-state 1, 2
nationalism 89, 109, 135, 137
Negri, Antonio 16
Negt, Oskar 15, 20, 26, 27–8, 47, 57, 83, 85

Index 145

neoliberal technocratisation 51–3, 135–6, 137
normalisation rhetoric 105

Obama, Barack 98–9, 120
Occupy Wall Street movement 61–2, 118, **119**, 120, 130n7, 137
Ogilvie, Corey: 'I am not moving' video 120
open aesthetic approach 98–9
opinion polls 110, 134
overall civil society publics 47, 50, 62, 63, 93; aesthetic characteristics of 96

panopticon 55
parliament-oriented mass media public *see* public of parliament-oriented mass media
parliamentarian institutions 36
parliamentary democracy 24, 27
Parsons, Talcott 19
partial civil society publics 47, 50, 62–3, 65–6, 93, 138; aesthetic characteristics of 94–6
participation 23, 24, 65–6, 126–7, 134–5; active 44, 46, 90n17; unequal opportunities for 2
particularism 21, 29, 30
party space 105–6
pathos 87
peasantry, Danish 8
personalization of politicians 12–14, 34, 56, 92, 97, 98, 110, 111n3
Peters, Bernhard 26, 49
phronesis 85
physical spaces of practice 54–5
pleasure/displeasure 81, 86, 87
polarising aesthetic intervention 99–103, 113–14, 133
political, the 19–20, 28, 47
political, and late modern identity work 29–32
political camps 49
political citizen identity 126
political commentators 110
political community, and aesthetic discourse 80–5
political consciousness 28
political discourse 34, 75, 76, 79, 80, 88, 89, 92, 110, 114, 115, 121, 122, 129, 133, 139
political identity 34, 95
political judgement 4, 85–8, 99, 110, 114, 124, 126, 127–8, 139

political power 3, 20, 79–80; aesthetic self-presentation of 3, 8–14; artistic representation of 3, 4–8
political power relations 22, 35
political practice 75–6, 79
political satire 115–17
political science 15
political *sensus communis* 86, 87, 117
political/cultural uprisings (1960s/70s) 109
politicians 53, 97; as civil society agents 48; harmonising public approaches 103–4; and mass media 13–14, 56, 97, 98; participation in entertainment programmes 106; personalised (self-) presentations 12–14, 34, 92, 94, 110, 111n3; and social media 14, 56; *see also* public of parliament-oriented mass media
politicisation 3, 45, 139; from below 28, 46, 95; and identity 30, 32–6, 37–8
politics 47; commodification of 56–7; definitions of 19
popular culture 76, 78, 113
populism 88, 99, 101, 109, 135, 136–8; emotional appeal of 137–8; interpretation of common good 137–8
post-factuality 60, 136, 137, 138
post-structuralist theory 16, 29
power: exercise of 109; and identity 29; symbolic 29
power relations 22, 44; economic 35; political 22, 35
power struggles 29, 30, 82, 83, 110; in civil society forums 67n11
power-mediation of the state 44, 46
power-oriented aesthetic interventions 92–112, 114; at artefact level 4, 98–105; at atmospheric level 4, 98, 105–10
precariousness 36, 136, 138
presidential election system, USA 120–1
prestige struggles 33
primitive accumulation 52
privacy 58
private judgement 81, 83–4, 99, 100
private sphere 27, 47
privatisation of knowledge 52
procedural consensus 26
Prokop, Dieter 78
proletarian public sphere 27–8
Provo Movement 117
provocative intervention 115, 123–4
public debate 23, 24, 25–6
public discourse 3, 24, 25–38, 43, 67n4; consumerist 28, 29, 44, 49, 54, 55, 57,

146   *Index*

public discourse *continued*
  59, 61, 66, 78, 80, 103–4, 106, 114;
  modalities of 26–9; *see also* democratic
  public discourse; subjective experience-
  reflecting public discourse; universally
  reasoning public discourse
public opinion formation 23–4, 44, 45, 47,
  57, 87, 92, 93, 110, 133–4, 135
public of parliament-oriented mass media
  4, 48–9, 50, 52, 75, 93, 133, 135;
  aesthetic characteristics of 97
public of parliament-oriented mass media,
  aesthetic intervention in 97–111,
  114–15; at artefact level 98–105; at
  atmospheric level 4, 98, 105–10;
  harmonising 99, 103–5, 113–14, 133;
  polarising 99–103, 113–14, 133
public space 3, 24; civil society-oriented
  use of 128; conditions of medial spaces
  of practice 55–9; conditions of physical
  spaces of practice 54–5; conditions of
  virtual spaces of practice 59–66;
  conflictual nature of 43–7; contemporary
  conditions of practice in 51–66; market
  competition in 53–4; neoliberal
  technocratisation 51–3; overall process
  of aestheticisation 53–4; participation in
  126–7; relational potential in 127
public sphere 2, 26–8, 47; bourgeois 25,
  26–7, 28; and deliberative democracy
  25–6; of production 28; proletarian
  27–8; transnational 2, 67n4
public(s): aesthetic characteristics of 93–7;
  expert 50; strong 47, 48; types of 47–51;
  weak 47–8; *see also* governmental
  decision-maker public; overall civil
  society publics; partial civil society
  publics; public of parliament-oriented
  mass media

Rancière, Jacques 16, 85
rational choice tradition 23
real estate bubble of late 2000s 108
reason 2, 5, 8, 15, 16, 25, 75, 97, 110, 113,
  137
reception aesthetics 15, 77–8, 93, 98
reflective judgement 84, 86, 87, 115, 117,
  124, 127, 129
reform rhetoric 104
relational aesthetics 127–9
republican concept of democracy 23
resistance 27, 28, 57, 65
revolutionary change 84–5
Rigaud, Hyacinthe: *Portrait of Louis XIV* **9**

satire 115–17
Schmitt, Carl 20
Schulze, Gerhard 16, 74
science 75
scientific practice 79
security policy 101
Seel, Martin 84
self-interest 44
self-organised activities 55
self-presentation of political power 3, 8–14
SelltheVote action 120–1
Sennett, Richard 2
sensationalism 58
senses 77; appeal to 2, 14, 53, 76, 78, 88,
  92–3, 97, 99, 110
sensory-based knowledge 57
sensus communis 81, 82, 125, 126, 127,
  128, 129; aesthetic 81, 82, 86, 126;
  ethical 82, 86, 87; political 86, 87, 117
sexual minorities 27
shitstorms 61, 65
Sierra, Santiago 123
Snowden, Edward 122, 123
social media 58, 61, 63–4, 69n42, 96, 126,
  136; and identity work 63–4; politicians
  use of 14, 56
social movements 22, 24, 36, 47, 53, 109,
  134, 137; *see also names of individual
  movements*
socialisation, in the family 27
Solvognen theatre group: 'Army of Santa
  Clauses' 121–2; Rebild action (1976)
  122
Soviet totalitarianism 12
special interests 23, 30, 43, 44, 82, 83, 100;
  versus common good 65, 86, 89, 136
spin 1, 49–50, 104, 133
spin-doctors 110
Staeck, Klaus 115
state 43, 44, 45, 46, 126, 127, 133, 135;
  power/legislation-mediated
  societalisation principle of 44, 46
Street Art 127
strong public 47, 48
subcultures 28, 47
subject: classic ideality conception of 16,
  17; post-structuralist conception of 16;
  secularised conception of 17
subjective experience-reflecting public
  discourse 28, 44, 46, 47, 55, 62, 78, 80,
  84, 103, 114, 129, 134, 138, 139; and
  aesthetic judgement 82; and aesthetic
  practice 76, 77; and Internet 59, 61, 65;
  and partial civil society publics 94–5

Index   147

sublime 84–5, 88, 102, 110, 113, 121, 123, 124
subversive intervention 115, 123–4
Superflex artist group 128
Superkilen, Copenhagen 128–9
surveillance 55, 59, 66, 102, 103, 122–3
symbolic power 29
system and life-world 44

taste 16, 33, 74, 75, 88; aesthetic judgement of 8, 81–4, 86, 88, 110, 113
technocratic neoliberalism 51–3, 135–6, 137
teleological judgement 87
terrorism 60, 102–3; military response to 109
time horizons: mass media 56; political process 56, 58
Tiravanija, Rikrit 127
totalitarianism 10, 12
tribal society 16, 74
trolling 65
Trump, Donald 56, 59, 69n37, 99
trust 55, 56, 64, 88
Twitter 63

Ubermorgen artist group 120–1
understanding 85, 86
Union of Consciously Work-Shy Elements 117
United States, presidential election system 120–1
universalism 21, 23, 29, 30
universally reasoning public discourse 28, 44, 46, 50, 54, 57, 78, 103, 114,

129, 133–4, 139; and aesthetic judgement 82; and aesthetic practice 76, 77; and Internet 59, 61, 65; and partial civil society publics 47; and public of parliament-oriented mass media 48
urban space: artistic interventions in 124; de-historicisation of 125; digital screens in 127; governmental surveillance activities in 55; public interaction in 54; relational interventions in 128–9; separation of groups in 54–5

values, policy of 52–3
Versailles **10**, 10
virtual spaces of practice 59–66
Vote-Auction action 120–1

weak public 47–8
wealth: concentration of 136; distribution of 36
Web 2.0 126
Weber, Max 19, 20
welfare state 36, 109; rolling back of 104
will formation 47, 48
World Social Forum 137
World Trade Organisation (WTO) 116
World Wide Web 59

Yes Men, The: Dow Chemical action 116–17; surveillance issue action 122–3; WTO action 116
YouTube 63

Zeitgeist 106–10, 138

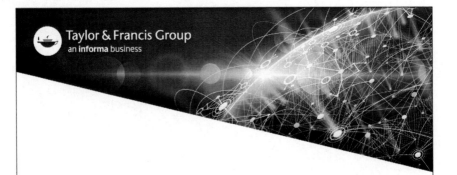